Race, Place, and Risk

SUNY Series in Afro-American Studies

John Howard and Robert C. Smith, Editors

Race, Place, and Risk

Black Homicide in Urban America

Harold M. Rose and Paula D. McClain

State University of New York Press

Published by
State University of New York Press, Albany

©1990 State University of New York

For information, address State University of New York
Press, State University Plaza, Albany, N.Y. 12246

Library of Congress Cataloging-in-Publication Data

Rose, Harold M.
    Race, place, and risk : Black homicide in urban America / Harold
  M. Rose and Paula D. McClain.
      p.   cm. — (SUNY series in Afro-American studies)
  Includes bibliographical references.
  ISBN 0-7914-0393-9. — ISBN 0-7914-0394-7 (pbk.)
    1. Homicide—United States. 2. Afro-American criminals. 3. Afro
  –Americans—Crimes against. 4. Discrimination in criminal justice
  administration—United States. I. McClain, Paula Denice.
  II. Title. III. Series.
  HV6529.R67 1990
  364. 1'52'08996073—dc20

10 9 8 7 6 5 4 3 2 1

In memory of our colleagues
Maxine L. Nimtz
Rodney J. Fruth

Contents

List of Tables

List of Figures

Preface

Blacks have long been the individuals most likely to be the victims and offenders in willfully motivated acts of lethal violence. The risk of homicide victimization in the nation's black communities waxes and wanes as an apparent result of a series of external shocks to those communities. But in both good times and bad times, the level of risk among blacks tends to be higher than that of any other racial or ethnic population. In spite of the seriousness of the problem, academic researchers seldom have chosen to focus on this phenomenon.

This lack of attention to black victimization may be attributed intuitively to a combination of factors. First, there has been a tendency to shy away from research that focused on stigmatizing individual behaviors, at least prior to the 1960s. Second, there has been a reluctance to pursue topics that focused direct attention on negative black behavior. But regardless of the motivation, black homicide risk seldom has been addressed in a holistic fashion. This investigation represents a serious effort to begin to fill the void.

In view of the paucity of research interest in this topic, we acknowledge that a single volume on the subject can focus in-depth only on selected aspects of the problem. Given our academic training (geography and political science), we are inclined to emphasize those aspects of which we are knowledgable. The emphasis of this book is on high-risk homicide environments within a sample of large black communities that are embedded in a regional cross-section of cities. We address a series of macro- and micro-structural forces within those environments that we contend abet both risk and structure of victimization. Thus, we do not confine our attention simply to individual-level flaws that lead to behavior in which victimization probabilities become attenuated, but to a series of forces, both external and internal to the community and the individual, that lead to heightened risk.

The most obvious realization growing out of such an approach is the complexity of the phenomena under review. The lowering of risk requires a comprehensive understanding of homicide as a multifaceted phenomenon for which easy solutions are not likely to be forthcoming. Therefore, we have strayed from attempting to provide easy solutions to a complex problem, and, instead, have attempted to provide a balanced treatment of those factors that contribute to elevated risk.

Rose's interest in the increased levels of black homicide was generated in the early 1970's by his brief stay in a midwestern metropolitan area in which homicide risk in the metropolitan black community had become extremely elevated. Nightly, media accounts made it quite clear who both the victims and offenders were—urban, black residents. Journalistic interest in these violent encounters far outstripped scholarly interest, and without the visual media's focus of attention on the despair within our midst, the problem would undoubtedly go unnoticed outside the confines of those high-risk environments. Thus, if he had not served as a visiting professor at a university located in this metropolitan area, the seed for this investigation may never have been planted.

It was only then that Rose began to discover the seriousness of the problem and the dearth of research exploring the topic. Upon returning to the University of Wisconsin-Milwaukee, he began to familiarize himself with the literature on the topic and began to work on the proposal that would allow a more rigorous grasp of the seriousness and nature of the problem, at least in a large urban context.

McClain became involved in the project in 1977 when she joined the faculty of the University of Wisconsin-Milwaukee. Rose wandered into her office shortly after her arrival and began to discuss his ideas for a proposal to study urban homicide. She caught Rose's enthusiasm for the topic and a research partnership was formed. The homicide project has been the driving force behind much of her later work on firearms and public policy, the urban environment and homicide, and, most recently, fieldwork with a police homicide detail. In 1982, she moved to Arizona State University, but the joint research on the project continued. This volume is the outcome of a collaboration extending over more than a decade.

Without extramural support, our proposed research effort would have never gotten off the ground. The Minority Mental Health Center of the National Institute of Mental Health (NIMH) provided financial support for the project, and the "Black Homicide Project" was initiated in the fall of 1977. The project was a large and complex undertaking that involved a large number of individuals performing a variety of tasks. With the assistance of staff, consultants, fieldworkers, and the unfaltering support of key individuals at the Minority Mental Health Center, the work was completed in the summer of 1980. The final report developed for the funding agency served as the groundwork for this much more extensive study.

Two individuals who contributed so much to the success of the earlier project but did not live to see this volume completed are Dr. Maxine L. Nimtz (anthropologist) and Dr. Rodney J. Fruth (psychiatrist). It is to them that we dedicate this book. Other persons involved with the project were Dr. Donald R. Deskins (geographer), Dr. Richard Henry (sociologist), Dr. Richard H. Patterson (psychiatrist), and Mrs. Elaine Fruth (social worker). Dr. Mary Harper of the National Institute of Mental Health, Dr. Franklin Zimring, Mrs. Gwendolyn Stephenson, and Mr. Leon Ashford also provided invaluable advice and counsel. We are extremely grateful for the dedication to the project displayed by our primary staff: Mrs. Diane Simons, project director, and Ms. Linda Johnson, project secretary. Numerous other persons were involved in making the research effort a success, but special thanks are extended to our interview teams in Detroit, Atlanta, and St. Louis.

Special thanks are also extended to the Phoenix Police Department for allowing McClain to follow its homicide detail for five months during the winter and spring of 1989. Although Phoenix is not one of the cities in this study, the experience and information gathered helped with the writing of parts of this book. She is particularly grateful to Assistant Chief Jerry Oliver, Capt. Jim Semenza, Lt. Sharon Kiyler, Sgt. Tim Bryant, and the detectives in the unit for their invaluable assistance.

Although the basic research for the homicide project was centered at the University of Wisconsin-Milwaukee, development of this manuscript was undertaken at Arizona State University. Without the assistance of Cherylene A. Schick of the School of Public Affairs and Marian Buckley, Keith Campbell, Tammy Stein, and Mary Cullen of the College of Public Programs' Auxiliary Resource Center, this manuscript would never have been completed. Their tolerance of and patience with our numerous revisions is greatly appreciated.

We are particularly grateful to Jacqueline Judd Udell for her superb editing of the manuscript, and to John S. Hall who suggested the title. We would also like to thank Robert C. Smith, coeditor of this SUNY series, for his helpful comments and continued support through the review process, as well as to Peggy Gifford, Acquisitions Editor for SUNY Press. Finally, we would like to thank our families—Ann Rose, and Paul C. Jacobson and Kristina L. McClain-Jacobson—for their continued support throughout the project and the subsequent writing of this book.

Black Homicide and the Urban Environment: An Introduction

In 1980, one out of every three hundred young-adult black males in St. Louis was a victim of homicide. In Detroit, one out of every four hundred fifty young-adult black males lost his life in a violent altercation. Similarly, one out of every four hundred young-adult black males in Los Angeles was a victim of homicide. In many cities throughout the nation, homicides are daily occurrences.

Violence resulting in death occurs at a higher rate in the United States than elsewhere in the developed world. A number of efforts to explain this phenomenon have been undertaken, but a general consensus regarding causation is lacking (Archer and Gartner, 1976; Wolfgang, 1986). Past and present researchers, however, have attributed the relatively high national homicide rate to the persistence of high levels of lethal violence among the nation's black population. Yet, seldom do these researchers partition risk in a way that would allow them to address directly its underlying causes. That is, few researchers have attempted to address elevated risk among the population at highest risk—the nation's black population.

To rationalize higher-than-average homicide rates in the nation at large by stigmatizing the population at highest risk represents a misdirected effort. However, some criminal justice researchers apparently find it easier to label black homicide offenders as "normal primitives" (see Swigert and Farrell, 1976) and/or to assign them other pejorative labels than to arrive at an objective assessment of the persistence of elevated risk in the nation's black communities. Thus, this effort represents an initial attempt at overcoming an apparent research void.

By skirting the issue of elevated risk among blacks, researchers are guilty of failing to address a serious issue in this country—the role of lethal violence on the life expectancy of selected segments of the black population (Dennis, 1977). Based on the neglect and the growing seriousness of the problem, Comer (1985) was led to urge the development of a more effective national public policy to combat the problem. Poussaint (1983), on the other hand, went so far as to recommend the creation of homicide prevention centers in selected communities characterized by exaggerated black risk. Nevertheless, until recently, the prevailing position has been, as stated by Thomas (1984:157), that ''Homicide has received a social reaction and public policy response that tends to normalize violence in the black community.'' That position undoubtedly is partially responsible for the lack of an ongoing objective assessment of the problem.

Although blacks are acknowledged to be the segment of the population with the greatest exposure to risk, it is ironic that we know so little about this phenomenon beyond an occasional anecdotal treatment. Therefore, the primary goal of this book is to shed light on a phenomenon that needs explanation, but, for a variety of reasons, has rarely been viewed as a high priority research area (Meredith, 1984; Rosenberg and Mercy, 1986; Hawkins, 1986).

THE STATUS OF BLACK HOMICIDE RESEARCH

To effectively address the issue of black homicide in the United States, a broad and extensive research base is needed. For the most part, past researchers have addressed only the general issue of the high level of lethal violence in the United States and not the specific topic of high risk among black Americans. Most of the research on homicide among blacks has been limited, and, in most instances, it is now outdated, although a recent volume edited by Hawkins (1986) represents an important effort to fill a void. A variety of explanations for the lack of research have been offered: 1) there is a general belief that violent interpersonal behavior involving lower-class blacks represents expected behavior; 2) researchers have limited interest in the negative behaviors of a pariah group, as long as these behaviors do not spill over into the larger population; and 3) obtaining race-specific victimization data, at least at local and/or neighborhood levels, is difficult.

Although previous research is limited, a small number of works can be cited that demonstrate there was interest in this topic in the early decades of this century (Brearley 1932; Barnhart, 1932). However, after the Great Depression, interest apparently waned until the post-World War II period (Bullock, 1955; Pettigrew and Spier, 1962). Because this research is dated, however, few insights into the changing nature of the problem are provided. Nevertheless, much is to be gained from these earlier efforts, particularly the ones from the post-World War II period. The timing of these earlier investigations is very important, for they serve as markers of the position of blacks in the national economy at specific points in time. We, too, will emphasize the position of blacks in national economic development, particularly since the middle 1960s, as a way of approaching the problem of persistent elevated homicide risk in the nation's larger black communities.

URBAN BLACK HOMICIDE

Our present investigation is limited to a single context from which to view changes in black homicide risk between 1960 and 1985—an urban context. Earlier homicide investigations essentially describe the behavior of blacks in rural areas and small towns. Yet, at the time, a small share of that population had already begun to seek its fortunes in the nation's larger cities in both the South and North. That also was the era in which the nation's economy was changing from agricultural dominance to industrial dominance. This economic transition was accompanied by subsequent shifts in values and lifestyles, and blacks were later participants in this transition. Prior to 1940, blacks were still overwhelmingly confined to rural environments where their hopes, outlooks, and values were circumscribed by their position in the economic and social scheme. As the nation moved from one stage of economic dominance to another, there were characteristic lags in the rate of regional shifts, which probably accounted for the persistence of rural southern values among blacks.

The Transitional Period—1930–1960

Exaggerated diversity and economic instability characterized the period from 1930 until World War II, which was followed by economic stability, the maturing of the urban economy, and the initiation of mass suburbanization. The dominant manufacturing economy had already begun to lose ground by the end of this transitional era. During that thirty-year interval, blacks from the American South poured into the nation's largest cities in unprecedented numbers. At the beginning of the period, blacks in large non-southern metropolises numbered 1.29 million, but after a single generation, they numbered 4.06 million, and the numbers continued to grow. By 1960, more than one-third of the nation's black population had some experience in large urban environments; yet, for most blacks, that experience seldom extended beyond a single generation. The three-fold increase in the number of blacks in major manufacturing cities was used by some academics to explain central-city decline (Lowry, 1980). Would not the transition to urban living have ameliorated exaggerated levels of homicide risk among black Americans if their persistence in maintaining southern rural values were the reason behind those levels?

The Urban Quarter Century—1960–1985

The largest number of blacks to seek a share of the urban American pie arrived too late to gain a foothold in the manufacturing economy. Nevertheless, they continued to move to urban areas. For that reason we have chosen to focus most of our attention on the "urban quarter century," 1960–1985. It was during this period that, for the first time, the vast majority of blacks resided in large cities throughout the nation. After declining slightly during the immediate postwar period, homicide risk again began to rise and reached a peak during the mid-1970s. Risk subsequently declined in the late 1970s. By the mid-1980s, an upturn in risk could again be seen, but not before risk levels had reached the low that marked the takeoff level that prevailed in the early 1960s (see Figure 1–1).

The twenty-five year span not only was a critical period in the transformation of the national economy in general, but was an even more crucial one for black Americans, who were the last to make the transition from a rural agricultural economy to an urban industrial one. Moreover, working-class whites with a one generation headstart had positioned themselves in the urban economy through ethnic politics, labor union dominance, and frugality to make certain their children would have ample opportunity to advance to the next higher rung on the social ladder. Thus, during the most recent period, young, middle-class whites of working class origin had left the central city to reside in the more desirable, child-rearing environments of the suburbs, and central cities in the American manufacturing belt were becoming the primary preserve of black Americans (see Table 1–1). Segments of central cities simultaneously were beginning to constitute some of the riskiest environments in America, and the primary victims of homicide were black Americans.

The Growth of Black Territorial Communities During a Period of Economic Transformation: The Consequences for Risk

During the urban quarter century, blacks, for the first time, began a concerted push beyond the margins of the central city in search of satisfactory residential accommodations. The pattern of black movement to the suburbs during this period has been described by a number of authors (Rose, 1976; Clark, 1979, Lake, 1981; Frey, 1985). This

FIGURE 1–1.

Black Homicide Risk Levels: 1960–1983

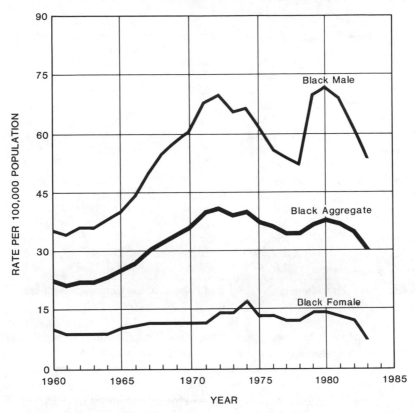

Source: Social Indicators, 1976, Bureau of the Census, U.S. Government
Printing Office, Washington, D.C., 1977.
Hawkins, Darnell F., editor, Homicide Among Black Americans,
University Press of America, New York, 1986.

movement to selected suburbs had the effect of reducing the level of heterogeneity that was observed earlier in central-city poverty neighborhoods (Wilson, 1987). Some researchers indirectly associate this change with the subsequent elevation in risk of victimization. Although the alteration in black urban settlement patterns could have fostered such an outcome, strong supporting evidence of that is difficult to come by. Nevertheless, Wilson (1987) suggested that the loss of middle class role models in neighborhoods that were previously heterogenous in character may have served to abet the development

TABLE 1–1

The Size of the Black Population in 15 Large Urban Centers
1970 and 1980

Urban Center	1970		1980	
	Black Population	% Black	Black Population	%Black
New York	1,666,636	21.2	1,784,121	25.2
Chicago	1,103,000	32.7	1,197,000	39.8
Detroit	660,000	43.7	758,939	63.1
Philadelphia	654,000	33.6	638,878	37.8
Los Angeles	503,606	17.9	505,208	17.0
Washington	537,712	71.1	448,229	70.3
Houston	316,551	25.7	440,257	27.6
Baltimore	420,210	46.4	431,151	54.8
New Orleans	267,308	45.0	308,136	55.3
Memphis	242,513	38.9	307,702	47.6
Atlanta	255,051	51.3	282,912	66.6
Dallas	210,038	24.9	265,594	29.4
Cleveland	238,000	38.3	251,347	43.8
St. Louis	254,000	40.9	206,386	45.6
Newark	207,000	54.2	191,743	58.2

Source: Data Users News, Oct. 1981 and Bureau of the Census of Population, 1970.

of maladaptive behaviors that the increases in crime and other illegal activities indicate. Although we acknowledge a link between these changes and changes in the character of the urban economy, we do so very cautiously.

There is some evidence of a lowering of intensity in patterns of residential segregation since 1970 (Clark, 1986), but there is little evidence suggesting a reduction in territorial scale of the black communities in major urban centers. On the contrary, existing evidence suggests the inverse. It is true, however, that spatial segmentation, based on social-class differences within expanding ghettos, has become more intense. To what extent does the level and scope of segmentation reflect the growth and/or decline in the urban economy? At this point we are unable to provide an unequivocal answer. But it is our contention that the size and intensity of segregation of lower-status populations within ghetto areas affects risk in ways that are not fully understood.

Beyond the fact of the changing scale of poor, urban, black communities, the question of the association of this phenomenon with changes in the character of the local and national economies becomes very important. Efforts to demonstrate the association between cyclical patterns of risk and their association with changes in business patterns is beginning to receive increased attention (Turner et al., 1981). This issue was recently addressed at an aggregate scale by Brenner and Swank (1986), but their approach has been sharply criticized (Cook and Zarkin, 1986). At a subaggregate level, Harries (1985), using region as the unit of analysis, also attempted to address the general issue, and the approach seems to be a valid one. To our knowledge, however, this approach has not been used to address the spatial-temporal dimension of risk. In this instance, blacks will represent the target population and changing ghetto environments the context. This approach has more merit than those that focus entirely on the endogenous traits of individual combatants viewed in isolation.

THE CHALLENGE OF THE ECOLOGICAL APPROACH

The ecological approach is the primary assessment tool we will use to begin to understand risk levels and patterns of risk among urban blacks during this period. This approach was strongly favored by Andrews (1985) as an appropriate method to be employed to examine risk intervention. Nonetheless, he cautioned that one should be aware of "a layering of risk factors, operating at different spatial scales, that interact in a complex ecological dynamic" (Andrews, 1985:372). Although Andrews was primarily interested in the assessment of the risk of disease among urban children, he clearly recognized the presence of a hierarchical set of identifiable spatial scales that are tied to the stimulation of ecological risk. The scales he employed are as follows: macro (region, municipality, urban area, community) meso (neighborhood); and micro (family environment, household). What was innovative about Andrew's approach was his attempt, at least conceptually, to demonstrate a linkage between the ecological layers. Most researchers employ a single ecological scale and rarely attempt to demonstrate the relationship between the ecological layers to provide a holistic picture of the factors that contribute to a given outcome. Generalizations made on the basis of a single scale tend to ignore influences occurring elsewhere in the ecological hierarchy.

Most ecological analyses are cross-sectional and static, and therefore do not address the forces and/or processes that are responsible for influencing the character of the data. Because of these and other shortcomings, ecological approaches have lost favor among some academics in disciplines in which such approaches have traditionally been used. Nevertheless, we contend that such models are useful as long as their shortcomings are acknowledged. Since our approach to black victimization is placed within a territorial context, the ecological approach, even with its shortcomings, is considered appropriate. Nevertheless, some attention will be devoted to individual-level treatment of risk in contradistinction to our primary emphasis on the use of aggregate level data in assessing black homicide risk. Individual-level approaches to the study of black risk are more frequently used (see Poussaint, 1983) than are ecological approaches. Yet there is little question that the context in which blacks play out their daily lives heavily influences risk patterns, and that context is poorly understood.

Units of Analysis

We will employ neighborhood-scale units of observation in the ecological assessment of risk. The choice of unit is dictated by our interest in black victimization and the need to utilize a spatial scale that will generate the minimum number of observations suitable for our purposes. The observations will be drawn from a sample of central cities that reflect differences in historic traditions, in black settlement history, in population growth rates, in character of their physical environment (low density, high density, and so on), and in the modal character of the urban economy (service economy, manufacturing economy, and so on). Each observation, however, will be drawn from the city's black community. By proceeding in this way we can keep in the forefront those forces operating at each ecological level and those at subsequent lower levels. Thus, an effort will be made to address both structural and cultural conditions that influence risk within a territorial framework.

DATA SOURCES

A broad array of data sources had to be employed in order to conduct this type of investigation. No single data base was adequate. The absence of official homicide data that identified the victim by race at the city and neighborhood scale seriously curbed earlier ecological efforts. Moreover, national-level data describing race of victim has been available only since early in the century (Holinger and Klemen, 1982). Thus the character of available data, their ease of access, and the multiplicity of sources needed all work against the conduct of ecologically oriented, black victimization investigations.

Primary Data Sources

Among the several data sources employed, we relied heavily upon a series of Federal Bureau of Investigation (F.B.I.) reports and state and local health department records. These two data sources make information available in a recurrent fashion, allowing for a temporal assessment. They do not, however, use a standardized unit in reporting victimizations, which is the source of some bias. Cantor and Cohen (1980) report that this bias is minimal when compared to that of other reporting agencies. The observed bias stems from the tendency of the F.B.I. to report victimizations by place of occurrence (e.g., police jurisdiction) whereas health departments report victimizations by place of victim residence. Therefore, the St. Louis Police Department could report 215 victimizations in a given year, and the St. Louis Health Department may report only 210. The differences in the two reports suggest that five of the persons killed in St. Louis during that year did not reside in the city. An additional source of bias is associated with slight differences in the definition of homicide employed by the two.

Secondary Data Sources

The above two data sources were supplemented by more detailed non-demographic information from local police departments, the Offices of Clerks of Courts, State Departments of Correction, the Social Security Administration, and ethnic newspapers. In addition, a sample survey was conducted in an effort to establish contact with a small sample of the next of kin of victims and a sample of offenders (n = 179). Unlike the other data sources, the survey was confined to a single year. Fortunately, however, it describes the circumstances of the actors in the homicide tragedy near the peak year of risk, 1975, and that is the phase of the risk cycle that is of greatest interest to us. Although each of the data sources have been immensely helpful, none are without their drawbacks. Besides the weaknesses and drawbacks already discussed, there are others—variations in the level of co-operation from one police jurisdiction to another, the absence of standardized reporting techniques, and the excessive costs involved in data assembly.

Because of these problems, as well as others, ecologically oriented black victimization studies utilizing the black community as the central foci are seldom undertaken. Micro-environmental assessments of risk require data at the neighborhood level which usually may be secured only from state and local health departments. These agencies are far more likely to collect data at the census-tract level (e.g., neighborhood scale) than are other agencies. By using neighborhood-scale data, it is possible to detect and subsequently explain variations in risk that occur within the nation's larger black communities.

URBAN TARGET COMMUNITIES

A number of investigators support the contention that elevated levels of homicide risk are an outgrowth of behavioral practices supposedly associated with socialization patterns common to the rural South (Hackney, 1969). While that explanation continues to be questioned, currently elevated risk is more dramatic in selected environments in the nation's larger cities. For this reason, we have chosen to focus on a small cross section of urban places in which blacks have been present during most of the twentieth century. Their residential tenure, however, varies greatly from place to place based on regional location. Nevertheless, the urban centers chosen are among the larger in the nation, both in terms of the metropolitan areas of which they are a part and the size of the population contained within their black communities. The ghettoization process and the subsequent territorial expression of that process indicate evidence of maturity at each of our sample locations.

Sample Selection

More than one third of the nation's black population resided in fewer than twenty of the nation's metropolitan areas in 1960, the beginning of our urban quarter century. Since elevated risk, at least at that point in history, appears to have been an essentially urban phenomenon, we have chosen to focus most of our attention on only six places drawn from the twenty largest places in 1960 (see Table 1–2). Our choice has been dictated by our interest in the impact of regional outlook and stage of development on risk, age of the black community and its demographic history, character of the urban economy, and prevailing risk levels at the beginning of the period. The communities included in our study are: Atlanta, Georgia; Houston, Texas; Pittsburgh, Pennsylvania; St. Louis, Missouri; Detroit, Michigan; and Los Angeles, California.

We did not include such historically important centers of urban black culture as Washington, D.C.; New Orleans, Louisiana; Baltimore, Maryland; Philadelphia, Pennsyvlania; and New York, New York. Because we are especially interested in patterns of micro-environmental risk, these larger cities have to be excluded on practical grounds; if they were chosen, the expense associated with gathering data at the census tract level for such cities would be overwhelming. Their exclusion

TABLE 1-2

Social, Economic, and Mobility Status Indicators at Beginning of Period

SMSA	SMSA Population[a] (1960)	Black Population (Central City)[b] (1960)	Net Migration 1960-70 (Black) (thousands)	Industrial Type	Stage in Economic Development Cycle	Segregation Index[b] (1960)	Homicide Rate (per 1000,000) (Aggregate)[c] 1964-65	Homicide Rate (per 1000,000) (Aggregate)[c] 1972
The South								
Atlanta	1,022,013	186,000	+33	Service	Growth	93.6	18.4	48.8
Houston	1,214,666	215,000	+111	Service	Growth	93.7	11.3	24.2
Northeast								
Pittsburgh	2,250,040	98,000	+6	Manufacturing	Decline	84.6	5.6	11.0
North Central								
Detroit	3,399,556	432,000	+98	Manufacturing	Stable	84.5	9.6	38.9
St. Louis	2,002,609	214,000	−1	Manufacturing	Decline	90.5	17.0	34.2
The West								
Los Angeles	6,129,683	335,000	+120	Manufacturing	Growth	81.8	8.4	16.6

Sources: [a]The Social and Economic Status of Negroes in the United States, 1970, Current Population Report, Series P-23, No. 38, U.S. Government Printing Office, Washington, DC, 1971.
[b]Taeuber, Karl E. and Taeuber, Alma F., Negroes in Cities, Aldine, Chicago, 1965.
[c]Barnett, Arnold; Kleiman, Daniel J. and Larson, Richard C., On Urban Homicide: A Statistical Analysis, March 1974, Operations Research Center, Massachusetts Institute of Technology, Cambridge, MA.

should have little influence on the conclusions we reach. Nevertheless, we will be mindful of the pattern of risk that prevails in these more classical ghetto centers.

Sample Referent

We have chosen the Harlem community as a referent for judging change in our sample cities. It appears that the recent upturn in risk got under way in New York City earlier than elsewhere. Nowhere was this early upturn more apparent than in an aging Harlem community. Clark (1965), viewing the Harlem situation during the early 1960s, explained elevated risk in the following way: 1) a tendency for victims of oppression to turn their aggression inward; 2) increased social abrasiveness stemming from conditions of high density; and 3) the absence of external control (e.g., poor police protection). Perhaps more notable are the observations made by Swersey (1981), who earlier detected a change in the structure of Harlem victimization. He presented evidence that showed a move from the more traditional structure of victimization to the less traditional. Early on, these structural changes received only weak and indirect attention by most scholars who had an interest in homicide. Nonetheless, it is now beginning to appear that interest in this aspect of risk is growing and, consequently, our understanding of risk has been enhanced. Moreover, it is especially evident that if we are to gain greater insight into changing patterns of risk in the larger ghetto clusters, more attention will need to be devoted to changes in the structure of victimization. The following observations appear to bear indirectly on aspects of both structure and risk (Boessel, 1970:268):

> The Harlem Youth represents a longer adjustment to the urban North, and exhibits more of the sophistication, frustration, and aggressiveness that emerged from contact with a freer environment which fails to provide chances to use that freer environment in a constructive way.

THE TARGET COMMUNITIES AND THE NATIONAL ECONOMY

The position of our sample cities in the national economy at the beginning of the urban quarter century and the changes that they have undergone in the years that followed establishes the macro context for the upturn in homicide risk. Although the peak risk period was delayed by almost a decade, there was an acceleration of the process during the latter years of the 1960s. A selected number of benchmarks were identified previously (see Table 1-2) that provide some insight into the operation of a diverse set of forces, varying by position in the ecological hierarchy, which are believed to have set the stage for the accelerration in homicide rates.

The state of the urban economy, the direction and level of functioning is thought by some to have prompted an upturn in aversive events, including lethal violence (Turner et al., 1981). The items selected for inclusion in Table 1-2 allow us to summarize where our sample communities were in the developmental hierarchy in 1960. These communities were all in metropolitan areas with populations of more than a million persons. Because of their size and position in the national economy, they were generally identified as the primary urban nodes that provided a broad range of employment opportunities in their respective regions. The Los Angeles metropolitan area, because of its greater size, is the only community in our sample to be identified as one of the nation's four national urban centers. Only Detroit and Pittsburgh at the earlier date could be described as more specialized production centers in which manufacturing activity outdistanced all others as a provider of employment. We have chosen a sample of places that had significant roles in the national economy and that followed varying economic pathways during the next twenty-five years.

Manufacturing Activity in the Sample Cities

Manufacturing activity represented a major source of employment in cities that varied in size and diversity. In two places it constituted the primary source of employment, but in our two southern labor market areas the importance of manufacturing was markedly smaller than at non-southern locations. The declining fortunes of manufacturing, at least in the American manufacturing belt, resulted in our identifying our non-southern metropolitan economies as stable or declining in the base year while economic growth was confined to the southern and western locations in our sample.

It should be reiterated at this point, however, that it was the promise of employment in durable goods manufacturing (i.e., steel, transportation equipment, and so on) that prompted black migration from the South in the prior two decades. Yet, declining opportunity in this economic sector was already evident to a growing number of blacks, as the volume of net migration to St. Louis and Pittsburgh in the following decade attests. When one considers that each of these labor markets constituted substantial targets of black migration during the 50s, the slowing of that migration and a reversal of that trend in at least one other city signaled that major change was under way.

A Note on Residential Segregation and Black Well-Being

One final point requiring emphasis is the intensity of residential segregation existing in each of our sample locations at the earlier date. The summary measures of segregation appearing in Table 1–2 are an indication of the prevailing level of racial isolation. Thus, large ghetto communities were present in each of the above locations in 1960, ranging in size from slightly fewer than 100,000 persons in Pittsburgh to just under 500,000 in Detroit. Moreover, the intensity of segregation varied only slightly as a function of regional location. The latter observation aside, we anticipate changes in the speed and direction of urban economic growth in the metropolitan areas in which our target communities exist to have a pervasive impact upon the quality of life available to the black population at each site. The direction of economic growth will be expected to influence the size of the poverty population within these compressed residential enclaves, as well as existing levels of inequality. Furthermore, it is anticipated that the severity of economic dislocation will be greatest in those communities in which the rate of ghetto expansion exceeds the rate of economic growth, revealing, in effect, what happens when the "promised land" no longer offers promise.

POST-1960 CHANGES IN THE URBAN ECONOMY: IS THERE A DIRECT ASSOCIATION WITH THE UPTURN IN HOMICIDE RISK?

The changing character of the urban economy in the post-1960s era seems to have set the stage, at least in a very general way, for the upturn in risk of homicide victimization. The upturn is generally thought to have gotten under way by mid-decade and to have peaked barely ten years later. Although no segment of the American public was immune from the rising risk of victimization, the nation's larger black communities were hardest hit (Block and Zimring, 1973; Block, 1976; Rushforth et al., 1977). Likewise, these communities suffered most from the suburbanization of jobs, especially manufacturing jobs, and the subsequent regional shift that eventually characterized selected segments of manufacturing employment (Sternlieb and Hughes, 1977; Estall, 1980). These and other overarching macroscale forces, however, are viewed in a variety of ways in terms of their linkage to the problem of risk escalation.

Differences in Perspective on Causes for the Upturn

The level of support assigned to the linkage between the state of the urban economy and rising homicide risk seems to be based on whether one's approach to the problem is criminological or non-criminological. We are aware that this represents an overly simplistic assumption, but it does identify, in a general way, a set of existing biases that are thought to influence one's view of reality. This view is further influenced by who is chosen as the primary focus of record—the victim or the offender. To highlight this, we will draw upon the views and/or orientations of a restricted set of researchers whose work is longitudinal rather than cross-sectional in nature.

Murray (1984:116), for instance, assumed the following posture: "The focus of our interest in the 1960s was not the crime but the criminal and the victim. Who was behind the sudden rise? Who was hurt?" Murray's position illustrated, in part, the weakness of part of our generalizing assumption, yet it sustains another part. His was an individual level assessment; thus he initiated his search for the answer in individual offender behavior devoid of the context in which this behavior occurred. Of the black contribution to rising homicide risk levels and crime in general, he stated, "There is reason to believe that, if anything, the increase in black criminal activity is considerably understated by the official data" (Murray, 1984:117). The implication of this statement suggested a lessening of social control in the nation's black communities during this period, a situation that Murray attributes to the passage of a series of liberal policies that were ill advised. Neither the validity of Murray's previous statement nor the implication that flow from it are being questioned; we are simply interested in illustrating a common approach to the problem.

The orientation employed by Murray has become increasingly popular over the last several years. Wilson and Herrnstein (1985), too, suggest that individual personality attributes are more important contributors to escalating crime rates than are external factors. According to Wilson (1985) this orientation has dominated social science treatment of the social dislocations occurring in the nation's larger black communities for more than a decade. Obviously, this approach is *not* the one to which we subscribe.

Brenner and Swank (1986), on the other hand, initiated the search for cyclical variation in aggregate homicide risk levels, including the period of interest, by focusing on business cycle behavior. They suggested that since the 1950s, homicide, as well as other crime, "increased as a result of recession and occasionally, even more strongly, as a result of specific factors historically associated with economic growth" (p. 85).

The previous discussion suggests that explanations for rising risk are likely to be highly dependent upon where one looks for answers, at least in an ecological sense. The failure to address the problem in this way casts doubt on our ability to directly intervene in creating order out of chaos. Undoubtedly, one could assume the posture that most problems of this sort tend to correct themselves over time. But that position fails to address the grief, hardship, and anxiety that is pervasive in households having had contact with such events. Likewise, it fails to address the concerns of those households situated in high-risk environments where the perceived threat of victimization is continually present (Rainwater, 1966). Our own position, however, tends to mirror that of Fusfeld and Bates (1984) who state that "signs of breakdown in the social fabric of low income urban black communities, although poorly understood, are undoubtedly exacerbated by labor market problems" (p. 113). Moreover, we contend that this condition is directly related to changing risk levels.

The Primary Targets of Risk Escalation

Nowhere was the social dislocation more evident than in the soaring levels of risk escalation observed in large ghetto communities across the nation, especially those located in the core of the American manufacturing belt. The upturn was first evidenced in these locations and also was slower to abate there. Table 1–2 illustrates that among our sample cities, risk doubled in most, almost tripled in Atlanta, and nearly quadrupled in Detroit in less than a decade. The aggregate changes in risk shown in the table demonstrate substantial variation in risk levels during the base period and similar variations after escalation was well under way. The observed variations in level of risk suggest differences in the extent to which blacks and/or other poor people were present in the population. Thus the aggregate data employed here partially disguise the changes that were taking place in central-city ghettos.

By employing data partitioned by the race of the victim, an effort will be made to address more directly changing patterns of risk in central-city black communities. It should be noted, however, that the quality of data was poor during the early years of the interval, but greatly improved during the latter years. Our treatment of this phenomenon will extend over the full quarter century (1960 to 1985), and the intensity of treatment will vary by five-year intervals. Our least intensive treatment will involve the five years before 1970 and after 1980.

MAJOR TOPICAL TREATMENTS

In order to achieve the twin goals of bringing to the reader's attention the importance of homicide as a primary cause of death among blacks in the nation's larger cities and to provide explanations for changes in risk levels in those communities, the book is organized in the following manner. Chapter 2 addresses the importance of culture, frequently asserted to represent an important intervening variable, in interactions leading to death. Cultural treatments have become commonplace in explanations of variations in risk, especially on a regional level; culture is viewed as a macroscale force that impacts risk by serving as a catalyst when other pertinent objective criteria are controlled for. Nevetheless, the influence of culture is difficult to measure, especially at a microenvironmental level (see Loftin and Hill, 1974; Baron and Straus, 1988).

The contribution of structural characteristics on risk is addressed in chapter 3. Structural characteristics are assessed through the development of a stress model. This treatment combines both analytical and descriptive efforts to demonstrate the impact of selected socioeconomic environmental attributes on risk. The scale is confined to the microenvironment within our individual sample cities. The choice of environmental scale is based on the need to be able to address questions of risk variation within black communities. If variations in risk are identified, are they persistent over time? Are there variations in patterns of risk unique to individual places? Can we generalize that risk varies, internally, in a rather fixed way? This is the area least understood, and the one to which we have devoted most of our effort. Nevertheless, we are fully aware that this simply represents one intermediate layer between individuals and the larger society of which they are a part. Yet this, as well as other layers, is often viewed in isolation, leading in some instances to unwarranted conclusions. To augment our understanding of microenvironmental influences on risk, we focus intense attention on high-risk environments as behavior settings.

Chapters 4 and 5 are devoted to the role of gender on risk. Differences in the propensity of individuals to engage in risk-taking behavior based on gender are well documented (Daly and Wilson, 1988; Wilson and Herrnstein, 1985). During the current period of risk escalation, the risk gap based on gender seems to have widened as risk among females increased more slowly and declined more rapidly than among males. On the other hand, young black males experienced levels of propagated risk not previously observed. Gibbs (1985), after reviewing a number of indicators of well being describing the situation of young black men, has labeled that population "an endangered species." What becomes evident over this period in terms of gender based risk behavior is the increasing role of age on the behavior influencing the likelihood of becoming a victim.

Chapter 6 shifts attention from aggregates and subaggregates to individuals. Unfortunately, only limited attention has been devoted to the individual in this investigation as an outgrowth of our strong ecological orientation. Yet we are aware of the serious shortcomings of investigations in which one generalizes to the level of the individual based on results derived from areal data. In order to minimize that possiblity, we have chosen to examine a small number of behavioral traits and/or life-styles that abet individual risk. Because our individual observations are small in number and are drawn from only three of our sample locations, we are cautious in attempting to generalize our findings.

Contact with a sample of offenders and the next of kin of victims was made possible through a grant from the National Institute of Mental Health. Those contacts were initiated in 1978 but involved homicide incidents occurring in 1975. Thus the information derived from interviews with offenders or family members of victims reflect the status of those persons near the peak period of victimization in large American cities. The number of persons willing to speak to us was small (n = 179), but the insight gained from these contacts was substantial. Although our contact with individual members of the sample was limited to a single meeting, we were able to monitor the behavior of those persons who had additional contact with the criminal justice system. Moreover, although we are strong supporters of a hierarchical perspective as a mechanism for gaining greater insight into changing levels of risk, we fully recognize that the bottom line must be based on altering individual-level behavior (see Poussaint, 1983).

In chapter 7 we address, in an abbreviated fashion, the general issue of deterrence. Our treatment focuses attention on only two dimensions—the availability of firearms and sentencing patterns. In this instance, we draw heavily upon the experiences of those individuals in our core city sample who were involved in fatal confrontations. We highlight differences observed across jurisdictions, especially as they relate to age and gender.

Finally, in chapter 8 we look backward and forward in an effort to accurately depict the future trajectory of lethal violence in the nation's larger black communities. To be sure, the picture has become more complex over time, but if we fail to get a grip on the problems that beset a growing share of blacks in the nation's larger cities, sections of those cities will become wastelands, as some already have, in which life is cheap and victimization targets become less predictable. It is in this chapter that we address the difficult question of what needs to be done if a segment of the nation's population is not to face a new century in which lethal violence will continue to play a critical influence on the number of life years lost.

Culture and Homicide Risk: The Black Experience

INTRODUCTION

The link between homicide risk and American culture is broadly acknowledged by scholars within a multiplicity of disciplines. Not all, however, agree on the relationship's level of importance, how it operates to influence risk, or how it might best be operationalized. Moreover, "culture" generally is viewed as a highly subjective phenomenon that indirectly rather than directly influences risk. Its influence is assumed to be more pervasive among the poor and the lower classes generally than among other classes; indeed, this culture is most often suggested as a contributor to the observed high levels of risk among black Americans. In this chapter, we will pursue a number of points, but our attention will be focused specifically on demonstrating the connection between American culture, the black subculture, and their respective associations with elements of violence. Subscribers to a similar perspective, Block (1981:747) summed up the situation by stating "A subculture of violence thus exists within the culture of violence." It is important that we try to understand the depth of the phenomenon if we are to make sense out of the association between culture and risk.

Ecologically oriented homicide investigations, employing some measure of association between risk and culture, have been conducted at a variety of spatial scales. These investigations generally indicate that the influence of culture on risk exists, but the influence varies depending on the level of observation: regional, urban (central city and/or metropolitan area), or subcommunity. The subcommunity has received the most attention in analysis of aspects of black risk (see Curtis, 1975). Yet regardless of the level chosen, the extent to which blacks are present in the population is consistently used as an indirect measure of the risk/culture association (see Sampson, 1986).

Many investigators tend to use this indicator as a standard way of measuring the influence of the subculture of violence on risk. A growing number of investigators, however, have questioned the practice. For instance, Erlanger (1976) expresses strong reservations regarding the validity of both the concept as well as surrogates employed to measure the concept. He utilizes survey data to demonstrate the questionable validity of the assumption that either southern black or white men place greater value on fighting than do men residing in the North. The primary point that emerges from Erlanger's dissent is best expressed in a comment he made in reference to Mexican-American males. He stated, "Chicano culture places a strong emphasis on values such as courage and dignity for males, but how these values are manifested in behavior depends heavily on the broader context in which people function" (Erlanger, 1976:246). We, too, contend that an examination of the spatial-temporal context is important to grasp more fully the role of culture on the propensity for violence among blacks.

ECOLOGICAL SCALE AND SUPPORT FOR THE USE OF VIOLENCE

Before addressing the more complex contributors to incidents of lethal violence, an effort will be made to outline the general context within which aspects of black violence are rooted. In keeping with our emphasis on the role of an ecological hierarchy on the risk-culture linkage, the following discussion will be cast within a place-based framework. Regardless of which of the varied definitions of culture one might choose, expressions of culture may differ in terms of the unit selected for examination. With that in mind we will now proceed to establish a general outline to assist us in understanding the culture, race, place, risk connection. If a black subculture of violence in fact exists, it should be best understood within this framework, rather than in isolation.

The Core Culture, Violence, and Scale

There is general consensus that a national core culture exists in the United States (Spindler, 1977; Ball-Rokeach, 1973) that varies across regions. The variations manifest themselves in differential emphases placed upon one set of core values rather than another set. From a violence perspective, however, it can be demonstrated that there exists a scale effect showing a differential commitment to the use of violence under a given set of constraints based on the scale of the observational unit (e.g., region). The constraints in this instance are associated with the legitimation of violence to uphold, maintain, or protect some valued resource. Thus an attack or threat imposed upon one set of core values or another might legitimately be thwarted through the use of violence.

At the national level, we defend ourselves against the prospect of foreign sovereigns who may wish to impose an alternative value system upon our populace, such as communism. In this instance, it is made clear that any external threat to individual liberty will be countered by the use of force. At the regional level, however, the threat may be viewed as internal. Given the unique economic and social histories of the nation's regions and the traditions that evolved out of their peculiar circumstances, the strength of commitment to the use of violence and the circumstances under which it is legitimated likely will vary from region to region. The South, for instance, is generally said to support a regional culture of violence (Hackney, 1969; Gastil, 1971; Reed, 1972), a culture that places great emphasis on the maintenance of a valued set of traditions, such as honor and white supremacy. Thus the Ku Klux Klan, as well as other paramilitary groups, have emerged over time in an effort to uphold those traditions. Although this example was not as valid in 1985 as in 1925, remnants of the agrarian values supportive of the use of violence continue to exist in the South.

Macroscale support for the use of violence to protect valued resources has not been lost on those operating essentially within a micro-environmental context. Although there is general agreement that culture evolves and spreads from a macroenvironmental base, its practitioners are individuals who largely function outside of a formal organizational base. Thus the legitimation of violence as a valued practice—in governing family relations (e.g., physical punishment of children) and in defense of individual honor (e.g., a fighting tradition)—varies greatly in terms of accepted practice from place to place. Nevertheless, a commitment to the use of violence manifests itself in different ways depending upon where the threat occurs within the ecological hierarchy. Moreover, intensity of support is conditional upon the individual's position in the social order. For example, a high-status southern white may be a strong supporter of the use of violence in defense of external threats to national security while holding the fighting tradition in disdain. On the other hand, a low-status white southerner might be more likely to support the use of violence at both a macro and microenvironmental scale. These examples demonstrate the complexity of the issue while drawing attention to the association between environmental scale and risk.

The Ecological Hierarchy and the Locus of Support for Black Violence

How does one best articulate the position of blacks along the risk-culture continuum, at least in terms of an ecological hierarchy? Given that, until recently, most of the nation's blacks had been socialized in the South, where it would appear that both their commitment to the use of violence and the circumstances under which its use might be considered appropriate were outgrowths of regional socialization practices. The macroscale cultural perspective of the southern region might best explain the general acceptance of the use of violence as a conflict resolution strategy. But the caste system that, until recently, prevailed in the region did much to establish the grounds under which violence constituted an appropriate response and to identify as well the appropriate objects of that response.

It is this situation from which Curtis (1975) derives his views supportive of the existence of a black subculture of violence, a point we will address in more detail later in this chapter. The compressed social world of blacks within a southern caste system gave them, even as free persons, a limited range of opportunity. But within that system a value hierarchy evolved that guided conduct and defined appropriate behavior both within and outside the black community. The violence that occurred within those communities, both within and outside of the South, is our interest.

Urbanization and Cultural Change

American culture has changed slowly in response to growing secular influence and corresponding decline in spiritual influence. This turn of events is in large measure associated with the speed of urbanization and its subsequent dominance as the principal environment of American residence. Within large urban environments, many traditions and practices that characterized life in rural America were gradually weakened and eventually displaced by cultural practices and styles more reflective of life in the new setting (see Figure 2–1). Yet Goldfield (1982) has suggested that southern population centers were slower to adopt urban values and styles than places outside the region. He contended that rural traditions continued to be very much in evidence in southern cities throughout the decade of the '60s. Moreover, when one considers that the South did not acquire an urban majority before 1950 and that, even then, there was continuing contact between the rural countryside and the city, it is little wonder that traditional values gave way much more slowly to emerging ones. This factor, we contend, did much to slow the escalation of homicide risk in the region during

FIGURE 2-1

A Temporal-Spatial Schema of White/Black Culture Contact

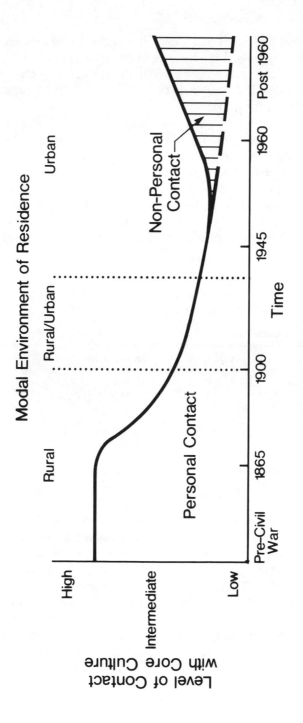

Modal Environment of Residence

the most recent upsurg in risk. Not only were rates of increase slower in the South generally, but changes in the structure of victimization were slower to take place as well. We think the latter phenomenon best reflects cultural changes in association with the propensity to engage in acts leading to death.

By the beginning of the urban quarter century (1960), northern urban centers differed from leading southern ones, both in their position in the nation's economy and in their position on the cultural continuum. Secular values had advanced more rapidly, and levels of violent behavior had reached new heights. Blacks outside of the South were active participants in the new round of violent acts leading northern black communities to reach levels of risk that had earlier been associated only with blacks in southern urban centers (see Table 2–1).

TABLE 2–1

Regional Comparisons of Black Homicide
Rates in a Selected Set of Urban Places: 1980

Southern Cities	Homicide Rate per 100,000	Nonsouthern Cities	Homicide Rate per 100,000
Birmingham, AL	40	Newark, NJ	66
Dallas, TX	55	Oakland, CA	58
Richmond, VA	39	Gary, IN	70
Nashville, TN	49	Cleveland, OH	77
Jackson, MS	35	Boston MA	32

Source: Computed by authors from FBI Supplementary Monthly Homicide
       Reports.

In light of these observations, the question that logically emerges is this: were the observed changes basically related to evolving cultural differences between blacks socialized outside of a formal caste system in the more secular North and those socialized in the more traditional context of the South? If the answer is affirmative, we should expect the evolving cultural differences to manifest themselves more readily in the structure of victimization than in the level of homicide risk per se. We will examine this thesis in some detail, employing data from our sample cities, later in this chapter. But before doing this, several reigning paradigms that address questions of risk, culture, and race will be examined more closely. Likewise, we will make an effort to demonstrate, in a cursory way, how a black subculture evolved that incorporated in its structure a set of conditions under which a violent response was considered appropriate. That is, we will take the long view and move forward to the present.

Black Homicide Risk and Culture of Violence Paradigms

The most often cited cultural explanations in support of the use of assaultive violence leading to lethal outcomes are those proposed by Wolfgang and Ferracuti (1967) and Gastil (1971). The former thesis has been labeled the "subculture of violence"; the latter is described most as the "regional culture of violence" thesis. Each is firmly grounded in culture of poverty theory. Gastil (1973), however, emphasized the importance of learned traditions in combination with a biosocial response to one's position at the bottom of the status hierarchy. Wolfgang and Ferracuti (1967) emphasized the role of the internalization of social norms of violence and the sanctioning of violent behavior by one's peers; they were not insensitive to the role of tradition.

The principal architects of cultural paradigms tend to emphasize that, in many instances, observed violence demonstrates an acting out by those considered to be carriers of a ghetto tradition. Beyond the similarities associated with these often-cited paradigms, however, it is evident that they tend to emphasize different strands of the culture package, such as individual vs. group, urban vs. rural, and north vs. south. An effort will be made to integrate these various strands into our ecological hierarchy. We will emphasize the effect of temporal change on the cultural strands because we recognize that its omission has been one of the major shortcomings of the previous paradigms.

In fairness to Gastil, his concept of culture demonstrates a temporal base, but it seems he has projected it forward in time without any apparent attempt to account for changes in the intensity of its elements. Wolfgang and Ferracuti, on the other hand, seem to have arrived at their position based almost entirely on cross-sectional observations. Neither, however, viewed the elevation of violence among blacks in the population as anything other than an example of the impact of culture on the tendency to respond to specific situations in previously learned and sanctioned ways.

In Gastil's view, the behavior of blacks was disproportionately a product of a regional culture of violence. Wolfgang and Ferracuti viewed black behavior as a product of the ghetto tradition that tends to sanction violence under prescribed circumstances. Blacks were more or less viewed as passive actors in subcultures that they fashioned or in a regional culture that heightened their vulnerability to involvement in situations requiring a violent solution. Neither, it seems, directly addressed the issue of the existence of a unique black subculture or the position of blacks vis-á-vis changes in the nation's core culture.

THE ROLE OF CULTURE ON THE BLACK PROPENSITY FOR VIOLENCE

To date there have been limited efforts to demonstrate the specific impact of culture on the propensity of blacks to engage in acts of violence. The work of Curtis (1975), however, represents one such effort. Curtis has done much to advance our understanding of the interaction between race and culture that leads to heightened levels of violent behavior. His work is an extension of that of Wolfgang and Ferracuti but he moved beyond the boundaries of that model to incorporate aspects of the approach proposed by Gastil. Curtis, unlike his predecessors, directly addressed a set of issues thought responsible for the elevated incidence of violence in urban black communities. By combining these two approaches, although focusing on a single population group, a clearer understanding of the problem is anticipated. Although his effort does advance our understanding of the problem, like previous research, it was grounded in the subculture of poverty paradigm, a perspective that has been criticized since it originated. Wilson (1987), a noted black scholar, rejected the culture of poverty position outright as unsuitable for describing the present plight of urban blacks.

The conceptual model, as defined by Curtis, although paying attention to the temporal dimension, fails to provide a meaningful distinction between the black poverty subculture and the violent contraculture, other than to inform us that it is possible for blacks to spend varying amounts of time in at least three cultural spheres. Curtis did, however, suggest that lower-status, blacks males who are attracted to the life of the streets are highly likely to adopt one or more ghetto traditions that intensify the likelihood of their involvement in violent interactions. But he failed to address, in other than a general way, why individuals adopt such lifestyles other than to state that they probably are following the path chosen by significant others.

On a more positive note, Curtis offered a schematic structure that addresses in a general fashion the contribution of both external and internal factors on the position of individual blacks in what he labeled "multidimensional value space." Thus his is the clearest statement yet developed on the interaction of race, culture, and violence in an urban setting. Nevertheless, although that treatment is more conceptually exhaustive than earlier works, the ecological layers of culture were not examined in other than a cursory fashion.

The Search for an Alternative Paradigm

The role of race, class, and culture are obvious contributors to situations in which lethal violence is an elicited response. But the question of where to place the emphasis is not easily answered. One approach to the problem begins with the mega-culture and proceeds slowly down the cultural continuum to highlight the effect of physical scale as well as position in the social order on the propensity for violence. Although such an approach represents the direction we would prefer to follow under optimal conditions, it is extremely time consuming. Needless to say, we will only be able to discuss in broad outline form the role of the suggested configuration on homicide risk. Thus some of the criticisms noted about previous approaches are also likely to be evident in the approach we have chosen to pursue.

The Black Subculture: Static or Dynamic?

Black culture in the United States is primarily a product of the variety of social experiences to which segments of that population have been exposed since their arrival in the early seventeenth century. Likewise, the larger American culture has been influenced by aspects of African culture as an outgrowth of an extended period of contact (Levine, 1977). Yet the social and physical isolation of blacks and their prescribed position in the social order has led to the evolution of a set of traditions and social norms thought to deviate from those of the larger society. The material and non-material expressions that emerged from that experience have extended from generation to generation. Nevertheless, valued traditions are modified over time in response to external changes in the environment. The observed changes occur at different rates from place to place as an outgrowth of their perceived utility. Thus, to better understand the impact of these changes on risk and subsequently the structure of victimization in urban black communities, it is important that we address selected elements of change.

We noted previously that the major cultural treatments of blacks in response to elevated homicide risk tend to emphasize the particular set of traits thought to represent the group's social position, such as the subculture of poverty and/or its residential isolation—the ghetto tradition. Both of these perspectives possess some merit, but the problem is that they are static, tending to emphasize only a condition of internal isolation and social position and the subsequent social disorganization thought to evolve from that position. Investigators subscribing to the previous perspective usually have validated it with case studies in which violent behavior was observed at a single point in time. Based on these investigations, we necessarily assume that such behavior cannot be linearly projected into the future without taking into account those external forces that are known to influence them.

THE NATIONAL CORE CULTURE AND THE AMERICAN EXPERIENCE

In order to more fully comprehend the role of culture on the homicidal propensities currently evident in the nation's larger black communities, one must, at a minimum, build upon the cultural history of the group within a framework of national cultural change. If we agree that culture represents valued traditions and practices, then it is only logical to contend that these traditions and practices are weakened or strengthened in response to their role in assisting in the survival process and/or the achievement of individual or group goals. Therefore, we start with the assumption that both the national core culture and elements of black culture have undergone major alteration over time.

We further contend that the most far-reaching changes have occurred during periods of transition from one major epoch to another (see Swidler, 1986). If this represents an accurate view of reality, then we are in a position to begin to examine, at least qualitatively, the role of culture on both the observed level (i.e., rate) and structural changes (i.e., victimization patterns) in black homicide behavior, particularly during the urban quarter century (1960–1985).

The core culture evolved in America during the Colonial era, basically reflecting a transfer of English and Scotch-Irish culture to the New World and its subsequent modification as an outgrowth of the American experience. During this period, however, the American experience was not homogeneous. Even though the nation was dominated by agrarian values during its early beginnings, these values were accorded different weights from one location to another. For instance, one could observe a differential weighting of strands in the value hierarchy in subsistence farming areas that distinguished them from commercial farming areas. Thus, in the plantation South, there emerged a different value hierarchy than that prevailing in the rural Northeast (see Wyatt-Brown, 1982).

The role of values in promoting the evolution of a unique southern culture is well chronicled. This differential weighting of values provided the foundation for the emergence of observed regional differences in culture that are frequently addressed by historians, anthropologists, literary writers, and others. Prior to the end of the Colonial period, a set of regional distinctions had emerged that were based on differences in the nature of the prevailing economies and the migrant origins of those settling in specific sections of the country. These distinctions were further enhanced by the evolution of the institution of slavery and the subsequent ethnic bonding of persons sold into slavery, persons whose origins were vested in a number of distinct African groups (Stuckey, 1987). The unique world associated with regional distinctions did much to alter the value rankings within the common core culture.

SOUTHERN REGIONAL CULTURE AND THE BLACK SUBCULTURE

To better understand the value system that has come to be identified as the black subculture, one must pay attention to the evolution of southern culture. Because the black subculture reflects long and continuing contact with the economic and social development of the southern region, a valid assessment of the black subculture, at least prior to 1940, could not be derived without addressing the existing relationship between the two. The extent to which African values continued to rank high among the emerging value mix cannot be specified, although it is evident that selected African traditions (e.g., dance, music, and so on) have been retained and incorporated into southern regional culture (Joyner, 1983) and into the national culture (Levine, 1977) as well.

The Question of Cultural Reciprocity

The development and institutionalization of the slave system in the American South did much to influence the subsequent world view of both those who were enslaved and those who directly and indirectly benefited from the system. Thus, our primary contention is that the system of values and subsequent behavioral repertoire that came to be identified as the black subculture stemmed in large measure from the constrained position of blacks in the southern social order— a factor considered by some to represent a key element in the evolution of a distinctive southern culture (Blassingame, 1972).

In the plantation South, where slavery reached its apex, a core culture evolved that tended to place undue emphasis on honor, gentility, and individualism (Cash, 1941; Franklin, 1956; Wyatt-Brown, 1982). Out of an inordinate adherence to these values, and the lifestyles they promoted, come support for the quick resort to violence as a means of resolving any conflict emanating from a perceived ethical breach. Not only was there a quick resort to violence in defense against the prospect of the loss of self-esteem, but violence also was employed as a means of regulating slave behavior in both a labor and social context.

An exaggerated sense of honor appeared to underlie most acts of white violence, and the fighting tradition was known to pervade the total social spectrum, occurring commonly among both the planter class and the yeoman backcountry dirt farmer. The primary distinguishing elements among combatants were the weapons used and the setting in which combat occurred. Throughout the antebellum period the up-country population was most likely to engage in what was described as "rough and tumble" combat, where eye-gouging and other crude tactics were commonplace (Gorn, 1983). The gentry chose to abandon the "rough and tumble" in favor of dueling, a form of combat that reflected their aristocratic position in southern social life. The questions that remain unanswered, however, are to what extent the prevalence of a fighting tradition among white southerners carried over to the slave population and to what extent that tradition was retained into the late twentieth century among southern and non-southern blacks in an urban context.

BLACK SUBCULTURAL DEVELOPMENT:
A REGIONAL EVOLUTIONARY PERSPECTIVE

The association between the black subculture and levels of lethal violence began to receive heightened attention during the early twentieth century. As blacks continued to abandon the countryside in favor of southern cities and towns, additional subcultural strands began to emerge. What became clear early, however, was evidence of exaggerated levels of lethal violence in the South's larger urban places (Barnhart, 1932). Obviously one sector of the urban black population found selected secular values more attractive than values admonishing persons to ignore the vices of city life. Yet the adoption of selected urban lifestyles placed individuals at a heightened exposure to risk. Barnhart (1932) reports that the black homicide rate in Birmingham, Alabama, in 1910 was 107 homicides per 100,000 blacks. Although this unusually high level prevailed in one of the South's newest urban industrial centers, elevated risk was demonstrated to exist in most lower-south urban places prior to 1930 (Brearly, 1932).

Direct evidence of elevated black homicide rates, at all ecological scales, within the southern region is growing and is providing support for the belief that risk was tied to selected aspects of the black variant of southern regional culture. Additional support for this position grew out of evidence that blacks residing in the Northeast, who were natives

of the region, experienced levels of risk much lower than those occurring among southern blacks. But the most obvious distinguishing
feature of risk was the extreme level it had reached in lower-South cities
and in those cities outside of the region that had been primary targets
of black migration after 1910.

Extreme variations in risk levels could be observed among
southern and non-southern cities alike during the first half of the
decade of the 1920s (see Table 2-2). Table 2-2 not only illustrates variations in risk among places, but when compared with Table 2-1, it offers a picture of the level of violence occurring in the same set of urban places at points in time separated by more than two generations.
What generally seems to have occurred is an elevation in risk among
non-southern cities and a depression in risk among southern places.
On the basis of the information displayed in Tables 2-1 and 2-2, one
may conclude that the observed outcome can be explained largely by
the continuing migration of blacks from high-risk environments in the
South to lower-risk environments outside the South. The subsequent
diffusion of values that sanctioned the use of violence under prescribed
conditions accompanied the migration process. Yet we think the situation is far more complicated, at least in terms of the cultural connection (for example, see Fig. 2-1).

TABLE 2-2

Selected Urban-Regional Differences in Black Homicide Levels: 1920/1925

Southern Cities	Homicide Rate per 100,000	Nonsouthern Cities	Homicide Rate per 100,000
Birmingham, AL	104	Newark, NJ	36
Dallas, TX	99	San Francisco, CA	18
Richmond, VA	28	Indianapolis, IN	57
Nashville, TN	46	Cleveland, OH	101
Jackson, MS	113	Boston MA	21

Source: Brearly, H. C. *Homicide in the United States*. Chapel Hill, NC: The
      University of North Carolina, 1932.

Subcultural Development in the Urban South

The frustration and the disappointment that accompanied black
reconstruction status, as well as other problems associated with share-
tenancy arrangements, led many blacks to abandon rural areas in favor
of life in the towns and cities of the South (Henri, 1975). Rural aban-

donment took place slowly; 90 percent of the region's black population continued to reside in rural environments for more than a generation after the freeing of the slaves. Thus it is only logical to assume that many of the values originating within the context of slavery persisted with similar intensity well into the next century. Urbanization, however, even though occurring slowly, made it possible for blacks to engage in private behaviors removed from the constant surveillance of white observers.

The semi-isolation that resulted from movement to the city facilitated an increase in emphasis on an exciting life and the growth of life-styles associated with that emphasis. Much of the behavior associated with acts of lethality during this period grew out of situations involving excessive alcohol consumption, participation in games of chance, and indiscreet sexual conduct. City life tended to abet a rise in risk of victimization, even before southern cities became very populous places. Hoffman (1923), describing the situation prevailing in Memphis, the city for which the black victimization rate was described as the highest in the South in 1920, was careful to point out that blacks seldom committed homicide that could be described as felony-related.

It was under these conditions that impulse control seemed to wane. But more importantly the consistent reinforcement of the appropriateness of the resort to violence as a means of resolving intergroup, as well as interpersonal, conflict was a paramount element in elevating the risk of death. The core values of the group dictated who the victims would most likely be, at least in terms of their relationship to their assailant. A challenge to one's honor, a denial of self-esteem, or the possibility of heightened social recognition could serve as a catalyst propelling individuals into mortal conflict. Thus the traditional structure of homicide victimization among blacks in the early twentieth century was overwhelmingly expressive. Moreover, the motivation leading individuals to engage in lethal acts was most often undergirded by emotional discord and/or anger.

The Movement North

By the end of the first decade of the twentieth century, it was thought that most blacks had made the necessary adjustments to the new modified caste system that had been developed in the South. Not all, however, were eager to adapt to a modified system of oppression. When beckoned to join others in search of improved economic opportunity, they did so by becoming part of migration streams leading north to such urban centers as Philadelphia, Pittsburgh, St. Louis, New

York, Chicago, and Detroit. The "great migration" that began in 1914–1917 set the stage for further modification of the black subculture. The emerging modifications that were most pronounced reflected contact with a diversity of European subcultures with value systems differing in many ways from those of white southerners. The northern industrial economy placed a different set of demands upon black workers and meted out a different set of rewards. However, black migrants most likely differed from non-migrants in their world view.

Movement to northern urban centers, like the earlier movement to southern cities, required major adjustments. For the first time blacks were in direct competition with whites for jobs, although mechanisms would soon be introducted that would favor whites in the competitive struggle (Lieberson, 1980, Harris, 1982). The "promised land" frequently offered less than was anticipated, leading some disaffected migrants to return to the region of origin. Those who remained, however, went about the business of attempting to ascertain what part of their previously acquired cultural repertoire would sustain them in the new environment and what new tools were needed to make a satisfactory adjustment to a new set of circumstances.

The Black Subculture in a Northern Context

Life in the urban North seemed to promote greater diversity within the population than had been the case in the rural South. The rise of a working-class population fostered the emergence of concerns that transcended mere survival and focused increasing attention on the attainment of a comfortable life. Emphasis on equality as a central value also increased. Yet, at the same time there was evidence of growing distrust, increasing hostility, and a greater willingness to exploit one another, especially among the poor, than had been the case in the previous environment. This might simply reflect a population-size effect; within a context of massive ghetto development there occurs a concentration of persons willing to engage in previously unsanctioned behaviors. Nevertheless, a continuous flow of migrants from the South, interrupted only by the depression of the 1930s, enabled the northern variant of the subculture to retain a continuous link with its source region.

By 1960, two generations of blacks had grown up in a set of northern industrial centers and their contact with the black core culture had undergone a substantial weakening. A number of the elements of the southern black subculture that interregional migrants had brought with them had undergone a major transformation. Reference to a unified black subculture probably was no longer valid. We are suggesting that there came a time when a threshold population, removed from direct contact with an original core, independently developed a set of modified world views in concert with other subcultures. The evolution of a variant strain of the original black subculture is believed to have subsequently had an impact on the structure of homicide victimization. Therefore, we anticipate, as a result of the maturation of the northern black subculture, an alteration in the risk-violence association. The greater speed with which blacks in the North adopted new values and engaged in a more diverse set of lifestyles led to an expansion of the circumstances under which violence became more commonplace, although the issue of legitimation appears unresolved at this point.

Value Shifts and Cultural Roots of Violence During the Urban Quarter Century

In chapter 1 we suggested that the urban quarter century was ushered in by cumulative changes that occurred in the national economy. But as we have attempted to demonstrate in the previous pages, such changes seldom occur in the economy without a subsequent alteration in one's system of values and, as a consquence, one's introduction to new ways of doing things. Life-style modifications generally follow observed shifts in national values. The urban quarter century wrought more far-reaching changes in the national culture than has any similar period in American history. From the perspective of a culture/violence nexus the most significant change is associated with an intense emphasis on individual gratification and waning support for communal well-being. Thus the national core culture tends to place undue emphasis on instrumental actions and the logical-rational behavior that serves as the bases for such action.

The black subculture, however, is overwhelmingly expressive in its orientation. Nevertheless, subcultural changes are responsive to changes in the national core culture, and during the period under investigation, instrumental behavior has taken on added importance within a black cultural context. The speed of adoption of instrumentally oriented values appears to have occurred more rapidly in nonsouthern urban areas, although southern urban areas have not been immune to their influence. The question of how these changes have influenced the circumstances associated with acts of lethal violence in the nation's larger urban centers is incompletely understood at best, and at worst, is totally misunderstood. The myopia to which we refer is an outgrowth of the tendency to cast the culture-violence link almost completely within a framework of exaggerated risk. Risk levels are probably the single most important dimension of urban violence, but it should be pointed out that they represent only one dimension of the culture-violence link.

VICTIMIZATION STRUCTURE AND CULTURAL CHANGE

To gain a more complete grasp of culture-violence link, the added dimension of victimization structure requires greater attention. Traditional patterns of black victimization were dominated by acts of interpersonal violence. These acts often grew out of the precarious position of individual blacks in the social order and their willingness to inflict pain and suffering upon those to whom they primarily related. The high homicide levels observed in southern cities in the early years of this century most often fit this description (i.e., lethal attacks against friends and family). This pattern best exemplifies the pattern associated with the black subculture of violence. Major changes were to take place in the structure of victimization in the nation's larger black communities after the changes that occurred during the urban quarter century. We propose a dichotomous schema that should assist in defining more precisely the culture-violence link in black communities throughout the country.

Structural Character of Victimization during Intervals of Elevated Risk

To anyone familiar with homicide risk levels in the nation's black population, two distinct windows of high risk can be shown to exist. One of these windows is the period extending from the second decade of this century to well into the fourth. This era of elevated risk appears to have been ushered in by the arrival of the first major movement of blacks from the countryside to the city, which reached its apex in 1934. The second window became evident during the mid 1960s and showed strong evidence of persistence througout the 1970s. During this interval of concentrated violence, the peak was recorded in 1972. These two periods of concentrated violence appear to have two things in common. They represent periods during which the volume of black migration to the cities was large, and they also were intervals of ferment associated with major changes in the character of the national economy. In the first instance, the nation was in the final throes of moving from an agricultural to an industrial economy, and during the more recent instance, the economy was undergoing a change from industrial dominance to incipient and subsequent early postindustrialism.

Most of our attention will be directed toward the latter window. Yet in order to guard against misreading available clues we will frequently refer to the earlier window as a means of maintaining proper bearing. These two windows, however, refer solely to periods in which homicide risk was elevated. Having already concluded that elevated risk provides an incomplete measure of the contribution of culture to the propensity of a group to employ violence as a goal attainment mechanism, it becomes necessary to look elsewhere for an explanation. Attention will now be directed to an examination of the place of victimization structure in the culture/violence linkage. A dichotomous schema incorporating both risk and structure is favored over the use of risk as a single measure of the culture-violence association. The proposed schema is illustrated below. Table 2–3 is composed of nine cells into which any identifiable urban place can be located. The positioning of each place describes its location along the cultural evolutionary continuum in terms of the risk-structure association. For instance, during much of the twentieth century, the nation's larger black communities could be placed in the upper left cell. Certainly, most such places would appear in that cell during the interval coinciding with the appearance of our first window.

TABLE 2–3

Proposed Risk-Structure Schema

		Victimization Structure		
		Traditional	Transitional	Emergent
Risk Level	High			
	Intermediate			
	Low			

The second window, which coincides with a substantial segment of the interval described as the urban quarter century, is characterized by a more diffuse distribution of black communities across the cells in the schema. The suggested positioning of individual places within identified cells reflects an adaptation of these places to external change. The more important of those changes are associated with cultural adjustments to stages of economic development. Because changes in the national economy affect individual places differently based on functional specialization, some places are presumed to have moved more slowly over the violence-risk-culture stage than others. Likewise, the existence of regional differences in commitment to particular strands of the national core culture or the black subculture should serve as a brake on the speed of movement from traditional victimizations (i.e, expressive)[1] to the emerging end (i.e., instrumental)[2] of the structural continuum, independent of level of risk. Risk, it is suggested, represents a response of persons concentrated in the lower reaches of the status hierarchy to aspects of life on a variety of dimensions. Whereas structure reflects a response to the rearrangement of important strands in the national core culture and, subsequently, in individual subcultures.

To demonstrate the effectiveness of the proposed schema, we must establish realistic boundaries that will allow us to distinguish between established categories. The problem of establishing rational boundaries as a means of identifying categories of risk, however, is less formidable than establishing comparable structural categories. A review of black risk levels prevailing during the initial window of escalating risk assists us in achieving the simpler goal. Based on that experience, we have chosen the following risk levels to distinguish between high-, intermediate-, and low-risk urban places respectively: Cluster A is ≥ 45 homicides per 100,000 persons; Cluster B is 35 to 45 homicides per 100,000 persons; and Cluster C is 20 to 35 homicides per 100,000 persons. By implication, any black community that maintained mean risk levels below that described in Cluster C for a sustained period, can no longer be said to include a substantial number of persons who engage in traditional black life-styles.

The problem of arriving at a set of satisfactory structural boundaries is a much more difficult challenge. Yet as one reviews the battery of case studies describing the circumstances under which a growing share of urban homicides occur, it would be difficult to ignore regional differences, especially during the more recent period (Block and Zimring, 1973; Zimring and Zuehl, 1986; Rushforth et al., 1977). Based on a review of previous investigations, we have decided to utilize the expressive/instrumental orientation mix as the most appropriate way of handling the second and more difficult goal. Those places in which 80 percent or more of all victimizations can be attributed to expressive motivations will be labeled environments of traditional patterns of dominance. It is in these environments that the traditional black subculture is most likely to manifest itself. Places in which fewer than 80 percent of the victimizations are an outgrowth of angry conflict, but wherein the pattern of victimization continues to represent expressive dominance, will be described as "transitional communites." Finally, we have chosen to classify those places in which instrumental motivations dominate ($\geq$ 50 percent) as "emergent communities." The rapid growth in instrumentally motivated victimization is a hallmark of the urban quarter century.

The Black Subculture and Altered Victimization Structures

Traditional elements of the black subculture have tended to manifest themselves in circumstances surrounding acts of lethal violence nationally, cross regionally, and locally throughout most of the twentieth century. But evidence of a shift in the national value hierarchy, ushered in by a maturing urban population and rapid changes in the structure of the national economy, were not lost on the nation's larger black communities. The initial evidence of a growing willingness of segments of the black community to employ acts of violence to support the achievement of instrumental goals is associated with the urban riots that flared, for a brief period, in a number of large American cities during the 1960s.

A more subtle and less noticed indicator of a shift towards instrumental behavior was the sharp increase in robbery involving black offenders and victims. Nationally, between 1960 and 1969 the number of black robbery victimizations increased from 14,821 to 42,980, for an increase of almost 200 percent (Savitz, 1973). However, regional differences in the rate of adoption of both rioting and robbing behaviors could be detected. The South lagged behind the rest of the nation in the use of violence to pursue instrumental ends, especially if those ends were not associated with long-held traditions. Therefore, we expect our six-city urban sample to conform to the regionally directed pattern of victimization previously discussed.

Like others who have expressed an interest in the culture-risk association, we encountered difficulty in efforts to operationalize that association. Moreover it becomes clear, from reviewing the FBI's Supplemental Monthly Reports (SMRs), that the circumstances under which death occurred varied substantially among our six-city sample. Yet at the time of the upturn in risk, each place in our sample could be placed squarely in the column of traditional dominance. Nevertheless, signs of incipient moves in an instrumental direction were seen in Pittsburgh, Detroit, and St. Louis as early as 1965.

Changes accelerated in the structural mix during the decade of the 1970s, such that by the end of the decade, instrumental or secondary victimizations had attained parity with expressive or primary victimizations in some locations. These changes could be detected at every ecological scale, but by focusing on regional changes, one can systematically address the role of value shifts in a way that would be more difficult outside of this context. Although structural differences were apparent in our sample cities as early as 1965, these differences were nominal at the earlier date. By 1970 structural differences were evident at both the regional and local scale. However, differences in the rate of adoption of new values were apparent. For instance, in 1970 almost 80 percent of the prevailing risk in the South was associated with expressive victimizations; ten years later this category accounted for fewer than 70 percent of the total. Yet in the Northeast, the contribution of expressive acts to risk declined from approximately two-thirds to slightly more than two-fifths over the same period.

The changes in national core values appear to have been the most far-reaching in the Northeast, with changes occurring more slowly in America's heartland. Based on these observations of regional change, we anticipate that our urban sample will manifest a similar pattern during this period of cultural instability. We anticipate the least change to have occurred in Atlanta and the most far-reaching change to have occurred in Detroit.

THE SUBCULTURAL CONTINUUM AND VICTIMIZATION PATTERNS IN AN URBAN SAMPLE

Before moving directly into a description of the changes occurring in the violence-subcultural support system in our sample cities, we will direct our attention to a pair of polar communities that tend to highlight differences along the risk-structure axis. The communities selected to illustrate cultural and/or subcultural orientations are New York's Manhattan and the city of Birmingham, Alabama. As blacks constitute the primary victims and offenders in high-homicide-risk urban places, the elevations in aggregate city risk tend to reflect the extreme seriousness of risk in a city's black community (e.g., Harlem). These places were chosen because of their position along the continuum of postindustrial development and some assumptions regarding their position along the race, culture, and violence continuum.

The Traditional Pattern—The Case of Birmingham

Birmingham, one of the South's earliest major manufacturing centers and a migration target of persons leaving rural Alabama during the early twentieth century, is an ideal location to examine for the purpose of demonstrating traditional dominance. Blacks in Birmingham grew up with the city; that is to say, black growth paralleled city growth throughout its several developmental stages. Likewise, it is well known that the social world of blacks in Birmingham was severely circumscribed prior to the 1960's (Moore, 1961). On that basis we assume early subcultural values were firmly entrenched and the homicide victimization structure, as well as characteristic risk levels, would roughly correspond to the observed stage of subcultural development. Thus we would hypothesize the persistence of traditional expressive victimizations throughout the entire period under review (1920 to 1980).

In the early decades of this century, homicide risk levels in Birmingham were among the highest in the nation. The observed levels were primarily influenced by the prevailing behavioral propensities of the city's black community (Barnhart, 1932). Conflict among poor blacks with an orientation toward an exciting life led to excessive alcohol consumption, brawling, and, subsequently, a higher-than-average number of deaths. This behavior was abhorred by the respectable citizens of the Birmingham black community, as the following comment suggests, "It just seems to me to be a real disgrace for Negroes to kill and cut each other up as they do. Something ought to be done about it" (Moore, 1961). Risk levels have abated over time in Birmingham, hovering around 45 per 100,000 persons in the city's black community in 1980. Structural indicators, on the other hand, fail to demonstrate a similar kind of alteration over the same lengthy interval.

A detailed assessment of the prevailing pattern of victimization in Birmingham, covering the years 1936–1944, can be employed as baseline data for establishing the normative structure. From these data it was ascertained that 85 percent of all victims were black and that 91 percent of all deaths could be attributed to expressive motivations (Harlan, 1950). Family and/or intersex homicides accounted for approximately 25 percent of all victimizations; arguments associated with gambling or other money-related activity accounted for another 30 percent; and arguments growing out of trivial insults were responsible for 36 percent of the victimizations. Thus during the period just prior to and including World War II, honor and respect seem to be the values most often invoked in lethal actions. In 1980, FBI data demonstrated that four-fifths of Birmingham's black victimizations continued to conform to the traditional pattern involving conflict between lovers and adversaries.

Manhattan's Harlem: An Example of the Emerging Pattern

Harlem, unlike Birmingham, has maintained a high profile throughout this century as a center of black culture in the United States.

It has been described as the "cultural mecca" of black achievement in the arts and entertainment. The vast outpouring of blacks from the upper South to this new mecca after World War I set the stage for the formation of a black subcultural variant that was eventually to distinguish between those persons socialized in a southern rural or small-town-south environment from those socialized in the urban north. Subcultural styles were adopted that were more in keeping with those in vogue in their new environment.

Manhattan, by 1940, contained the largest urban black population in the nation. It should be noted that the largest share of that population was concentrated in Harlem. Harlem, like its larger parent community, was not only a residential community but a provider of services as well. Many of the services available in Harlem were viewed as illicit and often tied to the high levels of criminal activity present there. For those whose values were secular rather than sprititual, and who likewise placed emphasis on comfort, pleasure, and the general tenets of an exciting life, the providers of illicit services were assured the existence of a stable market. Likewise, in the late post-World War II era, legitimate opportunity for Harlemites began to wane, and traditional values continued to weaken. Some attribute these changes to the emerging victimization pattern first noted by Swersey (1977). He noted that between 1968 and 1973 a sharp increase occurred in intentional killings, and after careful examination, he concluded that the observed phenomenon was drug-related. More recent work has verified the dominance of this pattern for the borough of Manhattan (Tardiff, et al., 1986). In 1981, blacks in Manhattan were killed more frequently during the commission of another crime than in interpersonal disputes. Almost 60 percent of all victimizations could be described as instrumentally motivated, with drug-related risk rising to levels almost twice those associated with robbery and other crimes. Within the period of a single decade the structure of victimization in Harlem apparently underwent a major change.

By 1980, the gap along the victimization axis separating our polar locations had widened abruptly, demonstrating a clear expressive dominance across all time periods in Birmingham but a move to instrumental dominance in Manhattan and its high-risk community of Harlem. Based on the changes in the structure of victimization in our two polar comunities, we would expect our sample communities to demonstrate patterns of change ranging from those resembling the pattern in Birmingham to those that bear a strong resemblance to Manhattan's Harlem.

The ten-year interval separating these two dates was a turbulent period in many of the nation's larger black communities. It was during this interval that the nation's black homicide rate peaked and subsequently started on its slow downward slide. But because our sample communities were exposed to different rates of cultural change, we subsequently expect their homicide victimization structures to reflect these differences. It should be reiterated, however, that 1965 FBI data demonstrate that traditional black subcultural influence on structure continued in evidence in each of our sample communities. Nevertheless, Detroit, St. Louis, and Pittsburgh were already closer to the traditional/transitional boundary than was true of the Sunbelt communities. Table 2–4 demonstrates that the sample communities did indeed move at different rates along the risk/structure continuum

TABLE 2–4

Changes in Risk/Structure Dominance in Urban
Community Sample: 1970, 1975, and 1980

Risk/Structure Clusters		1970	1975	1980
A	HT[1] IT LT	Los Angeles	Pittsburgh	
B	HT' IT' LT'	Houston, Atlanta Detroit, St. Louis Pittsburgh	Los Angeles, St. Louis Atlanta, Houston	Detroit Houston Pittsburgh, Atlanta
C	HE IE LE		Detroit	Los Angeles, St. Louis

Source: Risk Level and Structural Composition Computed by Authors.
[1]HT = high-risk traditional
IT   = intermediate-risk traditional
LT   = low-risk traditional
HT' = high-risk transitional
IT' = intermediate-risk transitional
LT' = low-risk transitional
HE   = high-risk emergent
IE   = Intermediate-risk emergent
LE   = low-risk emergent

during the decade. Not a single community was lodged in the high risk/traditional structure (HT) of Cluster A at the beginning of the period. This implies that rapid changes in the structure of victimization were taking place at each location during the late 1960s. In 1970, high-risk/trasitional structure (HT') had come to represent the modal pattern. By 1980, however, two communities had moved into the high-risk emergent category (HE), a fact that suggests the traditional black subculture was being seriously challenged in St. Louis and Los Angeles. Detroit represents an anomaly in this instance; it was located in the high-risk/emergent structure category in 1975, but was once again in the trasitional state in 1980. This point will be raised again in chapter 3.

The following questions now emerge: How do these patterns impact risk? What are the forces that sustain the observed pattern? Who is placed at greater risk? What are the policies required to permit us to bring existing risk levels in closer accord with those generally observed in developed nations? Although the current 6:1 ratio of black to white homicides represents a vast improvement over the 10:1 ratio observed during the first window of elevated risk, it should still be considered an unacceptable ratio. But possibly if we had a firmer grasp of the subcultural dimensions we would be in a more favorable position to address the risk gap identified above.

SUMMARY

Culture continues to be invoked as an important contributor to differences in observed homicide risk levels from place to place in the United States. Arguments abound, however, regarding which contributor to risk explains most of the variation. Structuralist and culturally oriented investigators continue to assume supportive or countervailing positions relative to the research findings of their peers vis-á-vis this issue. But to date these researchers have devoted only limited attention to issues of culture and elevated levels of black homicide. As indicated earlier, Curtis (1975) is one of the few investigators to address this issue on an urban scale. Recently, however, Huff-Corzine et al. (1986) raised questions regarding some of the traditional assumptions of ecological models of homicide and their suitability for explaining black risk. Although their findings provide support for the role of a southern subculture of violence, they contend that the subculture that supports white violence is not adequate to explain black violence. In this chapter, we have attempted to address that issue. More specifically, we think we have addressed a set of concerns that Huff-Corzine et al. (1986) acknowledge to be missing in their investigation.

They noted (p. 919), "Although our findings indicate the possible existence of subcultures of violence among blacks and southern whites, they provide little insight into their historical genesis, current content, or mechanisms of influence."

3

Stress and Homicide Risk in Urban Black Communities: A Microenvironmental Perspective on the Homicide Environment

INTRODUCTION

Since 1960, the urban economy has undergone a series of structural changes that have negatively impacted the character of life in the nation's larger black communities. Until recently the impact of these changes was ignored by researchers. Wilson's (1987) recent work, however, forcefully demonstrates the impact of structural changes on black economic well-being. Building on the work of Wilson, other researchers are beginning once again to display some interest in the problem. Yet, there is a tendency to concentrate on a single segment of the population, the poverty population. In order to more effectively demonstrate the impact of structural change, the *entire* black community will have to receive the attention of researchers, rather than simply focusing on the underclass. Failure to do this will make it extremely difficult to demonstrate a direct association between changes in the economic character of the community and various troubling behavior.

Each community's social well-being, while showing evidence of uniqueness, is affected by macroeconomic changes. We, therefore, argue that levels of homicide risk in the nation's larger black communities vary as a function of economic well-being. This position, however, differs from that of many researchers in this area. Nevertheless, there is growing evidence that researchers are beginning to favor community studies or an ecological approach.

Recent changes in the structure of the national economy have resulted in population losses in a number of primary black urban centers, and these areas generally have shown the greatest gains on the Bradbury and Downs Index of Distress (Bradbury, 1984). By 1980, a number of these manufacturing-belt cities had been replaced in the urban hierarchy by a growing number of burgeoning Sunbelt centers—Houston, Dallas, Phoenix, and San Diego. Nevertheless, large black communities have failed to evolve in these new growth centers which are outside of selected traditional southern Sunbelt locations and World War II West Coast migrant destinations. The net effect has been to leave a sizable share of the nation's black population trapped in inner-city communities of despair (Berry, 1979; Wilson, 1985). It is in these latter communities that levels of homicide risk have risen most sharply since the initiation of the national upturn in risk.

In this chapter our primary task is to assess patterns of internal risk distribution and describe the environmental context of a series of homicide environments drawn from our urban sample. Our primary target communities have experienced differing population and economic patterns since 1960. Nevertheless, in most instances, they have mirrored the fortunes of the central city and metropolitan areas in which they are situated. Based on these differences, we would expect those communities in which economic dislocation has been least severe (e.g., Houston) to experience the least change in risk since 1970, whereas places that have been hardest hit economically (e.g., St. Louis) should be expected to experience the most drastic change. One difficulty with an orientation of this kind is operationalizing the concept of level of economic development on the direction and intensity of risk. To that end, we employ a measure of environmental stress as an indicator of economic well-being.

High stress can indicate the lack of access to basic economic resources and is thought to be a precipitator of a number of pathological conditions, including elevated homicide risk (Herzog and Levy, 1978; Linsky and Straus, 1986; Kasl and Harlburg, 1972; Kelley, 1985), whereas low stress indicates the opposite. Not only are we concerned with the economic state of principally black urban aggregates, but we are extremely interested in spatial subaggregates that form the basic building block of such communities (i.e., neighborhood units). Nonetheless, at this or any other microenvironmental scale, it is extremely difficult to precisely specify factors that consititute the major contributors to risk, which partially explains why microenvironmental investigations of risk are seldom undertaken. Yet, there is a growing interest in these smaller units of analysis in ecological investigations of risk; however, few of these investigations have singled out black communities and/or segments of those communities for special scrutiny despite the elevated levels of risk within those communities (*see* Sampson, 1985; Messner and Tardiff, 1986; Massey and McKean, 1985;

Roncek, 1981). Therefore, we focus this segment of our investigation on the smallest unit of analysis for which data can be assembled—the neighborhood—in an effort to reveal the risk/stress association.

A word of caution should be interjected at this point; the concept of stress, especially microenvironmental stress, is not a precise concept, and surrogates employed to measure it are not easily assembled. This frequently leads to the utilization of variables that are imprecise and inconsistent measures of the behavior under study. Moveover, the concept has not been widely adopted by ecologically oriented investigators. Nevertheless, we think its strengths outweight its weaknesses. Among those strengths are the ability to derive both precise summary measures that facilitate comparison, as well as the ability to transform those measures into a series of nominal scale categories—high stress, low stress. Thus we should be able to indirectly establish the macroeconomic link to microecological responses upon which the risk of violent victimization is based.

Levels of stress within each of our units of observation are derived through an application of principal-components factor analysis. A series of variables employed previously by a number of investigators to delineate the internal spatial structure of American urban places is utilized to derive a set of common factors. In this instance, however, only the derived factors that best describe levels of stress are employed to demonstrate variations in social well-being within our sample communities. The derived factor scores for each neighborhood-level observation on stress, socioeconomic status and social disorganization, will be utilized to enable us to elicit a measure of stress for each observation.

STRESS AS A COMPARATIVE MEASURE OF BLACK COMMUNITY WELL-BEING

The black residential clusters in our urban sample have undergone a disparate set of experiences during the post-1960 period. The strength of a sense of community reflects how well they have staved off negative economic forces. Not all communities have been successful in their efforts, as most have not been able to provide their residents protection against external threat such as the loss of jobs through plant closings and/or other structural changes. Such threats often manifest themselves in a weakened opportunity structure. Where these threats occur, they are most often associated with declining employment opportunity, decreasing levels of compensation, and limited employment security on one side of the ledger. On the other side are questions of personal safety, an inability to guard against property loss, and increasing evidence of incivility—a factor that contributes to a loss of social cohesion (Skogan and Maxfield, 1981). The resources required to defend against the latter are loosely tied to a community's ability to stem the tide of economic instability.

Neighborhoods in which residents exhibit the greatest vulnerability to these conditions are those in which stress levels tend to be higher. Stress levels suggest the degree of difficulty that individual communities are expected to encounter in efforts to alter levels of violent expression. However, any number of nonstressor variables also are likely to be present in the environment that may interact with stressors to promote a synergistic effect. For example, we would expect a higher-than-average concentration of young adult males in a poor neighborhood to be characterized by higher homicide risk levels than a similarly situated neighborhood in which this group constitutes a smaller proportion of the population. Nevertheless, these are simply assumptions that may or may not be supported by the evidence.

Changes in Aggregate Stress Levels: 1970–1980

Stress scores were computed for each neighborhood in our sample for the years 1970 and 1980. (The method of computation will be described in a later section of this chapter.) After summing the individual scores, an aggregate mean score was derived for each of the black communities (see Table 3–1). This provided us with a means of measuring the extent to which expected alterations in levels and direction of risk might occur during the interval.

TABLE 3–1

Mean Stress Levels in Urban Sample: 1970 and 1980

Community	Stress Level—1970	Stress Level—1980
Detroit	499	474
St. Louis	501	490
Pittsburgh	476	540
Houston	557	560
Atlanta	501	514
Los Angeles	490	524

Source: Computed by the authors.

Not only does this procedure allow us to address aggregate changes in levels of stress, but also sheds light on how stress levels have been redistributed within the community over the same period.

The internal distribution of stress, to the extent that there is a strong association between stress and risk, should suggest how risk will be distributed within the community. It is quite possible, however, that the risk/stress link is a weak one and that risk varies in ways that exhibit little relationship to stress. If that is the case, it would seem to suggest that our specification of the measurement of stress is inadequate, or that nonstressor variables, when interacting with stress, produce a larger-than-expected effect. At this point, we examine the internal changes that occurred in a single sample community to illustrate our point.

Stress and the St. Louis Black Community

The St. Louis black community is utilized to illustrate the extent, direction, and pattern of stress redistribution during a decade in which risk was consistently high. St. Louis reached its population peak in 1950 and since that time has experienced a continuing population decline. During the 1960s, most new economic activity developed in the metropolitan ring, a factor that further disadvantaged individuals without access to new workplace locations. In that decade, the only new jobs in the city were low-income service jobs (Streiford, 1974). Yet, unskilled blacks continued to migrate into the city. Loury (1980) attributed the observed economic decline to a piling up of blacks in the city who where ill-prepared for participation in the urban economy. We will not debate that point here, but there is substantial evidence to illustrate a deterioration in the quality of life in the St. Louis black community (*see* Newman, 1980); a pattern that continued throughout much of the decade of the 1970s. By the end of the decade, the St. Louis black community had lost almost 50,000 persons, as middle-and upper-income blacks moved to the suburbs, a phenomenon rarely observed in the annals of urban community development.

The point of this description is twofold: first, it allows us to track the fortunes of individual neighborhoods and neighborhood groups; and second, it allows us to track the spread of dangerous environments and to identify the extent to which they are associated with neighborhoods in which stress was increasing in intensity. If culture is taken into account at this point, it would lead us to anticipate a continuing weakening of the association between stress and risk, since stress, as we have defined it, is more likely to bear a strong association with traditional subcultural responses than to emergent subcultural responses. Because St. Louis was described earlier as having moved farther along the cultural continuum than any of the other communities in our urban sample, we would expect it to demonstrate a risk/stress association that differs substantially from places located closer to the opposite end of the cultural continuum.

Given the massive alteration in observed stress levels during the 1970s, it becomes difficult to generalize the risk/stress association. Neighborhoods, as a rule, demonstrated a high level of instability in terms of their position on the stress contiuum. The greatest instability was associated with that cluster of neighborhoods that were described as intermediate stress areas in the initial time period. By 1980, more than half of those neighborhoods were in the high-stress category. This resulted in a doubling of high-stress neighborhoods between 1970 to 1980, a condition strongly associated with black population abandonment. In most such neighborhoods, the black population was one-third to one-half smaller in 1980 than it had been in 1970.

What seems to have occurred in St. Louis during the 1970s was an intensification in segregation between the black "haves" and "have nots." The black "haves" that did not leave the city for St. Louis county tended to concentrate in low-stress neighborhoods made available by racial residential turnover. When low-stress turnover neighborhoods are added to those maintaining the original low-stress levels throughout the decade, these neighborhoods serve as the place of residence of approximately one-fourth the black community's population. Thus, during the ten years under review, a spatial reorganization of segments of the population along social class lines occurred, with growing concentrations in high- and low-stress neighborhoods. Intermediate-stress neighborhoods experienced a decline in their share of the total population as well. This reorganization appears to have altered further the expected stress/risk association, such that one cannot depend upon low-stress neighborhoods to shield their occupants from elevated risk.

This point may be demonstrated by observing the risk levels associated with the new-entry and low- and intermediate-stress neighborhoods on the community's far northwest side (see Fig. 3–1). In a number of those neighborhoods, risk levels surpassed 100 homicides per 100,000 persons. These are not the levels of risk usually associated with low-stress environments in which a strong buffering influence is assumed to be present. In this instance, however, it appears that most residents were killed someplace other than in the neighborhood of residence. On the other hand, the spatial discordance between place of residence and place of victimization is far less obvious in those high-risk neighborhoods characterized by high stress. What is obvious, though, is that environments characterized by high stress at the beginning of the period were much more likely to be excessively high-risk neighborhoods at the end of the period. The risk/stress

FIGURE 3–1

Stress/Risk Association in the St. Louis Ghetto: 1970 and 1980

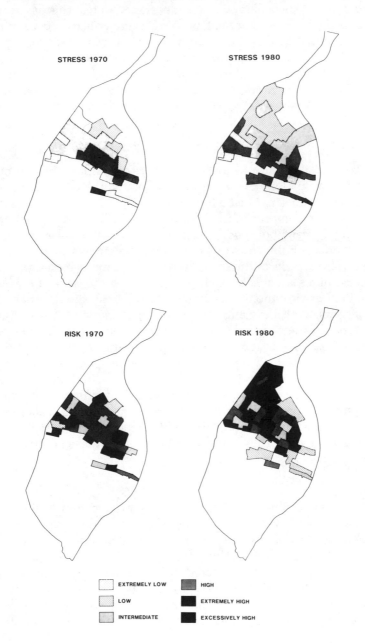

STRESS 1970

STRESS 1980

RISK 1970

RISK 1980

☐ EXTREMELY LOW	▨ HIGH
☐ LOW	■ EXTREMELY HIGH
☐ INTERMEDIATE	■ EXCESSIVELY HIGH

association in St. Louis is a complex one and is not easily explained by a static view of the observed spatial patterning of violent outcomes.

In order to provide a better understanding of the risk/stress association, a statistical model was developed to test this association with data drawn from our six-city sample. We anticipated variations in the strength of individual components to explain risk from place to place as a function of the strength of nonstressor variables on risk. Since our model was exploratory at this stage, we have limited our discussion of its performance. Nevertheless, we will explain its structure and identify the independent variables employed to operationalize the model.

The Social Environment, Risk, and the Stress Model

The social world of most blacks is circumscribed by the outer dimensions of the black community. For many, the circumference of their social world is restricted to a set of several contiguous neighborhoods. Although improved transportation and other social innovations are changing neighborhoods, we are uncertain how, if at all, these changes impact risk. Thus our environmental analysis was directed more toward aspects of the social, rather than physical, environment. A number of researchers have chosen to address the issue of the effect of the built environment on risk (Newman, 1980; Brantingham and Brantingham, 1981; Levy and Herzog, 1978). Although recognizing the importance of the physical environment, we do not assign the same weight to it that we assign to the social environment. We tend to agree with Moos (1976) and Aakster (1974) that the social environment represents a more influential contributor to the risk of deviance, as well as to other pathologies, than does the built environment. Moreover, it is within the context of restricted and/or constrained social environments that most interpersonal interactions take place; therefore, it is critical that we more fully understand the role of these environments on behavior.

Environmental Stress

In order to illustrate the importance of elements of the social environment on homicide risk, a set of socioecological stressors that are thought to influence risk have been chosen for inclusion in the general stress model. Stress research, including an identification of stressors, is most often conducted at the individual rather than the environmental level because this type of research is primarily conducted by psychologists. But a growing number of social scientists are beginning to exhibit an interest in aspects of environmental stress.

Much of this interest, however, revolves around concern with a series of identifiable events or actions that supposedly influence the health status of individuals (Dohrenwend and Dohrenwend, 1974; Levi and Anderson, 1975; Antonovsky, 1979; Moos, 1976; Kagan and Levi, 1974). More recently, some researchers have shown interest in the role of environmental stressors on violent behavior (Schlesinger and Revitch, 1980; Landau and Ravei, 1987; Lenski and Straus, 1986). Moreover, Revitch and Schlesinger (1981) implicate stress as an intervening variable in the commission of certain types of homicides.

Researchers have suggested that stress encourages individuals to develop a set of coping strategies that will enable them to overcome its unwanted and/or unpleasant consequences. When the intensity of stress is low, effective coping mechanisms may be easily adopted. But when stress levels become extremely high, effective coping is likely to become more difficult. Thus most persons may be able to overcome routine aspects of stress defined simply as a series of daily hassles (Baum et al., 1981). Yet they encounter severe difficulty when stress levels rise above some critical threshold. At that point, a variety of pathological outcomes are sometimes observed (see Brenner and Mooney, 1983; Aakster, 1974). In this chapter, however, our effort is restricted to an examination of the link between environmental stress, which is generally perceived to be associated with a specific social climate (Moos, 1976), and homicide risk within a set of urban microenvironments.

The Stress Model

The employment of socioecological stressors as a means of evaluating the environmental contribution to individual health status and behavioral disturbances has grown in importance during the prior two decades. Yet, we know of no previous effort to employ these indicators to evaluate homicide risk within a set of microenvironments contained totally within predominantly black subcommunities. Since various levels of enviromental stress are thought to lead to a range of individual behaviors, it therefore seems an appropriate construct for evaluating microenvironmetnal homicide risk levels. In order to test the validity of this notion, a stress model similar to that developed by Harburg et al. (1970) is utilized. They chose nine variables that were thought to contribute to stress and factor-analyzed them in order to derive a smaller number of common dimensions. Two dimensions that could be described as components of stress evolved from this exercise—socioeconomic status and social disorganization. Each census tract in the city of Detroit was then ranked in terms of the derived factor scores on each dimension (Harburg et al., 1970). By combining these rankings, the researchers were able to nominally identify each observation on a continuum of low stress to high stress.

Harburg et al.'s stress model was developed to satisfy a very different set of goals than those we have established. They were essentially concerned with identifying the hereditary and environmental contribution to risk of hypertension among a sample of Detroit blacks and whites. Our goal is much simpler. We are interested only in determing how effective a simple stress model is in explaining observed differences in homicide risk within individual black communities. Tests of the model will include all neighborhoods that make up the black community, although special attention will be devoted to those units we have identified as substantial-risk neighborhoods. Therefore, we will need only to identify an appropriate set of variables that qualify as surrogates of stressors to initiate the tests.

Data Source

Unlike the Harburg group, we have chosen to select our indicator variables from the U.S. Census Bureau's Census Tract publications. Among the twelve variables, several are analogs to those employed by the Harburg group. Others, however, represent selected variables utilized in the literature in which ecological variations in risk are examined.

Within the two dimensions of stress, socioeconomic status and social disorganization, some variables are so significant that they tend to function as either inducers of stress or buffers against stress, depending upon their value along the continuum. For instance, high income operates as a buffer, whereas low income acts to increase vulnerability. The Harburg model, however, also incorporated five crime variables. Crime variables were not included in our stress model because they were not available for each of our observations at the census-tract level. But, even with the exclusion of the crime variables, our model bears a stronger resemblance to that of Harburg and associates than other similar ecological models utilized to test the relationship of location on risk. Although there were some differences in the models, the results of the principal-components analysis led to an identification of the same primary dimensions as did Harburg et al.—social disorganization and socioeconomic status.

Instead of utilizing our derived stress measures to explain risk, we have used them as descriptors of the prevailing level of environmental stress at the neighborhood scale. Thus we are able to assess the manner in which resources are distributed within our sample communities while also being able to detect changes both within and between the sample communities during the interval. We take the position, however, that it is the individual components of stress that are the most meaningful, both from a theoretical and a policy perspective, in assisting us to better understand the risk/stress association. Therefore, aggregate stress measures were employed as markers of community and neighborhood well-being, whereas selected individual components of the stress model were employed to test a series of hypotheses bearing on risk. Selected variables were utilized in a least-squares regression model designed to explain microecological variations in homicide risk in our sample communities. Those variables thought to be less important were used as control variables in the analysis. This assemblage of stressors should allow us to address a series of issues thought to be important in understanding intracommunity variations in prevailing risk levels, as well as changes in levels of risk over time.

Choice of Model Variables

The variables selected to satisfy our twin goals of specifying levels of environmental stress and explaining ecological variations in homicide risk are as follows:

Percentage of the population that is black
Percentage black males aged 15–24
Percentage black male unemployment
Percentage of persons residing outside of SMSA 5 years earlier
Percentage of female-headed households
Percentage of females divorced or separated
Percentage crowded households
Percentage vacant residential units
Percentage of families with below poverty level incomes
Median family income
Median rent
Median educational attainment

Since our ecological analysis will include two time intervals, a slight modification in the description of one of our variables was necessary. In 1980, the Census Bureau discarded median years of education in favor of the percentage of persons with less than twelve years of schooling as an index of educational attainment. Moreover, one additional variable was added to the 1980 list—male labor-force participation rates. There is a theoretical basis for the choice of each of the above variables, both from the perspective of their contribution to levels of stress and levels of risk.

The twelve variables were used in varying combinations as independent variables in ordinary least squares regression models. The goal of the regressions was to test the explanatory power of the model on homicide risk. Although the variables employed have been utilized by other researchers in varying combinations, they have seldom been viewed as measures of ecological stress. The exception is the work of Levy and Herzog (1978) and Herzog et al. (1976); however, they were concerned with a broad range of pathologies impacting risk, covering mortality from specific disease to mortality as an outgrowth of social and psychological impairment.

The Link Between Macro- and Microscale Phenomena

We start with the assumption that in complex urban economies, a major source of microecological stress originates at the macrolevel. Individuals, in order to sustain themselves, must adopt a series of strategies to effectively cope with a battery of externally induced decisions. For instance, residents of selected Detroit black neighborhoods are known to have experienced immense distress as an outgrowth of economic structural decisions made during the period 1970 to 1980. The structural alteration associated with these decisions played an imporant role in increasing the proportion of all neighborhoods identified as high-stress neighborhoods in 1980. In 1970, only 30 percent were in this category, but in 1980, the share had reached 38 percent. Much of the change resulted from previously intermediate-stress neighborhoods becoming high-stress neighborhoods. The question that should now be raised is: What are the consequences of these changes for risk? We anticipate that the results of our regression model will assist in answering this question.

TESTING THE STRESS MODEL

A test of the stress model demonstrated that the relationship between stress and risk is less straightforward than we had earlier assumed. The inability of the stress model to explain more than modest variations in risk can be attributed both to shortcomings in the model itself, and to the nature of the phenomenon under investigation. The model, an ordinary least squares regression model, was initially plagued by high correlations among selected independent variables-multicollinearity—which led to subsequent difficulty in the interpretation of the initial results. Likewise, the use of census tracts as surrogates for neighborhood-scale units included a built-in weakness. That weakness is directly related to the instability associated with rare events, homicide frequency, when the units of observation are physically small. In such instances, units that possess similar objective attributes are more likely to differ greatly in the probability that a victim will reside in a given neighborhod. But since our primary objective is aimed at explaining variations in risk at a microecological scale, despite inherent weaknesses, we thought it worthwhile to adjust the model to enable us to achieve this goal.

The situation also was exacerbated by the dependent variable, "homicide risk," becoming structurally more complex over time and our inability to address this reality with the model. Although the stressor variables may have explained variations in risk based on a set of traditional motivations that contribute to fatal interpersonal interactions, they seemed inadequate to explain such variations when non-traditional stimuli were involved. These caveats should be kept in mind as we briefly review the success of the stress model in explaining variations in homicide risk in our sample communities.

The Scale and Character of Observational Units

The model was tested using all neighborhoods (census tracts) in each city in which the population was 50 percent or more black. In most of our sample cities, the mean black percentage at the neighborhood scale was in excess of 85 percent, an indication of only a nominal white presence. A subaggregate of substantial risk neighborhoods, however, represents our primary target of interest among this collectivity of neighborhoods. A minimum critical threshold of resident victimizations was selected, three (3) or more, to identify neighborhoods in this select group. This partitioning enabled us to gain insight into why the observed patterns of risk prevailing in individual black communities, as well as in subareas of those communities, took on specific characteristics. It also allowed us to address questions about the prevalence, as well as the intensity, of risk. Before we review the performance of the model, an additional commentary on the changes in stress levels and patterns in our individual black communities during the decade of the 1970s is in order.

Changes in Stress and the Redistribution of Resources

Our original sample communities included six places; however, we will limit our discussion to only five of those communites, excluding the smallest black community in our sample, Pittsburgh, because risk there was only moderately elevated in both 1970 and 1980. Consequently,

only a small number of substantial risk neighborhoods could be identified in Pittsburgh. In the remaining five communites, the volume of
resources available for individual black communities and their alloca-
tions showed a mixed pattern during the ten year interval, as did the
pattern of victimization. Regarding the latter, both Detroit and Atlanta
experienced a peak in both number of victimizations and risk after 1970,
but by 1980, an absolute decline in risk was evident. Risk also declined
in Houston, but in St. Louis and Los Angeles the inverse occurred.
Based on the assumptions of the model, the latter two communities
would be expected to have access to fewer resources in 1980 than they
did ten years before, whereas three of these communities would be
expected to have improved their resource access.

The above changes in the intensity of stress demonstrates the
A review of summary measures of stress levels in these communities in 1980 illustrates the weakness of the above assumptions.
The communities that experienced large increases in risk over the ten
year period—Los Angeles (112 percent) and St. Louis (28 percent)—
experienced changes in stress levels that moved in opposite directions
on the scale. In St. Louis, a nominal decrease in the absolute level of
stress occurred; to the contrary, however, Los Angeles experienced
the largest increase in its absolute level of stress than did any of its
peers. Inconsistency in the stress/risk association was also evident in
Atlanta's black community. Atlanta experienced a modest increase in
stress, but a sharp decline in risk. Only in Detroit and Houston did
our assumptions regarding stress and risk hold.

The above changes in the intensity of stress demonstrates the
fallacy of assuming that changes in the volume of resource availability
can be expected consistently to impact the direction of change in
homicide risk. A more sensitive index of risk behavior can be gleaned
from changes in the prevalence of differential levels of stress within
these communites than from single summary measures. Changes in
prevalence of high-, intermediate- and low-stress neighborhoods within
individual communities sheds some insight on changes in the general
direction of risk. The key to understanding such changes appears to
be directly related to rapid transitions in these communities, that is,
from intermediate to high stress. The intracommunity location of the
transition from one stress-level category to another is believed not only
to influence changes in level of risk, but changes in the structure of
risk as well.

The most dramatic changes in the internal allocation and/or
redistribution of resources within individual black communities were
those that occurred in St. Louis and Houston. In the former, one-half
of the neighborhoods that had been designated intermediate-stress

neighborhoods (i.e., working class) had been transformed into high-stress neighborhoods (lower class) by decade's end. Although we think the transition abetted risk, it serves only as a partial explanation of the changes under way. Houston, on the other hand, experienced an increase in the prevalence of low-stress neighborhoods, a situation that in part, indicates neighborhood upgrade. Likewise, Houston experienced a modest decline in the prevalence of high-stress neighborhoods. These two communities experienced the most prominent changes in the internal distribution of resources among our sample places.

In order for these changes to have meaning, the larger context in which they occur should be specified. Among the more important contextual changes thought to impact microecological patterns of risk are the changing character of individual metropolitan economies, the rate of metropolitan population growth, the size of the central city population, and its physical size as a ratio of the metropolitan total, and the extent to which the black population is moving to the suburbs. Each of these contextual factors is thought to impact both the volume of resources available to and in the black community and the transitional changes observed to be taking place within those communites.

The Structural Dimensions of the Model

The previous discussion provides the context within which the stress model was tested. Despite the weakness of a linear relationship between stress and risk at the neighborhood scale, we are nevertheless in a position to demonstrate the relative importance between stressor and nonstressor variables in explaining observed variations. The implications of such findings transcend the importance of attempting to demonstrate the greater significance of structural-versus-cultural contributors to risk. The results of the model allow us to identify which set of forces are most important in leading to variations in risk at the individual community level and within zones of elevated risk in each community.

At least three dimensions of risk enhancement are identified by the model as important to an understanding of risk. The stressors are often identified as contributing to conditions of deprivation, disintegration, or loss of social control (Williams and Flewelling, 1988; Sampson, 1987). Yet, other dimensions of risk enhancement, which are less often addressed, are included in our model. These were represented by a series of variables that directly or indirectly focus upon the status of black males. Thus, although our principal-components analysis revealed the expected dimensions of social rank and social disorganization, it also revealed a dimension that we have labeled "male economic instability" which was associated most often with male unemployment, male labor-force-participation rates, and vacancy rates. To distinguish these elements from our stressors, we have labeled them "elements of strain." It is this factor that we view as the primary promoter of maladaptive life-styles even in neighborhoods that extend beyond high-stress environments.

Stressors, however, dominated explained variations in risk across all communities, with "elements of strain" assuming a dominant posture only in St. Louis. It was only in the latter community that we were unable to reject the null hypothesis that stress was a non-significant explanation for observed variations in risk. Thus the abridged stress model, with all of its shortcomings, demonstrates a weak ability to explain variations in risk across places. The low-stress neighborhoods in most of our communities were physically remote from high-stress neighborhoods which often provided a buffer against risk.

By the same token, in high-stress neighborhoods, where poverty was widespread and single-parent households were prevalent, risk tended to be exaggerated. The latter phenomenon intensified during the interval from 1970 to 1980, leading to intensification of risk in neighborhoods that were unable to stave off these conditions. Intermediate-stress neighborhoods, in the initial time period, were at greatest risk of having their status downgraded and, as a consequence, of experiencing an alteration in their initial risk characteristics as well.

It should be noted, however, that social networks extend across all neighborhood types and thereby tend to cause distortion in the stress/risk association. For example, recent movers to low-stress neighborhoods continued to have ties to old high-and intermediate-stress neighborhoods where risk was higher. Therefore, individuals who continued to frequent exaggerated-risk settings did not substantially minimize their risk of victimization by simply changing their place of residence. The two-way movement of persons across neighborhood types as an outgrowth of social ties or economic linkages, therefore, complicates microecological efforts to explain variations in risk.

Within substantial-risk neighborhoods, however, some differences can be detected that distinguishes the way the model works in these environments from its workings in the larger black community. Whereas stressor variables were clearly dominant at the larger scale, it appears that strain (e.g., vacancy rates) become relatively more important in explaining variations in risk at a subaggregate level (see Tables 3–2 and 3–3). When redundant variables were removed from the model, a strain variable became the primary explanatory variable in Los Angeles, St. Louis, and Houston. When the black community is compressed and attention is focused solely on areas in which risk is exaggerated, strain variables assumed relatively more explanatory power. This suggests that elevated risk is associated more closely with the fate and behavioral propensities of black males in high- and selected intermediate-stress neighborhoods than is the loss of social control, a condition more often assumed to be associated with female-headed households. Moreover, these neighborhoods, based on attenuated vacancy rates, apparently represent the least-preferred neighborhoods within the black community. But when elements of strain are combined with weakening social control and lowered aspirations, the stage appears to be set for risk elevation. A central issue here, however, is the extent of the prevalence of such conditions across black communities and the subsequent impact on the loss of community cohesion. It is the latter factor that seems to promote the growth and development of pockets of attenuated risk, especially in nonsouthern settings.

The availability and distribution of resources in our sample communities accounts for a statistically significant level ($p = < .05$) of the variation in each of them, with the exception of St. Louis. Yet when log transformations were taken on the stressor variables, the situation was reversed. The strength of stressors in explaining variations in risk was greatest in Houston, followed by Atlanta, Los Angeles, Detroit, and St. Louis. Even after log transformations, a similar sequence emerged, differing only in a change in position between Houston and Atlanta. Thus, to the extent that traditional patterns of risk abetting behaviors were in place, the stress model was able to produce acceptable explanations in all but one of the communities. St. Louis continued to be an anomaly.

The situation differs somewhat within substantial-risk environments. Nevetheless, stressors, or their buffers, provide the best explanations in Houston and Atlanta. The high vacancy rates associated with down-and-out neighborhoods in the southern communities suggest that vacancy serves as an indicator of stress although it does not play a similar role in neighborhoods in nonsouthern cities. The speculated consequence of the above findings is that angry confrontation continues to play a more important role in producing pockets of elevated risk in southern cities, whereas a combination of angry confrontations and predatory behavior assumes a more prominent role in nonsouthern cities. In the latter situation, stressors tend to become secondary to strain variables in terms of their explanatory strength.

TABLE 3-2

An OLS Regression of Homicide Risk in a Selected Set of Substantial Risk Communities — 1980

Independent Variables	Detroit		Los Angeles		St. Louis		Atlanta		Houston	
	b	t-ratio	b	t-ratio	b	t-ratio	b	t-ratio	b	t-ratio
% Household Poverty	.78	1.40	.52	.39	−.83	−.16	−.143	−1.64	5.08	2.73 **
% Separated or Divorced	−1.00	−.34	2.73	.88	6.19	.55	−3.84	.54	4.94	−.153
% 12 Years of Education	.65	−1.33	1.24	.88	.54	.46	−.14	.19	−1.96	−2.16 *
% Male Unemployment	.002	.003	.94	.61	1.53	.55	−2.66	.88	−.72	−.28
Median Family Income	−.001	−1.08	.004	.78	.002	.93	−.005	−2.32*	.59	1.36
% Vacant Building Units	.44	.17	6.86	1.76	4.52	1.93	1.22	.48	6.49	3.47 ***
% 15-24 Year Old Males	−6.65	−2.79	2.27	.68	2.72	.53	−8.57	−3.47*	−2.36	−1.16
% Recent Migrants	.89	.38	−2.17	−1.19	−18.98	−2.29	−3.98	−1.87	−1.66	−.81

	Detroit		Los Angeles		St. Louis		Atlanta		Houston	
	n=53		n=42		n=30		n=25		n=46	
	adj	se	adj	se	adj	se	adj	se	adj	se
	R^2.18	43	R^2.29	42	R^2.19	59	R^2.36	64	R^2.29	46
	F ratio = 2.45		F ratio = 3.04		F ratio = 1.85		F ratio = 2.72		F ratio = 3.30	
	p=.05		p=.01		ns		p=.05		p=.001	

*p = .05
**p = .01
***p = .001

TABLE 3-3

An OLS Regression Model with Redundant Variables Removed — Substantial Risk Neighborhoods — 1980

Independent Variables	Detroit		Los Angeles		St. Louis		Atlanta		Houston	
	b	t-ratio	b	t-ratio	b	t-ratio	b	t-ratio	b	t-ratio
% Household Poverty	.62	1.40							3.52	2.02*
% Separated or Divorced										
% < 12 Years of Education					1.02	1.53				
Median Rent	-.30	-1.38	.50	-1.83						
Median Family Income							-.005	-2.1*	.01	2.51**
% Vacant Building Units			7.8	2.74**	3.7	2.19**	3.6	1.7	6.83	3.88***
% 15-24 Year Old Males	-6.18	-3.1**								
% Recent Migrants			-2.0	-1.55	-13.3	-2.38				
	adj	se	adj	se	adj	se	adj	se	adj	se
	R^2.25	41	R^2.38	39	R^2.27	56	R^2.31	67	R^2.25	48
	F ratio = 6.64		F ratio = 8.93		F ratio = 4.54		F ratio = 4.67		F ratio = 5.98	
	p = .001		p = .0001		p = .01		p = .01		p = .001	

*p = .05
**p = .01
***p = .001

Summary of the Risk/Stress Association

So far in this chapter our attention has been directed at explaining variation in homicide risk, at the neighborhood scale, within a sample of black communities. We chose to develop a statistical model that incorporated a number of surrogates of status, attitudes, and behaviors that were thought to impact risk. The stress model was moderately successful in providing an understanding of the differential way that stress impacted risk across places. The stress model was plagued by a number of shortcomings, some of which are inherent to the model while others are an outgrowth of the scale at which the investigation was conducted. Another shortcoming was our almost total reliance on the linear model. Although the shortcomings in the model are evident, future effort should be directed at improving model performance through partitioning the dependent variable homicide risk (see for instance, Williams and Flewelling, 1988; Sampson, 1987), the search for additional independent variables, such as a surrogate for culture (see for instance, Baron and Straus, 1988), and the employment of nonlinear formats. Although stress continues to constitute a viable explanation for variations in risk at a microecological level, it seems to diminish in importance in settings in which risk appears to be abetted by nontraditional behavior, a tendency which further weakens the linear association between risk and stress. Clearly, then, additional thought must be directed at how one should proceed in efforts to demonstrate both directly and indirectly the ties between microlevel variations in risk and meso- and macrolevel changes in stressors and nonstressors thought to be related to risk. Until understanding of these connections are better developed, effective buffers will not be provided.

THE MICROENVIRONMENTAL CHARACTER OF THE STRUCTURE OF RISK

We will now turn our attention to another dimension of microenvironmental risk—the life-style or behavioral dimension. Unlike our earlier focus, a nonquantitative assessment of variations in risk will be undertaken for four of our original six cities. A nonquantitative assessment, coupled with our quantitative analysis, provides us with greater insight into the problem. The four cities include Detroit, St. Louis, Atlanta, and Los Angeles. Fieldwork was conducted in the first three cities, but because changes in risk have escalated so quickly in Los Angeles we decided to include it as well in this phase of the assessment. As was the case in the earlier section, emphasis will be placed on evaluating risk in those environments that exceed a predetermined critical limit.

We previously concluded that the stress model, in its present form, failed to explain variations in risk in selected contexts, a factor that we attributed to a weakening of traditional life-styles. Furthermore, we were unable to partition risk in such a way that would have enabled us to address the effectiveness of individual independent variables on homicide risk growing out of varying victim-offender relationships, as was recently done by Williams and Flewelling (1987). Therefore, we decided that a nonquantitative assessment of these differences should complement our earlier quantitative effort and in the final analysis, provide us with greater insight into the problem than either alone would.

The emphasis in this section will be devoted to demonstrating how the modal structure of victimization manifests itself in variations in spatial patterns of risk. Attention will be directed toward demonstrating changes in microspatial patterns of risk as a partial outgrowth of the changing structure of victimization. In this way we should be in a better position to understand ultimately the impact of changes taking place at the macroscale on those taking place at the microscale. Failure to do that makes it unlikely that we would be able to introduce effective risk abatement strategies in a timely fashion.

Earlier we explained the logic underlying the identification of some neighborhoods as substantial risk environments. Seldom are those risk attenuated microenvironments the objects of research, probably because of the heuristic goals of most research. Needless to say, if we are to move from a heuristic level to a practical level, we must become more knowledgeable about the environmental context in which elevated risk is most often observed. The definition of homicide environments or substantial risk environments based on more than three victimizations per neighborhood is a construct better suited to evaluating risk in neighborhood clusters in which traditional victimization structures dominate. In those environments, the victim and offender are much more likely to be drawn from the same milieu. On the other hand, we expect the victim and offender to possess a greater likelihood of coming from different neighborhood types in areas where instrumental (violence designed to achieve a goal) victimizations respresent the modal form.

Neighborhood Contrasts in Victimization Structure

Data from Detroit are employed to illustrate this point. In 1973, Detroit witnessed the second highest number of homicides on record, and the highest number on record at that date. As might be expected, victims were drawn from many neighborhoods in the Detroit black community but were disproportionally from those labeled lower and working class. Yet, two neighborhoods stood out in that year as having almost a dozen victims each. One of these neighborhoods was situated in what Sinclair and Thompson (1977) identified as the city's inner zone, and the other in its middle zone. In a thumbnail sketch of these two zones, they stated the following:

> The inner zone is the domain of the poor and the downtrodden, those who are "rejected," "forgotten," or "left behind" by other elements of Detroit society. More than 25 percent of the zone's 37,000 families subsist on incomes below the poverty level (1977, p. 8).
> The middle zone contributes greatly to the city of Detroit's reputation as the nation's homicide capital... The high incidence of violent crime is related integrally to the tensions and frustrations created by social upheaval, but is also linked to Detroit's drug traffic and to exceedingly high handgun ownership (1977, p. 13).

These conditions should be expected to differentiate between the modal victim-offender relationships in our two high frequency neighborhoods, because our data reveal that stress levels are higher in the lower-status neighborhood than in the working-class neighborhood. Seldom do victimizations of this magnitude occur at the neighborhood scale during a single year. Though the absolute number of victimizations is small, it allows us to ascertain if differences in circumstances and motivations can be detected at this scale, given differences in neighborhood context.

Figure 3–2 graphically illustrates a number of important differences in the pattern of victimization occurring in these two substantial risk neighborhoods. It should be noted at this point, however, that though the incidence in the two neighborhoods was almost equal, an estimation of risk based on their respective 1970 populations indicates risk was substantially higher in the lower-status neighborhood. In the working-class neighborhood, felony and/or suspected felony homicides constituted the modal type, and eight out of ten victims were black males under age thirty. Moreover, felony-type killings were also evident in the lower-status neighborhood; one quarter of the bodies were found dead, and the assailant or assailants were unknown. But conflict emerging at drinking parties or over modest debt or intersex conflict was more commonplace. In the working-class neighborhood, drug-related conflict among acquaintances was more often evident. Likewise, victimizations occurring as an outgrowth of both robbery and breaking and entering were shown to have taken place. The most striking difference, however, as revealed by Figure 3-2, is the incongruence between neighborhood of victim and offender residence in our working-class neighborhood.

In the lower-status neighborhood, it appears that victim and offender were most often drawn from the same neighborhood (see Figure 3-2). A vector extending from place of victim residence outward provides some sense of the physical distance separating the residence of the victim from that of the offender. It is, therefore, apparent that assailants involved in instrumental transactions may travel a greater distance in search of an appropriate target. Location within an urban milieu is believed to influence not only risk of victimization, but the structure of victimization as well. It is evident that economic and cultural forces that extend beyond the confines of the territorial black community—nature of the economy, regional culture, and group subculture—influence both risk and structure. The impact of external forces in promoting variations is strongly associated with the position of individual neighborhoods in the internal structure of the black community. To demonstrate the validity of this position, we will selectively investigate the risk—structure dichotomy in our core city sample. Moreover, we will pay close attention to the risk-structure pattern in Los Angeles in 1980, because the greatest change during the decade occurred in that city.

Internal Spatial Variations in Risk and Structure

It is our contention that internal variations in the pattern of expressive/instrumental homicide mix is a function of a host of micro-environmental factors. Among those often singled out as contributors to observed variations are the following: 1) the presence of rooming house districts occupied primarily by single males; 2) low-income families with an orientation to the street life; 3) working-class districts in which youth are unable or unwilling to pursue the occupational opportunities that bestowed working-class status upon their fathers; 4) selected areas in which the well-off and not-so-well-off are juxtaposed; and 5) the concentration of poor youth in highrise public housing complexes. In areas in which the first set of characteristics prevail, we would expect high-risk neighborhood clusters to demonstrate a strong expresive dominance. A more balanced mix should be expected in the second category, and instrumental killings will be found growing in importance in the latter three areas.

FIGURE 3-2

Homicide Circumstances in Two High Incidence Homicide Neighborhoods

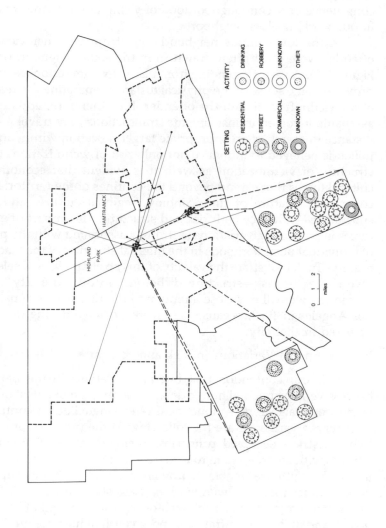

In Detroit, for instance, risk was found to be highest in those neighborhoods near downtown and to gradually decline with movement toward the periphery of the black community. But the structural pattern of risk did not conform to the same general spatial format. For instance, the instrumental contribution to risk appears to be less in the highest-risk sector and reaches a peak four to six miles from the city center before once again giving way to expressive dominance. What was most striking about this finding was the demonstration that the largest share of all homicides occurs in the zone of instrumental dominance, after which there is a sharp drop in the zonal share of total victimizations (see Figure 3–3). This observed pattern leads one to conclude that instrumental risk, when piled atop expressive risk, produces a higher concentration of risk than would ordinarily occur at this location within the black community. We, therefore, tentatively conclude that the observed spatial risk-structure observed in Detroit may well serve as a prototype of the internal pattern of risk and structure in large black communities that have begun to feel the influence of the transi-

FIGURE 3–3

Modal Type of Lethal Violence by Zone

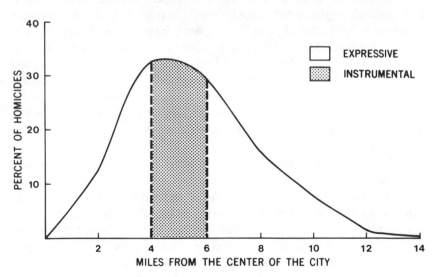

DISTRIBUTION OF BLACK HOMICIDE VICTIMIZATIONS
WITHIN TWO MILE DISTANCE BANDS
DETROIT 1970 – 1975

tional economy, the shift from industrial to postindustrial dominance. Hypothetically, we would describe that pattern in the following way (see Figure 3–3).

Figure 3–3 suggests that the level of expressive risk is highest near the downtown edge of the black community, and it diminishes as one proceeds toward the community's outer edge. The pattern of instrumental risk, however, is thought to increase with distance, peaking at some distance near the center of the community and showing evidence of decline thereafter. The above pattern should be less in evidence in the Sunbelt cities in our sample or at least in those where the traditional subculture is thought to be stronger than outside of the region. The unique spatial characteristics of individual places may produce distortions in this arrangement, if indeed it represents a realistic appraisal of the internal pattern of risk-structure variation.

A NEIGHBORHOOD SCALE ASSESSMENT OF RISK

Neighborhood scale assessments of risk are fraught with difficulty. These difficulties manifest themselves in small numbers of neighborhood-scale observations and victimizations; changing neighborhood boundaries, such as changing census tract scale between censuses; changing congruence between frequency and risk—changes in size of neighborhood populations; and the growing divergence between victim residence, offender residence, and site of victimization. Having adopted the definition of homicide environments discussed previously, however, we continue to support its utility. We are cognizant of its shortcomings but contend it continues to represent a useful construct for our purposes. As the etiology of victimization becomes more complex, the need for a complementary construct becomes more apparent.

To overcome some of these problems, a series of spatially contiguous neighborhoods were identified in which each neighborhood scale unit satisfied the threshold level of victimizations: three or more. Therefore, the identified clusters are assumed to be more likely to conform, in a real sense, to what one has in mind when the image of homicide environment is conjured up. This, however, does not overcome the problem of few observations, although it increases the probability that the victim and offender will be drawn from the same milieu. Yet, subjectively, the cluster construct provides us with a more useful tool as we attempt to enhance our understanding of the microenvironmental factors that contribute to risk. We have chosen to focus our attention on selected clusters occurring in our core sample at different time intervals.

Neighborhood Scale Differences Among Sample Cities

The Detroit black community, which encompassed the largest number of neighborhood scale units in each time period, is best suited for this kind of exercise. Atlanta and Los Angeles also possess neighborhood scale attributes that make it easy to perform the kind of subjective assessment we have in mind. On the other hand, St. Louis, Houston, and Pittsburgh environments, for one reason or another, are assessed less easily. The basic shortcoming associated with the St. Louis case is the problem of few observations, coupled with the compactness of the total community, making it difficult to identify distinguishable clusters. However, St. Louis is much too important a place to ignore as we grapple with an assessment of microenvironmental changes in risk and structure. Census boundary changes in Houston have created special problems. The physical character of the black community in Pittsburgh, coupled with a limited number of observations, has resulted in our eliminating it from this part of the analysis.

MICROENVIRONMENTAL DIFFERENCES IN RISK STRUCTURE

The number of identifiable clusters show a tendency to wax and wane as a function of the annual number of victimizations. Clustering also is influenced by the extent of territorial expansion of the black community during the period of observation. For instance, the number of black homicides occurring in Detroit in 1970 and 1980 were quite similar. But the occurrence of high frequency clusters was more prominent during 1970 than during 1980 (see Figure 3–4). During the latter year, a single primary cluster embraced fourteen neighborhood units. Three secondary clusters occurred in relatively close proximity. In 1970, however, there were seven identifiable clusters in the city, five of which could be classified as primary. As the number of homicides in Detroit increased during the first five years of the decade of the 1970s, so did the extent of clustering (see Figure 3–5.) Thus, by 1975, fourteen high frequency clusters existed in the city, but only five of these contained the minimum number of neighborhood scale units to be viewed as primary clusters; the rest could be described more or less as pockets of risk.

FIGURE 3-4

Detroit: Primary High Incidence Homicide Clusters: 1970

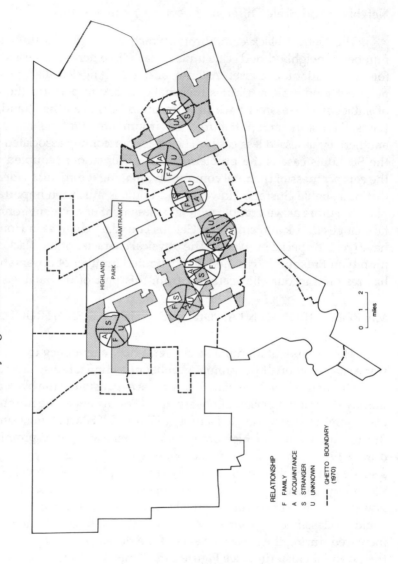

RELATIONSHIP

F FAMILY
A ACQUAINTANCE
S STRANGER
U UNKNOWN

——— GHETTO BOUNDARY
        (1970)

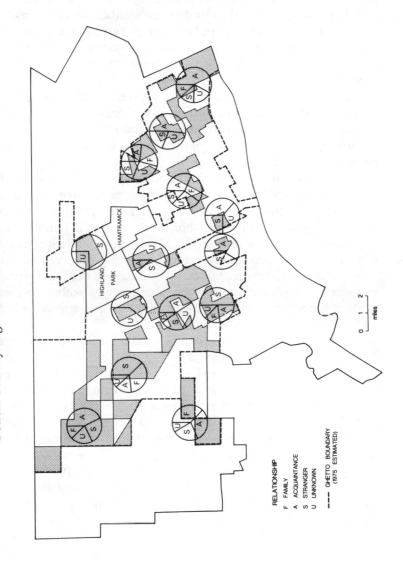

FIGURE 3-5

Detroit: Primary High Incidence Homicide Clusters: 1975

Clustering and Territorial Expansion

On the question of territorial expansion, the Detroit black community engulfed an additional 45 neighborhoods during the 1970s, for a 25 percent increase in the number of neighborhoods in which blacks constituted the majority population. This territorial expansion led to a thinning of population in previously high-density areas, because the population increased by only 13 percent during the period under investigation. However, residential mobility of segments of the population could possibly account for a substantial reduction in clustering without a substantial reduction in risk. If this is in fact the case, we would expect high risk to continue to be present in some previous high-frequency clusters, even though the clusters themselves, by definition, have disappeared.

We expect the above pattern to manifest itself in down-and-out non-family oriented neighborhoods, where expressive violence is commonplace. The question of how these dynamics influence the pattern of clustering in growth neighborhoods is less apparent. Nor is it apparent how the role of a structural mix, independent of population dynamics, influenced the pattern of clustering observed in Detroit in 1980. Intuitively, however, we would suggest that, as instrumental victimizations grow in importance, clustering is likely to become less evident under conditions of a decline in the annual number of victimizations.

Our sample cities are characterized by a high level of diversity based on population change occurring within the confines of an expanding black community. In Detroit, Houston, and Atlanta, population growth was occurring on an already-substantial population base. There was virtually no change in the size of the Los Angeles black population during the interval, although several additional neighborhoods were added to the zone of black population dominance. In St. Louis, the black community was characterized by major depopulation; almost 20 percent fewer blacks were present in the city in 1980 than had been present in 1970. Yet , the physical area dominated by blacks expanded during the interval. Ordinarily, one might have expected frequencies to diminish at the neighborhood scale in St. Louis, but the only evidence of this having occurred was in the older eastern neighborhoods where abandonment had reached an advanced stage. Both frequency and risk declined in those older neighborhoods but there was evidence of increase in recently annexed neighborhoods, which, incidentally, were among the higher-status neighborhoods in the community.

It should be clear from this discussion that neighborhood clusters characterized by substantial risk at the beginning of the period experienced a variety of changes during the decade. The direction of change, as well as the character of the clusters varied from one locality to another. Based on these observations, the internal process or a combination of processes that led to the evolving patterns is difficult to generalize. What we can do to help clarify the problem is delve more deeply into the role of major contributors to risk, at least in terms of structural character and circumstances leading to death in a selected set of primary risk configurations. In a few instances we will employ data drawn from the larger zone in which a given cluster is situated to gain greater insight into the process.

DETROIT: THE NEAR NORTHWEST CLUSTER

Because we know less about instrumental risk and its contribution to substantial-risk neighborhood clusters, we have chosen to focus our initial attention on one such Detroit cluster, at least as a point of departure. The cluster or zone we have chosen is situated on the city's near-northwest side. Blacks began entering the zone for the first time during the 1950s. At that time, higher-status households occupied the area, but as an outgrowth of the city's massive urban renewal program, the status composition began to change. According to Henderson (1964), by 1960, the area had come to be viewed as a marginal one because of both class conflict and an increase in crime. Nevertheless, it was this zone that formed the initial conduit for continued northwest-side entry in the decades that followed. Likewise, it was in this zone that nonconflict-motivated homicides (e.g., instrumental) became predominant early (Wilt and Bannon, 1974).

The Increasing Importance of Robbery-Homicide

Robbery and robbery-homicide increased dramatically in Detroit during 1965–1970 before beginning to taper off. Yet, Zimring (1979) contends that the sharp rise in robberies during this interval fails to account for the even sharper increase in robbery-homicide, which he attributes to a weapons effect. The situation prevailing in the city at that time has been described as follows:

> Detroit has always been known as a violent city, but by 1970 the situation was clearly out of hand. There were over 23,000 reported robberies, which meant that one out of every sixty-five Detroiters had been a victim. An army of drug addicts lived in the remains

of 15,000 inner-city houses abandoned for an urban renewal program which never materialized. Over a million guns were in the hands of the population, and union officials estimated that half the workers came to the plants armed with one weapon or another (Georgakas and Surkin, 1975, p. 202).

There is little question that by 1970, robbery had become a much stronger motive prompting individuals to kill one another than had been true only a few years earlier. Not only had robbery become more important, but so had the planning of robbery-homicides (Dietz, 1983). Dope pads and other residences supporting illicit activity were frequent sites of planned robbery-homicides. Unlike in St. Louis, where most robberies tended to take place on the street, in Detroit, residential robberies were becoming commonplace. With the growth of the irregular economy and the subsequent competition among distributors for the more lucrative markets, contract killings also were becoming more common (Dietz, 1983).

The city's near-northwest side is unique among high-risk clusters in that it represents a zone in which risk was detected to be high during each observation period. In 1980, it contained the largest set of contiguous high risk neighborhoods in the city. The clusters that previously existed on the city's east side had virtually disappeared, at least in terms of satisfying our homicide density criteria. The most unique feature that characterizes the zone in which this cluster exists is its earlier display of a violent orientation that was at odds with traditional patterns.

In 1965, the police district in which this cluster was located was the only district in the city to report more robberies than aggravated assaults. Because homicide and aggravated assault generally are thought to represent the traditional violence orientation of the southern region, it is important to note that a breach of that association was first observed within this district. The first generation of young black males to come of age on the city's near-northwest side displayed a taste for violence that distinguished them from previous cohorts socialized in other city environments. Within a few short years, the pattern of victimization that had developed there had spread across all police districts in which blacks comprised the majority of the population.

It is possible that the observed decrease in robberies during the second half of the 1970s impacted the city's volume of robbery homicide. The choice of victims possibly could have led to improved case closures and a corresponding increase in the probability that assailants would be incarcerated. The number of reported robberies showed a decrease across all of the city's police districts, but homicide frequencies fluctuated from year to year. Yet, the police district containing the near-northwest-side cluster, which had been the district accounting for the largest number of homicides and robberies during the 1970–1975 interval, saw the totals drop by more than 10 percent during the second half of the decade. Although robbery decreased significantly, homicide risk in this zone was not appreciably altered. Of course, one must keep in mind the distinction between frequency (the number of occurrences) and risk (probabilities of vicitmization). We are uncertain at this point if the robbery contribution to risk had been altered. During the first six years of the decade, the mean percentage of robbery-homicides to the total was 16 percent, but it ranged from 13 percent in the low-percentage years to 21 percent in the high-percentage years. The percentage tends to be influenced by the changing ratio of home invasions to street robberies. This point is addressed more fully in the following section.

The Victim-Offender Relation and Robbery-Homicide

Earlier, we mentioned the possibility that a change in the choice of victim could have influenced the decrease in the frequency of both reported robberies and subsequently robbery-homicides. Because robbery is traditionally an act involving strangers (Zimring, 1984), and the likelihood of such transactions leading to death is said to be a function of the degree of victim resistance (Luckenbill, 1984; Block, 1977), less resistant victims might have been selected. The percentage of all robberies ending in death, however, is variously estimated. Zimring and Zuehl (1986) report that less than one-half of one percent of all robberies lead to death in Chicago, but the certainty is increased as a function of context. For instance, in Chicago, residential robberies were found to have a higher likelihood of leading to death than those occurring in other settings (Zimring and Zuehl, 1986). These robberies were found more often to be drug-related. The pattern observed in Chicago by Zimring and Zuehl bears a striking resemblance to the pattern we observed in Detroit, particularly as it relates to the relative importance of home invasions and robberies involving acquaintances.

We previously noted the growing weakness of the assumption that all acquaintance homicides grow out of angry confrontations. By 1979, there was growing evidence that black robbery homicide offenders were beginning to display hardened attitudes toward their victims, a growing number of whom were known to them. Dietz (1983), in addressing the point of hardening of attitudes, indicates that interviews with persons who chose to prey upon individuals whom they knew, acknowledged depersonalizing the interaction so that it did not interfere with the goal of acquiring money. Such killings almost always involve two or more assailants and, according to Dietz (1983), the core members of the assailant team have no aversion to killing the target and/or targets. She states that drug houses and gambling houses are viewed as prime targets. The predator group is said often to view themselves as courageous individuals because the targets themselves are heavily armed.

Drug Houses as Robbery Targets

Drug houses appear to provide lucrative targets for would-be robbers, because money, drugs, and, in some instances, other items of value are available. In many instances, at least one individual making up the robbery team acquires entry to the house because he or she is known to the operator or the guard. The initial entrant then assists his confederates in gaining entry. Once inside, the stage is set for the confrontation to follow. Yet, the outcome is highly unpredictable. In some instances, the outcome leads to the death of multiple victims who are killed by multiple offenders, and in other instances, multiple offenders kill a single victim. In small husband-and-wife drug operations, both are usually killed by young black male assailants. In other instances, the drug-house operator prevails and kills or injures one or more persons involved in the attempted robbery. The one apparent difference that distinguishes many drug-house attacks from other residential robberies is the combination of multiple victims and multiple offenders. Montforte and Spitz (1975) suggest that if victimizations such as these were defined as drug-related, rather than relying solely on the presence of morphine in the victim's blood or track marks on their arms to satisfy the definition, the share of all homicides described as drug-related would increase dramatically.

Another example from our Detroit file further reveals a hardening of attitudes among selected young adults. Such individuals frequently become involved in violent solo interactions with peers, which grow into more complex and ambiguous behaviors that defy easy classification. The example that follows is a description of one of our 1975 sample victimizations. The description was taken from the Detroit police case files. The case involved a young adult victim in our victim sample and the hardened behavior exhibited by his assailant. The transaction starts out as a typical street altercation in which tempers flair and de-escalation of the conflict is made difficult by the presence of peer onlookers. We think the following description illustrates the point:

The deceased (age 23) and the defendant (age 19) were engaged in a pool game, when a disagreement occurred between them as to the size of the bet on the game. The defendant refused to continue to play and walked around the pool table where a scuffle ensued. The scuffle was broken up by other patrons. The defendant took his own cue and coat and walked towards the door. The defendant then drew his revolver from his back pants pocket and fired one shot, striking the deceased in the abdomen. The deceased fell to the floor and the defendant bent over the deceased, rolled him over and took an unknown amount of money from his pockets. The deceased's brother (age 19) then went to the deceased and the defendant pointed his revolver at him and demanded, "How much money do you have?" Upon being told, the defendant said, "Give it to me." The brother gave the defendant about $85 and the defendant ran out the door.

In its early and middle phases, the confrontation had all of the earmarks of a commonplace ghetto conflict growing out of a gambling argument. In the final phase, it appears to deviate from the run-of-the-mill conflict motivated argument and takes on the characteristics of an instrumental act. The callousness with which the act was committed and the orderliness with which the offender acted in taking the money illustrates that this was more than a typical street-corner confrontation. The defendant, it seems, can be more appropriately described as a hustler whose prime objective was to secure monetary reward and any act that would ensure the successful achievement of that goal could be performed. The defendant was brought to trial on the charge of murder in the second degree but was found not guilty for "lack of sufficient evidence."

In the early 1970s, commercial businesses represented major targets among youthful robbers. But these targets turned out to be highly dangerous for the robber because the robber was as likely to become the victim as the robbed. This realization probably prompted an increase in street and residential robberies. Moreover, the residential structures that had become the prime targets of predatory invasions—drug houses—also were well defended, making them dangerous targets as well. It is unclear whether these locations became more impregnable during the latter 1970s, or if it was the police crackdown on distributors that reduced their presence in the environment and led to the reduction in total robbery-homicides. Another possibility is that the involvement of multiple offenders led to one or more offenders implicating the triggerman, thus allowing the state to convict a larger share of perpetrators and thereby remove them from the streets.

Changes in a Cluster of Persistent Risk

The Detroit homicide environment, as defined by our residence-frequency index, became more diffuse between 1970 and 1980. The formation of high-risk clusters reached a peak in 1975, when fourteen primary clusters were detected. But the physical expansion of the community and the subsequent decline in homicide frequency eliminated a number of high-risk clusters. Moreover, the near-northwest-side cluster, which persisted throughout the interval, underwent a slight modification in structure, although risk levels appear quite similar in both 1970 and 1980. Possibly because of a shift in the age structure of victimization, with males aged over thirty years predominating, expressive dominance was evident. Only one in seven residents of the cluster were described as robbery-homicide victims in 1980. Although the risk level in our persistent-risk cluster changed little over the decade, the quality of life changed greatly. What was a predominantly intermediate-stress zone in 1970 had become a zone in which high-stress levels predominated in 1980, a factor that might possibly have led to a stronger expressive contribution to risk.

The role of robbery-homicide as a contributor to risk levels in Detroit was emphasized in this discussion because of its relative importance in the escalation of risk in the city. It touched most neighborhood clusters in which risk was high, but it tended to vary in importance from cluster to cluster as a function of opportunity. When juxtaposed against middle-income districts and districts characterized by high levels of residential mobility, incidents of robbery-homicides peaked in working-class districts.

THE ST. LOUIS HOMICIDE ENVIRONMENT

The St. Louis black community is much smaller than that of Detroit, but the problem of homicide risk is more severe. Unlike Detroit, which registered a mild relaxation of the problem during the late 1970s, the problem in St. Louis grew more severe with risk climbing even higher than had been the case during the initial observation year. The physical character of the St. Louis black community experienced a variety of changes during the 1970s. Among the more notable of those changes were widespread housing abandonment and the destruction of a major public housing complex—Pruit-Igoe. Black St. Louisans who could afford to abandoned their city at a rapid clip during the decade for residence in a series of suburban communities along the western edge of the city.

There are those who contend the changes did much to . homogenize the northside population and subsequently contributed to the observed levels of high risk that prevailed throughout the period. Yet, Meyers (1954) contends that high risk prevailed in the river city prior to the most recent period. He likewise noted that it was in those districts in which blacks resided that homicide risk reached its peak. We, too, are interested in whether substantial differences in risk and structure can be detected in the city's primary black-occupancy zone during the most recent decade.

Adopting an Appropriate Cluster Threshold

The difficulty in identifying distinct high risk clusters in St. Louis in both 1970 and 1975 was discussed previously. It was not because high risk did not exist, but rather because so many observations in the black community satisfied the threshold of three or more resident victims in any given year that cluster boundaries were difficult to delineate (see Figure 3–6). It is obvious that under high-frequency conditions, in a spatially compact but declining community, risk has remained high. Despite the difficulties, three primary clusters were identified in both 1970 and 1975.

One way to overcome the problem of boundary delineation is to impose a higher frequency threshold. A modified threshold should prove beneficial in this instance to overcome the unique set of physical circumstances that characterize St. Louis (see Figure 3–6). Thus, to more clearly distinguish the existence of high-risk clusters, a modified threshold in fact was established. Nevertheless, problems associated with the establishment of boundaries between clusters did not automatically disappear, but the modified threshold did produce greater congruence between frequency and risk.

The Structural Mix in High-Risk Neighborhoods

St. Louis, as earlier noted, manifested incipient evidence of weakening subcultural traditions as early as 1965. By 1970, however, its structural mix was already moving precipitously in the direction of instrumental dominance. At that date, the traditional conflict-motivated confrontations between black males over age thirty tended to slow the instrumental advance. In the aggregation of neighborhood scale units in which risk, defined in terms of frequency, was thought to be highest, contributions to risk from acquaintance killings and killings in which the offender was unknown to authorities accounted for more than 70

FIGURE 3–6

St. Louis: Primary High Incidence Homicide Clusters: 1975

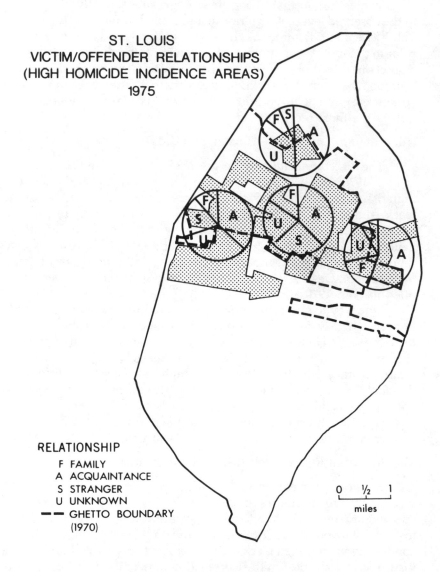

ST. LOUIS
VICTIM/OFFENDER RELATIONSHIPS
(HIGH HOMICIDE INCIDENCE AREAS)
1975

RELATIONSHIP
F FAMILY
A ACQUAINTANCE
S STRANGER
U UNKNOWN
— — GHETTO BOUNDARY
(1970)

0   ½   1
miles

percent of the total risk (see Table 3–4). The structure of victimization shown in Table 3–4 enables us to distinguish the St. Louis structure from that describing Detroit.

TABLE 3-4

The Structure and Level of Substantial Risk in
St. Louis Black Neighborhoods - 1970

Structure	Level	Percent of Total Risk
Acquaintance	34.2 per 100,000	35.8
Unknown	33.5 per 100,000	35.2
Family	17.2 per 100,000	18.0
Stranger	9.9 per 100,000	11.0

Source: Computed on the basis of number of deaths reported by FBI, by victim-
offender relationship, and the size of the population (U.S. Bureau of
the Census, 1970).

In Detroit, victimizations of strangers accounted for a larger share
of the risk than they did in St. Louis at the same date. Although both
places were becoming important instrumental-victimization environments, it is quite possible that a different set of circumstances
served as the primary motivation for the killings. The solution to the
puzzle is obscured by the ambiguity associated with unknown victimizations. Yet, when structurally specific risk (e.g., victims who were
unknown to the offenders) was regressed against selected
neighborhood-scale independent variables, those variables that most
often proved significant were significant for both acquaintance risk and
unknown risk. This suggests, at least in St. Louis, that the environmental attributes that support acquaintance killings also support
unknown victimizations. On the surface, this appears to be counter
intuitive judgment. Nevertheless, we are interested in ascertaining if
distinctions in the risk-structure association reveal themselves at the
cluster level.

By modifying the risk threshold, we were able to demonstrate
the existence of core risk locations within our initially defined clusters.
In most instances, however, the loss of neighborhood units from the
original cluster was minimal. The easternmost cluster, which originated
on the border of the central business district, was characterized by the
highest risk level. But even here, the largest share of the victimizations were dominated by acquaintance and unknown killings (see
Figure 3-7). This cluster included some of the worst housing in the
city, as well as the Pruit-Igoe housing complex. Family killings occurred
less frequently in this cluster than elsewhere. The mature male constituted the modal victim. The life-styles of aging men confined to an
environment of extreme poverty, which included excessive drinking,

games of chance, and conflict between the sexes, often led to death. But young men were also frequent victims, and it is among this group that high levels of instrumental violence was exhibited. The estimated victimization rate attributed to instrumental killings was 49 homicides per 100,000 persons, whereas that associated with expressive killings was 46 homicides per 100,000 persons. This represents a departure from the hypothetical expected pattern previously described. This deviation from the expected pattern possibly reflects the presence of a high-rise public housing complex in the zone.

Two additional primary clusters were identified in which risk levels deviated somewhat from the expected pattern. The central cluster, which was an extension of the cluster described above, was characterized by risk levels approximately one-third lower than those in the eastern cluster. In this cluster, expressive victimizations were relatively more important because family killings occurred much more frequently than they had in the eastern zone. Yet, the highest risk continued to be associated with acquaintance and unknown deaths. Given the contribution of family killings to total risk, females were almost twice as likely to become victims as they were in the previous cluster. Likewise, there was a balance in victimization between young adult males and mature males. In the city's second primary cluster, risk was lower and structure more variegated, an outgrowth of both life-style and demographic differences which distinguished it from its eastern neighbor.

The westernmost cluster, representing the most recent black occupancy zone, had intermediate-risk levels between those prevailing in the previous two clusters—81 homicides per 100,000 persons. Since the western zone was characterized by lower levels of stress than those associated with the previous cluster, one would intuitively assume risk levels would be lower. This was not the case. The major distinction between the western cluster and its central neighbor was the much higher risk associated with acquaintance killings and the somewhat higher level of stranger victimizations. There was virtually no difference in risk among unknown and family victimizations.

Conflict among acquaintances and among individuals unknown to the assailants provided the primary basis for sustaining high levels of risk in the previously identified clusters. In these neighborhoods, a strong statistical association existed among the two ($r = .743$), although some differences could be detected between the contributions of individual variables toward an explanation of levels of acquaintance risk and unknown risk. The variable that was the most important contributor to both types of risk was vacancy rate. In neighborhoods in

FIGURE 3–7

Population Change on St. Louis' Northside: 1970–1975

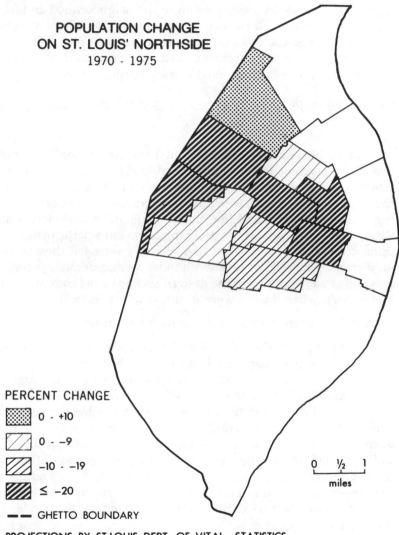

**POPULATION CHANGE
ON ST. LOUIS' NORTHSIDE**
1970 - 1975

PERCENT CHANGE

0 - +10

0 - −9

−10 - −19

≤ −20

GHETTO BOUNDARY

PROJECTIONS BY ST.LOUIS DEPT. OF VITAL STATISTICS

0   ½   1
miles

which housing abandonment, high levels of residential mobility, and declining social cohesion were in evidence, so were high levels of risk among these two risk types. Although unemployment and poverty also were positively associated with acquaintance killings, the secondary contributors to high levels of unknown victimization were the percentage of 15–24 year-old-males present in the neighborhood and family income. It is unclear if these two victimization types bring into contact persons who possess a dichotomous set of orientations, hailing from distinctly different neighborhoods, but for whom death at the hands of another represents their most glaring commonality.

ST. LOUIS POPULATION DYNAMICS AND ENVIRONMENTS OF RISK

In the interval between 1970 and 1980, the St. Louis black community underwent major change, especially demographic change, which possibly aggravated risk conditions. As previously noted, among the more notable changes were the abandonment of the city by a growing number of blacks and the economic plight of those left behind. Rising unemployment levels, declining labor-force-participation rates, intensification of poverty, and high vacancy rates left their mark on an increasing number of neighborhoods. By mid-decade, population loss had already decimated the eastern section of the community (see Figure 3–7), where blacks were in the majority in 1970.

Shift in the Location of Substantial Risk Structures

The population shifts altered the location of substantial risk clusters. The eastern cluster disappeared, the central cluster became elongated and segmented, and the western cluster expanded slightly, edging its way toward the city's western edge. Most apparent was the increase in the number of resident victimizations in cluster neighborhoods. As was true in the initial time period, cluster risk continued to be firmly anchored in acquaintance behavior and victimizations involving unknown offenders. The most striking difference, aside from the intensification of risk, was the composition of risk. Young adult black males were victimized at least twice as often as others in each cluster.

St. Louis' south central cluster emerged as the city's most dangerous by 1975. It is not known if, as a primary settlement target of persons who formerly resided in the eastern cluster, it represented a simple transfer of life-styles to another location, or if some other more complex set of factors was responsible for the deepening of risk. What was evident in this cluster was the growing influence of drug-related incidents and robbery on elevating risk. Mature adults most often were the victimized. By 1975, homicide had become firmly established as a leading cause of death in the black community and, though risk was highest in the south central cluster, it was only slightly lower in the north central and western clusters.

A crude estimate of the increase in risk among clusters indicates an approximate 50 percent increase. Many more neighborhoods had become places in which risk was essentially gratuitous. Increasingly, the target and the perpetrator were not previously known to one another. But, equally disturbing, when victim and offender were known to each other, a victimization was as likely to evolve from instrumental circumstances as expressive, especially among young adult males. The nature of these transactions resulted in a disproportionately small number of victimizations resulting in indictment. (This point will be discussed in greater detail in a later chapter.) Moreover, street justice often seemed to prevail; victimizers in one or more incidents became victims in a later incident.

The carnage in St. Louis in 1975 had not subsided by the beginning of the new decade. What had changed, however, was further modification of the pattern of high-risk clusters. Both the south central cluster and the western cluster experienced only modest change in the outline of their respective configurations. What was surprising was the emergence of a full blown cluster that embodied a series of neighborhoods that had not been a part of the St. Louis black community ten years earlier. This cluster was characterized by lower stress levels and higher status than any other set of neighborhoods in the city's black community. Yet, in 1980, homicide risk in that set of neighborhoods paralleled that prevailing in the eastern cluster in 1970.

Available data will not permit us to make precise structural comparisons as we did earlier, but it should be noted that the ratio of place of victimization to residence of victim was lower here than in the other two primary clusters. This suggests a large share of cluster victims met their fate in neighborhoods in which they had previous ties. If this was in fact the case, it weakens the validity of our construct for establishing the prevalence of high-risk environments. As instrumental victimizations grow in importance, it will become necessary for us to establish criteria that will enable us to distinguish high-risk victimization neighborhoods from high-risk offender neighborhoods. It is unclear at this point to what extent the two diverge in location. The problem is made more difficult by the ever-increasing share of offenders motivated by instrumental concerns. The number of such offenders unknown to the authorities tends to be growing.

THE DETROIT/ST. LOUIS COMPARISONS

High-risk homicide environments in Detroit and St. Louis moved in different directions during the 1970s. In Detroit, they expanded in number during the first half of the decade but diminished during the final half. Risk had become more diffuse, and by 1980, clustering had virtually disappeared on the city's east side. We are aware that the latter point may simply describe an ephemeral situation. Although risk had abated somewhat by 1980, robbery-homicide continued to represent a substantial contributor to risk.

St. Louis, on the other hand was plagued by rising risk levels throughout the period, and young adults were the primary targets of victimization. Robbery was also an important contributor to risk in the River City, but it appears that drug-related deaths were even more important. The growth of the drug business in the St. Louis community seemed to perpetuate continuing conflict between warring factions for distributional rights in specific local markets. These factions often were headed by several members from a common kinship group. Family leaders tended to be eliminated, or incarcerated over a rather brief interval, and were then replaced by other families, usually composed of brothers, who repeated the ritual. Drug-related deaths in St. Louis are more often outcomes inherent to the nature of the business; therefore, they differ from robbery deaths in Detroit in which drug houses constitute a prime target. In these two nonsouthern locations, we have observed a dramatic increase in the role of instrumental victimizations to total risk. Based on these observations it becomes obvious that some of the generalizations based on traditional risk structures do not hold in communities where economic change has had a pervasive negative impact on the local black community.

ATLANTA: THE PERSISTENCE OF TRADITIONAL RISK

No other city in the South, in the post civil rights era, has made an effort to alter its race relations image to the extent that Atlanta has. Many young black profesionals from around the nation view it as the new cultural capital of black America. Even though Atlanta has outwardly undergone a metamorphosis, the subcultural tradition of violence is still in evidence in the neighborhoods. At the beginning of the period, Atlanta maintained the highest homicide risk level among the nation's fifty largest cities; a position that it had not surrendered by the early 1970s (Barnett et al., 1975). By 1980, however, it ranked below St. Louis, Detroit, and Cleveland, and possessed a level of risk that was similar to that prevailing in other major southern cities. Although risk in Atlanta's black community declined during the decade, some evidence supported an incipient pattern of instrumental victimization.

The Location of High Risk Clusters

Patterns of black victimization in Atlanta have received less attention than those in some other high homicide risk communities, although the work of Imes (1972) and Munford et al. (1976) shed some light on the situation. Aside from the notoriety associated with the recent Atlanta child killings (Baldwin, 1985, and Headley, 1985), the phenomenon of black risk in this southern metropolis has received only limited attention. As a traditional southern city, high levels of victimization have long been pervasive in the city's down-and-out neighborhoods, a condition that has simply come to be expected.

As we have seen elsewhere, crimes of opportunity escalated during the 1960s, and Atlanta also had an increase, although its increase in opportunity crimes has not approached the level occurring in Detroit and St. Louis. Yet Munford et al. (1976) demonstrated that public killings involving unknown individuals were on the rise in Atlanta as early as 1971-1972. Some of these killings seem to have tarnished the city's image, because both the local and national media have highlighted these events as evidence of increasing criminality. Though evidence grows in support of incipient instrumental victimization, victimization is more stable in Atlanta than in communities outside the region. The question is, have changing risk levels combined with an alteration in the structure of victimization influenced the location of high-risk clusters?

That Atlanta has undergone a major spatial rearrangement of population within the black community is apparent. Many old established neighborhoods lost population while growth was taking place along the margins of the 1970 enclave. But, unlike its nonsouthern counterpart, St. Louis, it did not experience an absolute decline; it experienced modest growth instead. At the beginning of the period, high risk extended over a large number of neighborhoods. At this time, only high-status areas within the black community proved more or less invulnerable. Thus the association between risk and stress was moderate to strong, which indirectly suggests that emerging high-risk clusters were an outgrowth of frequent conflict-motivated actions involving acquaintances and family members.

As long as frequencies remained high and community expansion occurred at a slow pace, high-frequency/high-risk clusters embraced a large share of the community's poor and near-poor neighborhoods. One unique feature of selected Atlanta clusters was the greater frequency of female victimizations, an outcome associated with the greater relative importance of family homicides. Although Atlanta in 1970 attained unusually high levels of risk in its black community, the structure of victimization did not differ substantially from the traditional pattern that prevailed in Birmingham in the late 1930s and early 1940s (Harlan, 1950).

Changing Risk Levels in Atlanta

Because much of the homicide research historically has been oriented toward explaining the traditional pattern of victimization, that pattern is well known. Therefore, we will devote far less effort to explaining risk structures in Atlanta than was devoted to this phenomenon in our other two core city samples. What clearly occurred during the last six years of the decade was a sharp lowering of risk growing out of conflict among acquaintances. Risk levels associated with acquaintance killings were reduced by more than one-half between 1970 and 1980. For some reason, young adult black males reduced their propensity to engage in mortal combat, a factor primarily responsible for the lower observed aggregate risk in 1980.

Major headway was also made in reducing the incidence of family homicide. In the initial time period, family homicide risk in Atlanta was substantially higher than levels prevailing in any of our other sample cities. This specific victim pattern distinguished Atlanta from its peers. Whereas robbery killings were becoming routine events in Detroit and shoot-outs among drug dealers were much in the news in St. Louis, family killings struck a raw nerve in Atlanta. Growing concern over this matter led to the development of a crisis intervention counseling center within the police department. The work of the center has been given some credit in reducing family-victimization levels since its inception. Needless to say, unknown victimizations have increased in Atlanta, as has been true nationally. By 1980, that category of killings was only slightly less risky than acquaintance killings.

The precipitous drop in the annual number of homicides in the city's black community after 1974 resulted in diminishing the scale of homicide clusters, although the 1980 cluster pattern bore a strong resemblance to that prevailing in 1975 (see Figure 3–8). Population loss in older neighborhoods bordering downtown eliminated them from the high-risk category based on frequency. Yet, actual risk levels remained high and, in some instances, intensified. In that case, to more

realistically define substantial-risk clusters, we shifted the threshold
upward. Yet, in Atlanta, it appears that a downward shift would have
been more appropriate, especially in those neighborhoods in which
the most severe population losses occurred.

FIGURE 3–8

Atlanta
Primary High Incidence Homicide Clusters: 1975

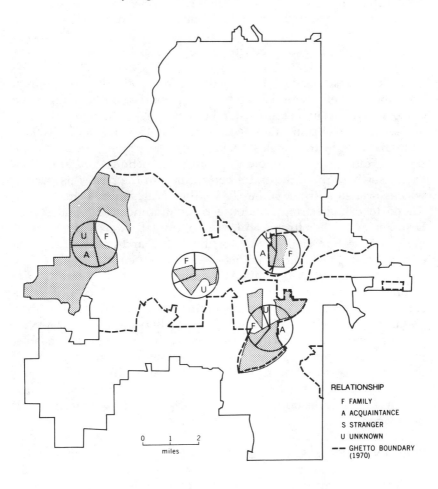

RELATIONSHIP

F FAMILY
A ACQUAINTANCE
S STRANGER
U UNKNOWN
−− GHETTO BOUNDARY
(1970)

One of the most striking differences in the evolving pattern of
high-risk environments occurring between 1975 and 1980 was the
substantial expansion of the southeastern cluster. Almost two-fifths

of all victims resided in this cluster by 1980. Lower levels of environmental stress and a smaller share of persons falling below the poverty line distinguished this cluster from others where a similar level of risk was manifested. Risk had been elevated in an environment in which lower levels previously prevailed. As a zone in the process of racial residential change during the interval, it had come to house both black and white populations at higher-than-average risk of victimization. In 1980, 22 percent of the victims in the cluster were white, and most had been victimized by a same-race offender. Moreover, it should be noted that white victims were more often the target of instrumental victimization than were black victims. However, nationally, white victims are more likely to be targets of instrumentally motivated killings, than are black victims.

Other clusters evolved during the last half of the decade, but high frequency universally translated into high risk. The traditional pattern of risk was dominant in this cluster, but not by a large margin. Stranger and unknown victimizations accounted for 45 percent of all black victimizations, with females constituting the primary instrumental target. Women were more often the target of victimization in Atlanta than elsewhere throughout the period, but, in the past, this pattern was associated with lethal family conflict. Males in this cluster continued to exhibit strong evidence of continuing traditional styles. Disputes and other forms of angry confrontation occurring during periods of leisure at the home of the victim and/or offender were commonplace. Male street killings were infrequent.

Why Atlanta victimizations declined over the interval is not completely understood. Apparently, however, the local economy was able to accommodate a larger share of the young adult population than was possible in Detroit or St. Louis. Young adults socialized in a service economy might have been more receptive to the kinds of jobs available. For whatever reason, the risk of acquaintance death declined dramatically, the decline revealing itself most vividly among young adults. The primary cluster of risk prevailing in 1980 was one in which the modal victimizations were concentrated in the mature adult population.

LOS ANGELES: A CASE OF EXTREME RISK INTENSIFICATION

The western region has been the target of black migration for a shorter period than have other regions. Rapid growth in the urban west was largely a response to World War II labor needs. Los Angeles now contains the fifth largest black community in the nation and, if we add to that its suburban extension, it is rapidly approaching the metropolitan Detroit population in size. The black population of Los Angeles is somewhat more diverse than that in Frostbelt cities because a large share of its population has migrated from elsewhere in the nation; those attracted to this market have come in search of a wide range of opportunities. Los Angeles is more cosmopolitan and less parochial, as demonstrated by its role as a major trend-setter of fashions and life-styles.

A Comparison with Core City Sample

At the beginning of the period, blacks in Los Angeles appeared to have escaped the rising tide of escalating personal violence. Risk levels in the city were much lower than those prevailing in other large black communities around the country. But that assessment would be short-lived; evidence of increasing risk was present by mid-decade. Because we view Los Angeles as the anomalous case, we have chosen to add it to our core-city sample to detect how it differed from the other cities by the decade's end.

Though differing from each of the members of the core city sample at the beginning of the period, Los Angeles also possessed a number of commonalities. Its large population, spread over an expansive area, bore some similarity to Detroit, as did the large percentage of the population born elsewhere. Its strong dependence on a service economy and the presence of a high-status black enclave within the larger enclave reminds us of Atlanta. Moreover, the fleeing of large numbers of persons to adjoining suburbs brings to mind the pattern occurring in St. Louis during the same interval. Like Detroit, it was the site of a major riot during the 1960s, but, unlike Detroit, it was not a single-industry town. Los Angeles is a multi-ethnic new immigrant center and the only one of our sample cities in which blacks are neither the largest single-ethnic minority, nor the most recently arrived new ethnic population. To what extent these differences have influenced the level and pattern of victimization in this somewhat tranquil setting is not well understood.

A Doubling in Risk in a Single Decade

Our detailing of changes in level and pattern of victimization in this western urban center will, of necessity, be more circumspect. However, some additional attention should be focused on this peripheral sample case. To date, few analysts have pursued the topic of homicide risk in Los Angeles. With the exception of the work by Allen and her associates (1980), little previous work exists upon which to build. Nevertheless, there is cause for alarm when the homicide incidence among a large population subgroup almost doubles within a single decade, from a level of 41 per 100,000 to 87 per 100,000.

In this situation, unlike that in our previously discussed cases, a strong link appears to exist between violence in the city and its extension beyond the city. For instance, there were 441 blacks killed in the city in 1980, but only 60 percent of the victims resided in the city. Unfortunately, we are not in a position to differentiate between victim origins and circumstances of death and are therefore unable to specify the nature of the violence chain. Yet, in Los Angeles, movement to the suburbs clearly does not lessen the probability of risk in the way it appears to do in St. Louis.

An Alteration in Structural Orientation

What is apparent in the Los Angeles case is the dramatic increase in the number of unknown killings described. The size of the absolute increase in victimizations occurring in this population between 1975 and 1980 is almost totally accounted for by the size of unknown victimizations in the latter year. Eventually, many cases described initially as unknowns are closed and the actual relationships and circumstances revealed. But in the absence of this verifying information, it is not illogical to assume a large percentage of the killings in this category were felony-related. With that in mind, an expressive pattern of victimization similar to that prevailing in Atlanta apparently was altered and, by 1980, had taken on the broad general structural outline more typical of St. Louis. The grafting onto a pattern of traditional dominance, one that is largely instrumental in orientation, has led to a takeoff in levels of violence not visible in the early 1970s. For instance, robberies increased substantially in two police districts in which blacks constituted the majority population (1975–1980), whereas aggravated assaults showed much less change. The next question, therefore, is, just how have changes in incidence manifested themselves in a micro-environmental context?

Evidence of Change in Cluster Patterns

Several pockets of substantial risk were in evidence in 1970. But individual neighborhoods within these pockets could most often be described as environments of intermediate risk. The level of risk that prevailed in Los Angeles' substantial-risk neighborhoods was, on average, 20 percent lower than substantial-risk neighborhoods in St. Louis, Detroit, and Atlanta at the same date (see Table 3–5). In 1970, fewer than 25 percent of all predominantly black neighborhoods qualified as substantial-risk environments. By 1980, the proportion had risen to almost one-third. Yet, the increase in the number of substantial-risk neighborhoods was less than the level of increased risk in all substantial-risk neighborhoods. Thus, by 1980, the mean risk in substantial-risk neighborhoods was more nearly akin to that of other locations in the sample than it had been ten years earlier. Yet the mean risk differed from all but St. Louis in its change in pattern and scale of high-risk clusters over the interval.

TABLE 3-5

The Mean Homicide Risk in Substantial Risk Neighborhoods
— 1970 and 1980 —

	Homicide Rate (per 100,000)	
City	1970	1980
Atlanta	119	126
Houston	73	117
St. Louis	103	130
Los Angeles	86	120
Detroit	105	107

Source: Computed from FBI Monthly Homicide Reports and Census of Population Reports, 1970 and 1980.

The primary high-risk clusters merged at the beginning of the 1970–1980 period. The initial expansion was basically to the west, but since 1975, the strongest movement has been to the south. The primary central and southern cluster, by 1980, essentially had come to represent a single cluster extending from the northern edge of the community to its southern edge. Thus the dramatic increase in frequency of victimization generally intensified, and neighborhoods that had not earlier qualified for substantial risk designation were drawn into the fold. The offenders in this evolving high-risk corridor showed a tendency to favor youthful victims and victims who were male more than 80 percent of the time. In the absence of direct structural data, one would speculate that instrumental motives contributed heavily to the evolving substantial-risk configuration observed in 1980. This position is buttressed by data from annual police reports detailing the substantial increase in robbery between 1975 and 1980 in the two police districts embracing the cluster. The FBI monthly homicide report for Los Angeles shows that the largest share of young adult black male victimizations were motivated by instrumental concerns.

The increase in victimization levels in Los Angeles had the effect of expanding and coalescing two previously existing substantial-risk clusters. At least one previously existing secondary cluster retained its former status, although that cluster appears to be in the process of transition from predominantly black to predominatly Hispanic. This seems to have had little effect, however, on its substantial-risk status. The ethnic mix of the victims shows a tendency to reflect the neighborhood mix. Yet, the general increase in risk in that city during the latter half of the decade was primarily associated with excessive victimizations involving blacks and Hispanics, as pointed out by Loya et al. (1986). But the posited city-level explanation of changing aggregate risk does not explain the level of risk that was evolving in these respective ethnic communities.

Some of the more logical explanations of observed changes in risk at the microecological level are growth in gang activity, increased propensity to commit robbery, and a general tendency to adopt maladaptive values and styles. But, at a slightly higher level of resolution, it would be shortsighted of us to ignore the role of inter-ethnic conflict in the job market (Oliver and Johnson, 1984) on the prospect for an increase in risk. This situation is partially an outgrowth of large-scale new immigration to the city. These views, however, must be considered tentative, because they have not been tested thoroughly. Nevertheless, by 1980, risk of victimization in the Los Angeles black community seemed to possess more in common with St. Louis than Atlanta, a condition that should provoke a careful re-examination of situational factors.

POST–1980 CHANGES IN AGGREGATE RISK AND THE EFFECT AT THE MICROLEVEL

Detroit, by 1985, had once again assumed the position as a ranking high-risk victimization center. Five years earlier, the trend of contagious assaultive violence that had been prevalent throughout the period 1964–1974 appeared to have been reversed (Loftin, 1986). The observed downward movement in risk was short-lived, however; an incipient upturn was under way as early as 1984. The renewal of the earlier pattern appears to be continuing, and Detroit can once again be placed in the emergent high-risk end of the risk-structural continuum. However, of central importance here is how the neighborhoods have been affected by the most recent upturn. At the neighborhood level, a number of earlier identified pockets of substantial risk had seemingly disappeared. Nowhere was that more in evidence than on the city's eastside. But a 22 percent increase in black victimization between 1980 and 1985 led to re-emergence of some former clusters and an intensification of risk in the city's near northwest-side cluster. Of the 100 additional black homicides occurring in Detroit in 1985, a disproportionate share involved residents in a zone contiguous to the primary near-northwest-side cluster, which constituted the city's foremost high-density cluster in 1980. By 1985, this zone served as the place of residence of approximately 25 percent of all homicide victims in the city.

The near-northwest-side's zone of expansion was over-whelmingly composed of neighborhoods that in 1980, could best be described as predominately intermediate-stress neighborhoods, but low-stress neighborhoods also existed. This situation seems to further suggest a weakening of the stress/risk tie. Just what forces were at work to provoke such a sharp increase in risk in a single cluster is not easily explained, but the continuing decline in this complex of contiguous neighborhoods and the subsequent juxtaposition of a different mix of poor and nonpoor populations might stimulate an intensification of predatory behavior.

In each of our remaining sample cities, the absolute level of victimization declined between 1980 and 1985. However, an absolute lowering of the level of victimization does not necesaily lead to a reduction in risk. Based on our population estimates for the latter years it appears that risk reductions did in fact occur at each location except St. Louis. In St. Louis a slight increase in risk was recorded, even though there was an 11.0 percent decrease in the number of victimizations.

At each place, changes in the observed level of victimization were revealed in altered patterns of homicide density at the neighborhood level. Nowhere was this more apparent than in Atlanta (see Figures 3–9 and 3–10). The continuing decline in both risk and absolute levels of victimization in this traditional high-risk center led to the disappearance of two primary clusters of substantial risk that existed in 1980. The city's third primary substantial risk cluster also demonstrated a substantial decline in its intensity of victimization. A similar pattern could be detected in St. Louis and Los Angeles. But in each of those places, islands of substantial risk remained that appeared to be affected little by evidence of aggregate declines in risk. Therefore, attention should now be directed to those microenvironments where high risk continues to persist even as overall risk patterns show evidence of decline.

FIGURE 3-9

Atlanta: High Incidence Homicide Clusters: 1980

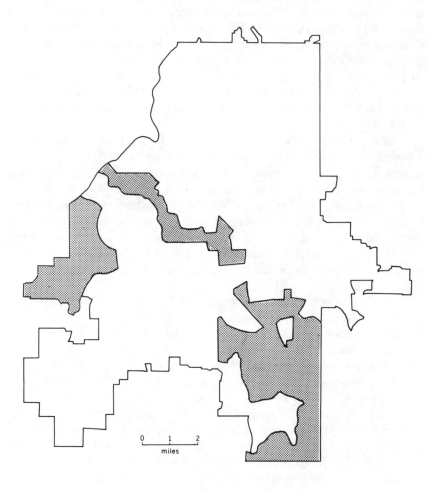

CONCLUSIONS

Homicide risk varies greatly within individual black communities, as well as between them. Internal variations in risk, needless to say, illustrate variations in the distribution of resources within those communities. Neverthless, stress—resource deficit—and risk show only a weak linear relationship. The strength of that relationship appears to be loosely tied to the regional location of our sample observations.

FIGURE 3–10

Changes in Homicide Density in Atlanta's Southeastern Cluster: 1980–1985

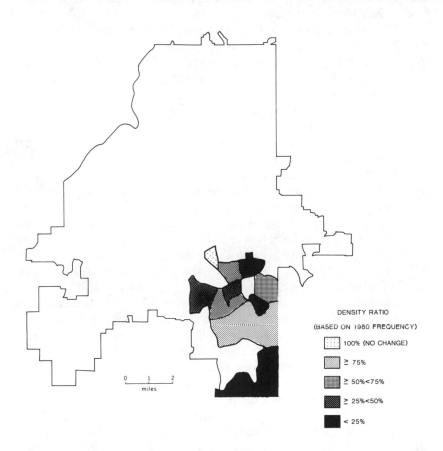

Thus, apparently we have failed to conclusively demonstrate the direct ties between the impact of macroeconomic forces and micro-environmental functioning.

We conclude, however, that although our crude modeling attempt produced only weak statistical evidence of this association, it did point the way toward improved modeling efforts and, we hope, the possibility of gaining more substantive insight into an association that is frequently overlooked. The work of a growing number of ecologically oriented researchers suggests that some of the weaknesses that we encountered in the modeling process can be overcome (see Sampson, 1986; Williams and Flewelling, 1988; Baron and Straus, 1988;

Messner and Tardiff, 1986; Huff-Corzine et al., 1986). Therefore, we will continue to rework the model in the hope that it will assist us to understand more fully a problem that requires much more attention than it has heretofore received.

Substantial risk environments expand and contract as a function of alterations in levels of risk. But the modal behaviors that abet risk in one setting are not necessarily those that abet risk in alternate settings. Therefore, not only is it necessary to attempt to model a set of processes that demonstrate the macro-micro link, but it is equally important that we understand how groups adapt to their microenvironment in a specific context. The failure to do this will lead us to generalize without taking into consideration the character of the contextual environment.

In the latter half of this chapter, we have attempted to demonstrate the importance of context. But clearly, much additional work is required if we are to develop a sounder understanding of why selected microenvironments appear vulnerable to sustained high risk during intervals of both growth and decline. Thus it is imperative that we become more knowledgeable about the organizational structure of individual black communities, about the development of strands of black culture in face of changes in the larger culture, and about the institutional support base required to offset risk under conditions of both community economic growth and decline. As long as the nations' black communities are viewed monolithically by those outside, it is unlikely that the kind of public policy concerns raised by Comer (1985) will be addressed. He was concerned that the serious problem of unacceptable levels of violence that pervades segments of the nation's larger black communities will continue unless appropriate public policy is fashioned to address the many issues that confront these communities. Similar concerns have been expressed by Wilson (1987), although his focus is much broader. Wilson generally agreed that these issues might best be addressed through the formulation of a series of well-thought-out non-race-specific policies. Nonetheless, we have reservations that non-race-specific policies will be adequate to address this issue. Such policies are likely to be formulated without an adequate understanding of the micro-environmental contexts in which these negative behaviors are taking place.

4

Black Males: The Primary Target of Risk

INTRODUCTION

Homicide within the black community has been concentrated historically among males. Since 1914, when data by race were first available, official records showed that black males ran a much higher risk of victimization than any other race-sex group (Holinger and Klemen, 1977). That distinction continues into the present, although it is now beginning to show some abatement (Ueshima et al., 1984). Nevertheless, the lowering of risk at the national level provides little comfort as long as a sizable segment of that population continues to represent a high risk group—young black urban males. Moreover, aggregate statistics can distract from the situation prevailing in individual high-risk communities, and thereby lead attention away from settings in which the problem continues to remain serious. In this chapter and the next, we will review the changing level of seriousness in our sample communities with emphasis placed on the role of gender on risk.

During the decade of the 1970s risk levels reached their peak, and then began to abate; however, a slight upturn was beginning to appear before the decade ended (Cook and Zarkin, 1985). Among our sample cities a variety of patterns of risk could be observed at the beginning of both the 1970s and the 1980s (see Table 4–1). Risk declined in Atlanta, Houston, Pittsburgh, and Detroit, whereas it increased in Los Angeles and St. Louis. The observed changes do not neatly fit a pattern of association based on the direction of population change. A black population growth rate of approximately 39 percent, 14 percent, and 9 percent characterized Houston, Detroit, and Atlanta, respectively. Yet in Atlanta, a substantial reduction in risk occurred whereas in the other two communities declines in risk were more nominal. The anomalous situation involves Los Angeles, which showed very little change in population size, and St. Louis, which had a substantial loss in black population (see Table 4–2). Thus we need to look beyond simple demographic trends in order to explain observed changes in risk.

TABLE 4–1

Black Risk Levels in 1970 and 1980
in Six City Sample, Per 100,000 Persons

City	Risk Level (1970)	Risk Level (1980)
Atlanta	82	46
St. Louis	67	92
Detroit	68	59
Houston	56	46
Pittsburgh	38	33
Los Angeles	41	87

Source: Based on 1970 and 1980 Census Population counts and the number of homicides reported by individual city health departments.

TABLE 4–2

Black Population Change in the Sample Cities: 1970–1980

City	1970	1980	Percent Change	1985 (Estimate)
Atlanta	253,000	274,000	8.7%	290,000
St. Louis	254,000	206,000	– 18.9%	196,000
Detroit	660,000	753,000	14.0%	796,000
Houston	316,000	440,000	38.9%	484,000
Pittsburgh	104,000	101,000	– 2.8%	——
Los Angeles	505,000	505,000	——	492,000

Source: *Census of Population, 1970 and 1980*. Estimates computed by authors.

Likewise, on the surface the regional Sunbelt/Frostbelt dichotomy does not appear to be influential in contributing to the changes. For instance, the communities at the lower end of the risk continuum in 1970, Pittsburgh and Los Angeles, moved in opposite directions during the interval. Pittsburgh experienced a 13 percent decline in risk, whereas Los Angeles registered an amazing 110 percent increase in risk. With aggregate patterns of black risk conforming to no obvious pattern, the task of logically attempting to develop an explanation will not be easy. But because the observed levels are so heavily weighted by black male behavior (see Table 4–3), it is with that segment of the population that we must begin to search for answers.

TABLE 4-3

Male Victims as a Share of Total Victims
(In Percentages)

City	1970	1975	1980	1985
Atlanta	79.0%	74.0%	74.1%	83.3%
St. Louis	83.3%	70.9%	86.2%	85.4%
Detroit	76.3%	74.2%	77.8%	81.6%
Houston	86.6%	74.9%	80.7%	80.0%
Pittsburgh	78.9%	92.3%	81.8%	80.0%
Los Angeles	69.2%	77.1%	85.8%	82.9%

Source: FBI Monthly Homicide Reports, 1970, 1975, 1980, and 1985.

Age constitutes a critical element influencing the onset and ter-
mination of a variety of risk enhancing behaviors; therefore, we will
pay close attention to the age structure of the population generally as
we search for clues. We also will examine the differences in risk
observed throughout the age structure of our sample cities.

POPULATION AGE AND THE RISK OF VICTIMIZATION

The risk of black male victimization is strongly associated with
age, rising during late adolescence, peaking during early maturity, and
declining at the onset of late maturity. The exact location of peaking
within these broad developmental stages varies temporally as well as
from one place to another. During the most recent interval of risk
escalation, peaking was observed moving down the age spectrum, such
that at individual locations, high risk was associated with early maturity
rather than late maturity. Traditionally, however, the age structure of
victimization was characterized by peaking in the third decade of life.
That peaking age is associated with the strong predominance of primary
homicides, whereas the earlier peaking pattern is thought to be
associated with the growing contribution of nonprimary homicides to
aggregate risk (Greenberg, 1985).

An Emerging Cluster of Vulnerability

During the most recent period of risk escalation, the 15–24 year
old segment of the population was discovered to be the most vulnerable
to changing risk levels, especially in complex urban environments
(Klebba, 1975). For instance, in Chicago, among this segment of the
black male population, a 257 percent increase in risk occurred between

1965 and 1970 (Block and Zimring, 1973). At the beginning of the period, the age specific rate for this population was estimated to be 54 deaths per 100,000 population, whereas at the end of the period the level was 192.9 per 100,000. Block and Zimring partially attribute this extreme elevation in risk to the changing behavior of males in this age category, because 60 percent of the aggregate increase in risk in the city could be associated with the altered offense rate of this age group. Young adult black males had become much more inclined to engage in behavior that increased the risk of death to members of their peer group and others. A greater willingness appears to exist on the part of this segment of the population to become involved in activity that frequently leads to felony murder. Other age segments seem less inclined to engage in risky behavior.

A number of attempts have been made to explain this emerging phenomenon. Waldron and Eyer (1975) attribute it to an increase in alcohol consumption, impulsive rage, and a breakdown in respect for societal values. Others associate it with an easy access to guns and substance abuse (Weiss, 1976). The observed increase in nonprimary homicide involving youthful offenders could possibly reflect the gap in the participants' subjective assessment of needs and the ability to satisfy those needs (Greenberg, 1985). Explanations of the latter type are rejected by Hirschi and Gottfredson (1983).

What is clear is that the risk of victimization among this age segment varies substantially among our sample urban places, at least during the base year (see Table 4–4). In our core sample elevated risk can be detected in late adolescence, whereas risk is much lower among this group in the peripheral sample. But black males in this age segment in St. Louis attain a level of risk that places them in a class by themselves (one person in approximately 200). Nevertheless, Shin (1981) clearly illustrates that the prevalence of lower-risk levels in our peripheral sample locations deviates from that describing the national average among 15–19 year olds. But in each place, the 20–24 year old group exceeded the national average, and in most instances, by a large margin. Thus young adult blacks in St. Louis, Detroit, and Houston were, at a minimum, twice as likely to become homicide victims as their peers nationally. The Atlanta and Los Angeles groups were only somewhat less likely to become victims.

There is little question that young adult males in our sample were negatively compelled by some unspecified force or forces to engage in a set of behaviors that were dangerous to their health. To what extent have these forces continued to ignite or offset the levels of risk observed above? By examining risk levels among those 25–34 years old, we

TABLE 4–4

A Comparison of Risk among 15–24
Year Old Black Males—1970 (per 100,000)

City	Risk Level	
	15–19 Year Old	20–24 Year Old
Atlanta	194	265
St. Louis	140	452
Detroit	136	313
Houston	61	293
Pittsburgh	20	196
Los Angeles	52	234

Sources: Computed by Authors.

should be able to determine how well the original cohort has fared in negotiating a risky environment in the process of aging. Likewise, we will examine the differences in risk among those 15–24 years of age in 1980 as a means of comparing them with their peers ten years earlier.

THE TEMPORAL DIMENSION OF YOUNG ADULT RISK

The increases in risk initiated during the mid-1960s seemed to peak after about ten years of steady increase. The peak year varied by individual place, but 1974 apparently was the turning point in the nation at large. The mean level of decline since the initial peak was attained seems nominal for blacks. Yet a substantial decline in risk among black males between the age 15–24 had occurred by 1978 (Center for Disease Control, 1983).

The same source that reported the decline was careful to point out that levels of risk in the North Central region were almost double those prevailing in other regions. No attempt was made to explain this discrepancy. This raises questions regarding regional differences in rate of decline. The most obvious question that comes to mind is, what is the impact of economic decline on risk within this segment of the population? Another subsidiary issue and one previously raised by Silberman (1978) is, what has been the effect of black suburbanization on emerging behavioral traits? Mature ghetto centers lead to a greater class homogenization within central-city black communities. Some attention will be devoted to these issues in the following review of changes in risk.

Risk and Cohort Aging

The risky 15–24 year old black male population in 1970 was 25–34 years old in 1980, the period in which risk was highest. Given that this population was characterized by higher levels of risk at an earlier age than usual, should we expect a continuing elevation in risk among this cohort in the intervening interval? The answer to this question in large measure depends on the extent to which individuals in the sample communities maintained the life-styles evident at the earlier date. As previously noted, one of the features that distinguished white and black juvenile patterns is the point at which delinquent behavior ceases. Black patterns often persist for an extended period of time. If the forces responsible for initiating a pattern of conduct that proves risky do not abate, or if persons previously enamored of specific life-style orientations continue in risky life-styles, then elevated risk would be expected to persist. One life-style modification that normally occurs during this interval is associated with family formation. A delay in the formation of a stable personal relationship provides one with a longer interval in which to engage in acts of irresponsibility.

The 15–24 year old cohort of ten years earlier displayed a great deal of similarity in their 1980 risk levels to that which prevailed in 1970 in Detroit and Houston (see Table 4–5). Although the levels did not change appreciably, the direction of movement did change: it was down in Houston and manifested a slight upward movement in Detroit. In Atlanta, a substantial downward movement was detected whereas the inverse of this trend was noted for Los Angeles. The most dramatic change was observed in St. Louis, where the earlier pattern had intensified, leading to a more than 90 percent increase in risk level over the interval. Young adults in Houston and Detroit apparently continued the life-style orientations they exhibited at the beginning of the 1970s, whereas those in Atlanta and Los Angeles appear to have made some mid-course changes in direction. It is not clear at this point how these changes manifested themselves. But young adults in St. Louis seemed to have increased their involvement in risk-taking activity as they entered the late maturing phase of development. Therefore, it would be difficult to argue that the risk pattern observed simply represents a random fluctuation, at least in the case of St. Louis, Los Angeles, and Atlanta.

In none of those locations was there a net addition to the young adult population during the seventies, a situation that could have led to greater ingroup competition for scarce resources. To the contrary, the original base population apparently diminished in each instance,

TABLE 4–5

Changes in Risk in the Young Adult Cohort
1970 and 1980 (per 100,000)

City	15–24 Year Old	25–34 Year Old
	1970	1980
Atlanta	205	140
St. Louis	296	529
Detroit	224	249
Houston	177	152
Pittsburgh	108	116
Los Angeles	143	263

Source: Computed from FBI Monthly Homicide Report and data from the
Census of Population, 1970 and 1980.

a condition that might be expected if the volume of migration was inadequate to promote growth. In Detroit and Los Angeles the extent of the reduction was nominal (approximately one percent). The Atlanta decrease was larger but less than 4 percent. The major decline in the size of this cohort occurred in St. Louis, where a more than 40 percent decrease was noted. This decrease among young adults in St. Louis was more than double the negative percentage change that occurred in the city's total black population.

On the surface, risk among this segment of the population would seem to be lower during the interval, but as noted above, the inverse actually occurred. One must assume that in St. Louis an intensification of the forces responsible for a risk increase occurred, at least in terms of their impact on this vulnerable group. In Los Angeles, some new force apparently was unleashed, based on the side of the increase in risk. Both the Houston and Detroit population experienced only modest change, although their respective economies were moving in the opposite direction. Positive change was occurring in Atlanta without any apparent explanation.

In Los Angeles, St. Louis, and Atlanta, movement to the suburbs escalated during the 19⁷ᴜs. The young adult population, in each instance, was the primary contributor to that process. Assuming that selective persons with higher income and a greater number of years of educational attainment were those moving to the suburbs, those left behind would likely be persons with less income and fewer years of education. The movement to the suburbs, when coupled with net out-migration from the metropolitan area, produces a population leveling effect that is most easily observed at the neighborhood level. Yet it is not possible to speak confidently in support of the position that this process leads to a loss of influential role models. The position taken by a number of analysts is that the process contributes to a decline in social control, which some feel undergirds the current escalation in violent behavior. We acknowledge that the ongoing process of population movement seems to have the effect of concentrating a disproportionate share of the metropolitan poor in the city, but no definitive link to observed risk levels can be substantiated without further scrutiny. What is it about the Atlanta situation that is producing the opposite effect?

Young adults in our sample cities obviously were confronted by a different series of life-course events and adapted to those events by choosing to participate in a variety of life-styles. Where maladaptive life-styles more often were chosen, risk escalated. The inverse of this occurred when existing maladaptive life-styles were abandoned. In Atlanta and St. Louis, one would logically assume either the prevalence of quite different life-styles and/or a contrast in the way resources are allocated. In these places the young adult population maintained similar levels of risk at the beginning of the interval, but the levels changed during the course of the interval. The Los Angeles situation appears even more baffling at this point, but we will look at the situation more closely at a later point.

Risk and the 1980 Young Adult Cohort

Attention now will be directed to the same-age population in 1980. Changes in external circumstances and/or the adoption of life-styles characteristic of those of the previously described group should be expected to impact the risk experienced by the younger population. In this instance, positive changes in risk were noted in Houston and Atlanta. A positive change connotes a major decline in risk. At the beginning of the new decade the young adult population in Atlanta was operating in an environment in which risk levels were more than two-thirds lower than they had been ten years earlier, and those in Houston were more than one-half lower (see Table 4–6). The inverse of that pattern can be observed in Los Angeles, where risk levels among young adult males increased more than 70 percent.

In Detroit and St. Louis, young adults were confronted by similar levels of risk in the initial year in both decades. Thus the forces at work in the earlier year continued to operate in the latter year in the North Central cities. Likewise, a positive change was under way in the two southern cities, whereas the western city had taken on the risk characteristics of the North Central cities.

TABLE 4-6

Young Adult Risk Characteristics in the Sample Cities—1980
(Number of Deaths of 15–24 Year Old Black Males per 100,000)

City	Risk Level	Direction of Change in Risk
	(1980)	(1980)
Atlanta	63	–
St. Louis	303	+
Detroit	227	+
Houston	82	–
Pittsburgh	38	–
Los Angeles	252	+

Source: Computed from FBI Monthly Homicide Report and data from the
Census of Population, 1980.

The origins of this observed pattern of risk can be addressed in
a variety of ways. The perspective we have chosen in exploring these
origins will emphasize the role of the economy and the experience of
blacks in general. Emphasis will be placed on the success adults have
had in penetrating local economies. Each of the above labor markets
was in some way affected by changes occurring in the national
economy. It is well known that St. Louis and Detroit were hardest hit
by these changes, whereas the Sunbelt urban locations were experiencing the positive feedback associated with regional economic growth.
If a strong positive association exists between structural conditions and
risk, then the above pattern of risk seems generally in keeping with
changes known to be under way. Yet the changes in risk occurring
among young adults in Los Angeles do not conform to the expected
pattern.

Young Adults in the Labor Force

Black male labor force participation rates since 1960 have been
characterized by a downward movement, even after one removes
young eligibles from the pool (Farley, 1985). The young eligibles are
those aged 16–24 whose entry into the market may be delayed by
involvement in school or a less demanding responsibility. The unstable
work experience of this group provides them with excessive discretionary time, time that facilitates the development of poor work habits
and also allows them an opportunity to become familiar with the workings of the irregular economy. For this group, especially its younger

members, the underground economy represents its primary source of income (Mangum and Seniger, 1978). Whereas one segment of black male workers has progressed since 1960, white-collar workers, others have had far less success and are known to have lost ground.

In our sample cities changes in labor-force-participation rates provide a crude index of the experience this population has had in the market (see Table 4–7). In 1980, in only one of our sample cities did black male labor force participation rates exceed the national level of 71 percent for the group. Houston, the rapidly growing Sunbelt metropolis, held that distinction. Atlanta, on the other hand, registered participation rates more akin to north central cities than to Houston. Even Los Angeles experienced unexpected low levels of participation, whereas Detroit, as expected, had the smallest share of its eligible males in the labor force. Only St. Louis in the earlier period was characterized by subpar rates, and this condition continued into the next decade.

TABLE 4–7

Black Male Labor Force Participation Rate — 1970 and 1980

City	1970	1980
Atlanta	81.8	56.9
St. Louis	67.1	57.1
Detroit	88.0	49.6
Houston	84.3	73.4
Pittsburgh	63.7	57.7
Los Angeles	72.7	61.9

Source: Census of Population, 1970 and 1980.

With substantial declines taking place in black male participation in the labor force in general, failure to enter is an even more serious problem confronting young adults. The greater entry difficulties were enumerated recently by Mare and Winship (1984) and include the following: minimum wage legislation; absolute size of cohort; intensification of competition in the market from women and immigrants; changing location and composition of industry; and an increasing unwillingness to accept lower-status jobs. Each of the above explanations is no doubt at work in our sample cities, varying in intensity with the unique circumstances of location. Nevertheless, it is evident that black rates have declined, and because younger adults and new entrants traditionally have had lower rates than others, we expect that an increasing share of this population had more discretionary time at its disposal, a share extending over an increasing range along the young adult age continuum.

Increased Availability of Discretionary Time

With an increase in discretionary time, the critical issue becomes how one spends one's time, and/or how life-style orientations are influenced by lessening time constraints. Traditional age-graded patterns of behavior have become blurred (Meyrowitz, 1984), leading young persons to engage in behaviors and to adopt styles earlier thought appropriate only for adults. When these changes are accompained by those described above, absent other constraints, the stage appears to be set for an acceleration in risk.

We are aware that persons committed to a criminal life-style (e.g., the professional robber and burglar) may continue to practice that life-style while employed full time (Holzman, 1983). Therefore, we are not suggesting that acts of violence are primarily associated with being in or out of the labor force. Traditionally, however, low-income workers have been known to engage in acts that often cause tempers to flare during limited periods of leisure (e.g., weekends), such that it is during those periods that acts of lethality reached their peak (Bullock, 1955). Needless to say, neither of these arguments should deter us from attempting to establish a link between increased leisure and the escalation in homicide risk among young adult black males.

Work History: Data Sources and Other Observations

Two available data sets should provide insight into the question of the extent to which black, young adult male victims were employed at the time of their death. The first data set describes the work history of persons drawn into our sample of 1975 victims. Data were not available for all the victims in our sample. For instance, a record of the work history of victims was impossible to secure when a social security number did not appear on death certificates. The work history data are confidential; therefore, researchers are provided anonymous histories only that are based on social security numbers submitted to the Social Security Administration. We were, however, able to have the individual files identified in broad age categories. In that way we are able to identify individuals whom we have defined as young adults.

The death certificates indicate whether or not the victim was employed at the time of death and what the victim's usual occupation was. Traditionally, most black homicide victims have occupied the lowest rung on the occupational ladder, and their deaths are expected to occur during the weekend leisure period (Bullock, 1955). Any substantial deviation from that pattern would suggest a breach with tradition. As indicated in an earlier chapter, we believe that the cultures in our sample communities are positioned differently along the traditional/nontraditional structural axis. The closer a community is to the traditional end of the spectrum, the more weekend peaking patterns are expected to prevail. A more nearly random occurrence of victimizations should be expected to prevail in those communities in which cultures have moved farthest from the traditional end of the continuum. These patterns should be especially pronounced among young adults, who are most easily influenced by changing styles and values.

One final piece of evidence should provide corroboration, albeit indirectly, of whether the victimization was motivated by anger or instrumental behavior. This evidence is the differential frequency of occurrence of single-offender or multiple-offender offenses. The latter has been suggested as the hallmark of the nontraditional pattern (Block and Zimring, 1973; Block, 1965). Offender demographic characteristics were not included in the F.B.I. Monthly Homicide reports prior to 1977. Thus we employ these data to describe 1980 offender patterns only. We expect to find a greater prevalence of multiple-offender offenses involving young adults in those cities in which male labor-force-participation rates are lowest. Potential offenders in these communities are expected to have available to them an increasing amount of discretionary time; thus, there should be a tendency for them to band together for the purpose of committing property crimes.

Most young adult victims from each of our sample locations were identified as labor force participants at the time of death. The level of participation was high in all locations except in St. Louis, where only one-half of the victims appeared to have a labor force affiliation at the time of death. Some individuals were identified as students who had not yet entered the labor market. Others, out of school, seemed not to have become members of the work force simply because of a physical disability or other unspecified reasons. Only in St. Louis did there appear to exist a weak link between the world of work and young adult status.

The average number of quarters worked during any year varied little from place to place. The mean for the group hovered around two quarters out of the year for those earning an income. The most glaring distinction between these individual city representatives was the difference in average income earned by young adult males during their labor market tenure. Young adult workers in St. Louis averaged less than $800.00 annually, whereas those in Detroit averaged closer to $1,900.00. The remaining workers averaged less than $2,000.00 annually as well. If the labor market characteristics of the St. Louis victim sample are spread widely among similarly situated individuals, then is it unreasonable to think that risk levels would not rise under the circumstances? If those involved in the lethal act are ill-prepared to compete in a declining economy, they are unlikely to have a strong commitment to the regular economy.

Weekend/Non-Weekend Homicide Peaking Patterns

The weekend/non-weekend peaking pattern is easily discernible for the total sample and in many ways conforms to expectation. The two southern cities in our sample were expected to demonstrate a stronger association with traditional victimization patterns, and, indeed, they had the strongest weekend peaks (see Table 4–8). Houston and Atlanta can be said, then, to anchor one end of the traditional/non-traditional axis, and Los Angeles and St. Louis to anchor the other. The young adult male sample shows a strong similarity to the total sample in the peaking pattern.

TABLE 4–8

The Weekly Black Homicide Cycle
(Weekend/Non-Weekend Peaking Pattern)

City	Weekend	Non-Weekend
Atlanta	56.0%	44.0%
St. Louis	46.7%	53.3%
Detroit	52.8%	47.2%
Houston	61.1%	38.9%
Pittsburgh	50.0%	50.0%
Los Angeles	45.5%	54.5%

Source: Computed from information appearing on individual death certificates.

But slightly more than half of the black young adult males in Atlanta were killed during the weekend. In St. Louis 47 percent were weekend victims and a similar percentage of the Los Angeles victims were killed during this interval. Therefore, young adult male victims are apparently somewhat less likely than older cohorts to die during weekend confrontations. Because of the small number of observations, however, caution is advised. If this pattern could be detected over a much larger number of observations, then we would feel comfortable in saying that it represents the combined contribution of increased discretionary time in those locations where economic decline is manifest

most severely in the local black community. The other principal contributor is the adoption of life-styles thought to assist in adapting to
an emerging set of circumstances, but which often prove maladaptive
in the long run.

The pattern of victimization that evolves under conditions of
economic decline can be attributed in large measure to the violence-
specific behavior of young adult black males, especially those whose
marketable skills are deficient. With an increase in the skill requirements
necessary to qualify for the more highly remunerative positions in the
transitional economy and an intensification in the competition for jobs
requiring little skill, the skill-deficient population finds itself in limbo.
As a way out of their dilemma, some adopt a crime-oriented life-style.
For some, this simply is a continuation of behaviors adopted as a
juvenile, whereas for others, it is a deliberate decision to engage in
non-normative behavior. Such decisions often tend to be viewed as
rational by the decision maker.

The behavior of young adult males has played an important role
in moving an ever-increasing number of homicide victimizations into
the felony murder column. This behavior has led to an increase in
victimizations among peers as well as increasing age discordance between victim and offender, a condition that is revealed by the increase
in the number of lethal assaults on older males perpetrated by younger
males. An increase in the age discordance pattern also is apparent by
the increase in justifiable homicides committed by older adults against
younger adults. For the moment, however, we will devote attention
to the growing number of victimizations involving multiple offenders
and single victims. As indicated previously, this pattern seldom revealed itself in the traditional structure of victimization, because it is
primarily instrumentally motivated.

The Growth in Multiple-Offender Offenses

We would expect the above dimension of the non-traditional
structure to have become more commonplace by 1980 as an element
in lethal confrontations. Likewise, we would expect the locations
hardest hit by economic decline to demonstrate a greater prevalence
of multiple-offender confrontations than communities that have been
offered greater economic protection. As it turns out, our assumptions
are only partially correct. It should be noted, however, that the
hypothesized relationship refers only to the prevalence of multiple-
offenders who assault other young adult males. Among our sample
locations, St. Louis, Detroit, and Los Angeles were characterized by
a higher frequency of multiple-offender attacks than were the remaining

sample locations (see Table 4–9). In 1980, blacks in Houston appeared to be the most economically secure based on median family income, male labor force participation rates, and male unemployment. Moreover, multiple-offender victimizations were not shown to be associated with the death of a single young black male victim during that year. Yet in St. Louis more than one-third of such victims were involved in confrontations involving multiple-offenders. St. Louis should be described as the least economically secure community. Both Detroit and Los Angeles appear to be moving in the direction of St. Louis, at least in how the local economy impacts the black community. Multiple-offender killings have come to represent a growing force, but we are aware that the rise of multiple-offender offenses cannot be explained away simply in terms of community economic security, although we contend that it is a prime contributor to our emerging pattern of victimization.

TABLE 4–9

Multiple-Offender Assaults as a
Share of All Lethal Confrontations 1980

City	Percent Multiple Offender
Atlanta	1.0
St. Louis	35.6
Detroit	18.7
Houston	0
Pittsburgh	1.0
Los Angeles	15.4

Source: Based on data extracted from 1980 FBI Monthly Homicide Reports.

An Overview on the Travails of Young Adult Black Males

During the most recent interval of escalating risk, young adult black males have constituted the primary victim and offender population. In urban areas generally, homicide risk has shifted down the age pyramid, peaking at earlier ages. In our sample cities, however, peaking seemed to be associated with the increasing importance of non-traditional victimization patterns. Between 1970–1980, a decline in the intensity of peaking was observed to have occurred at those locations where traditional victimization patterns remained strongest. Likewise it was observed that young adult risk levels appeared to be directly linked to economic well-being in the local black community. Male labor-force-participation rates, male unemployment, and median income were employed in establishing economic well-being. It also was noted that the life-style orientation of the 1970 cohort of young adult males seemed to have continued throughout the decade because that cohort continued to manifest a similar risk pattern ten years later, especially at locations characterized by economic decline. It appears that elevated risk among young adult males is likely to be sustained in those communities in which economic decline is evident and the prevalence of maladaptive life-styles is widespread.

The younger segment of the adult male population (15–24 years) was the focus of attention in this section of the chapter. Yet the 25–29 year old group usually is included in this population. It is not that we have failed to recognize that, we simply wished to focus attention on that segment of the group thought to be potentially at greater risk, especially in declining economies. By the time they reach the more advanced stage of young adulthood, there is a greater likelihood that individuals will have abandoned the parental home, settled into stable employment, formed a family, and demonstrated a lower affinity for high-risk life-styles. Our data, however, indicate less support for that position in places characterized by declining economies. In the following section of this chapter, we will simply dichotomize the at-risk population into two groups—under thirty years of age and over thirty years of age—following the lead of Herjanic and Meyer (1976). This dichotomy allows us to distinguish between the patterns and motivations associated with the victimization of young adults and mature adults.

In the section that follows much attention will be focused on victim-offender relationships. Those relationships in the past have revealed strong associations with age, life-style orientations, and practices that are partially tied to the life-cycle. Not only will we focus on victim-offender relationships, we will single out for closer inspection several behavioral traits believed to foster circumstances that heighten the risk of victimization.

MATURE ADULTS

The previous treatment of young adult males was thought to be an essential element in this chapter because they are the most likely to engage in destructive behavior. Destructive behavior, in some instances, is thought to occur in response to a decline in perceived opportunity in local declining economies. There is little question that the changing economy, coupled with changing social attitudes, has enabled some young adult black males to move into high-level mainstream occupations and, subsequently, to seek residential accommodations beyond previous zones of quasi restriction. These new race heroes are often hailed for their achievements, especially those who occupy positions of high visibility, such as entertainers, professional athletes, and so forth. But for those who are deficient in talent and/or skills, opportunities available to their fathers and other relatives during previous generations will not be available to them.

Gibbs (1985) recently suggested that all other identifiable demographic groups have experienced progress in the last twenty years except black 15–24 year olds. The behavior of this segment of the population bears a heavy responsibility for the growing number of life years lost in the nation's larger black communities. The question now becomes, how have older cohorts fared in this era of high homicide risk, such that their life chances differ from those of young adult blacks?

Mature adults comprise the largest potential pool of homicide victims if we exclude those who have not yet reached age fifteen. It should be noted, however, that the recent increase in child abuse has placed a larger number of young children at risk. But the convention among some analysts is to remove those younger than fifteen from the pool because they are infrequent victims (Munford et al., 1976). The label "mature adult" is probably too all-inclusive because it embraces persons representing at least two or three generations. Yet one logically expects risk to decline as a function of age. Moreover, risk levels remain relatively high during early maturity but show a sharp drop after age forty-four, because persons previously committed to action-oriented life-styles begin to gradually withdraw from those styles. We expect late mature populations to adopt a more sedentary existence. The national aggregate pattern of black male risk indeed demonstrates the previously described age-graded pattern of risk (Klebba, 1975; Shin, 1981). A review of the record of risk characterizing our sample communities, however, demonstrates less consistency than one would be led to expect (see Table 4–10).

Mature Adult Patterns of Risk in Sample Locations

In those locations where risk was high in 1970, it seems to have been felt across all ages. But it was among the lower-risk communities that the age pattern of risk demonstrated the greatest inconsistency. For instance, there is little in the way of logic that would explain the higher level of risk in Houston at age 60–64. Nor is it obvious why the highest level of risk among the lower-risk communities in Los Angeles occurs during the ages of 40–44. However, one might start by examining the social-class position of the population by age, as well as age-

TABLE 4–10

Age Graded Patterns of Homicide Risk among
a Sample of Mature Black Adult Males—1970
(Deaths per 100,000 population)

Age	Atlanta	St. Louis	Detroit	Houston	Pittsburgh	Los Angeles
30–34	303	403	206	195	47	96
35–39	276	222	192	186	135	89
40–44	241	272	183	131	110	120
45–49	215	285	169	68	70	39
50–54	213	239	130	118	159	55
55–59	210	62	104	80	84	66
60–64	120	48	69	195	——	130
65	103	99	78	41	40	18

Source: Computed from FBI Monthly Homicide Reports and Census of
Population, 1970.

based migration patterns, both in terms of regional origin and social
class mix. Needless to say we are unable to provide such a detailed
assessment and therefore will confine much of our discussion to the
broad general category of mature adult (☐ thirty years) while recognizing the limitations of this decision.

Homicide risk among mature adults, just as among young adults,
underwent a variety of changes in the interval between 1970 and 1980.
In St. Louis risk remained unusually high through age forty-four after
which risk fluctuated during subsequent five-year intervals. Atlanta
stands in stark contrast to St. Louis because risk was reduced during
early maturity and declined precipitously during late maturity. Los
Angeles' pattern of age structure of risk bore a strong resemblance to
that prevailing in Detroit, a pattern quite dissimilar to that in place ten
years earlier. Apparently, the dynamics of risk vary greatly from community to community. But it should also be understood that variations
in risk by five-year age groups in the mature adult population often
reflect the variety of motives that impact the lethal confrontation.

When traditional motives explained the vast majority of all victimizations, the age-risk gradient described earlier was likely to prevail.
But Cook (1986) informed us that the emerging pattern of victimization,
said to have attained equilibrium status in 1973, now accounts for
approximately forty percent of all victimizations. The emergent non-
traditional pattern is motivated by instrumental concerns dominated
by robbery. Risk of instrumental victimization increases with age (Block,

1985), because those who are likely to have greater financial resources and less ability to protect themselves from attack tend to be older persons. Thus, in those locations where youthful offenders have proliferated, a secondary rise in the mature adult risk gradient often can be observed after age 54. Moreover, both victim-offender relationships and the motives surrounding the confrontation strongly influence the height and shape of the risk gradient in this somewhat less risky segment of the adult black male population.

VICTIM-OFFENDER RELATIONSHIPS

The relationship among persons involved in fatal interactions often provides a key to understanding the circumstances leading to death. Were the persons engaged in the fatal confrontation emotionally bonded, part of the social network that places great emphasis on honor, or simply ships passing in the night? The value system that one adopts can be expected to define the appropriate rules of conduct that govern relationships under a variety of circumstances. Individuals are known to confine their associations to persons or groups whose behavioral cues are familiar to them, thereby enabling them to anticipate a specific response in a given situation or setting. The relationship between victim and offender may take on a wide variety of forms, but police agencies have reduced the multiplicity of relationships to four general categories. Those categories include family relations, acquaintances, strangers, and a general catchall category labeled "unknown." These four officially sanctioned categories will be employed here in detailing the nature of the association among interacting dyads. One of the shortcomings of this classificatory scheme is its failure to convey the circumstances leading to death, although improvements in this area were made during the late 1970s.

Homicide Categories

The first of these categories, Family and Acquaintance homicides, has traditionally accounted for the vast majority of annual homicide deaths. Anger is generally identified as the primary precipitator of the lethal confrontation, concern with self being believed to be primary (Luckenbill, 1984). Anger growing out of a threat to one's self image has historically served as the basis for what are called primary confrontations. Between 1976 and 1979 a primary relationship was said to exist between 82 percent (20 percent family homicides and 62 percent acquaintance homicides) of black male victims and their assailants nationally (Jason, Flock and Tyler, 1983). This information, extracted from official documents, points to the weakness of blind dependence on aggregate statistics based on these categories.

To accept on face value the above-reported results would have us ignore the changing trends in the pattern of relationships between victims and offenders. Changes in the circumstances leading to death call into question some of the prior associations implied by the standard typology. For instance, the primary and secondary identities traditionally allocated to the categories "family" and "acquaintance" homicides, and "stranger" and "unknown" homicides, respectively, are no longer as clear cut as in the past. This is especially true of the category "acquaintance," which presently simply indicates that the victim and offender were not unknown to one another. A careful review of official records indicates that one can no longer be certain that the lethal confrontation among persons so designated grew out of a situation in which anger was the basic precipitant of aggressive behavior.

Likewise, the category designated as "unknown" presents many problems. Yet the growing importance of this category suggests a complex set of circumstances that make case closure more difficult, implying that the case was most likely one involving the commission of a felony. Moreover, because of the many unanswered questions relative to both the relationship and the circumstances leading to death, one must exercise caution in assigning relationships. Nevertheless, Zimring and Zuehl (1986) are of the opinion that in most cases classified as unknown, at least in Chicago, robbery was the primary motive. They contend that many of the more difficult to classify cases are thought to be associated with drug robberies. Because the circumstances surrounding them include fewer of the elements that would normally lead them to be classified by the police as robberies, they are classified as "circumstances undesignated."

An Alternative Categorization Schema

The growing fuzziness in the relationship between victim and offender has led to the use of a substitute schema by the New York Police Department. Tardiff et al. (1986) report that this new schema, introduced in 1981 includes three categories. Those categories have been labeled "disputes," "robberies," and "drug-related." Apparently these categories provide a more accurate description of the circumstances surrounding death, and at the same time, they allow one to distinguish between homicides that were primarily drug-related, though possibly involving robbery, from those that were primarily robbery-motivated. These two motivations are now thought to account for the majority of all homicides that take place in Manhattan. The New

York Police continue to classify homicides in the traditional way but seem to agree that a direct focus on circumstances is likely to prove more productive. Yet this recent emphasis on circumstances does not appear to address the issue of relationship and/or circumstances unknown.

Victim-Offender Relationships as a
Tentative Index of Cultural Orientation

Throughout this book we have suggested the existence of a pervasive but not always visible link between risk of victimization and structure of victimization. Aggregate shifts in risk often disguise changes in structure, and the effect of structural change on observed risk is not readily apparent. For instance, Tardiff et al. (1986) demonstrated that about two-thirds of the observed risk in Manhattan in 1981 could be allocated to felony murder. Yet the structure of victimization that characterized Birmingham at the same time stood in sharp contrast, although manifesting similar risk characteristics. Therefore, we assume that observed changes in the victim-offender relationship among our sample cities will serve as an index of the movement from a more traditional cultural orientation to an emerging cultural orientation. Moreover, we expect black males to exhibit a weaker commitment to traditional values in settings hardest hit by the transition in stage of economic development. Yet over time we would expect a convergence of behaviors irrespective of location because the national visual media is an efficient propagator of emerging values.

Prior to the most recent upturn in risk in the United States, expressive victimizations motivated by anger clearly were responsible for the vast majority of homicide victimizations. In 1963 family homicides accounted for 31 percent of the total whereas those among acquaintances totaled 50 percent (Iskrant and Joliet, 1968). Homicides classified as "unknown relationship" made up only 5 percent of the total. By 1973-1974 the victim-offender picture had undergone a change such that family homicides then accounted for about 25 percent of the total, and those among acquaintances had experienced a slight decline. But at the latter date, killings occurring during crimes of violence constituted approximately 30 percent of the total (Metropolitan Life Statistical Bulletin, November 1974). In one decade felony murder had established itself as a substantial contributor to homicides during a period in which there was evidence of a general escalation in risk. This pattern also showed itself among blacks in our six urban locations.

Evidence of Incipient Change

Reviewing 1965 victim-offender data for our sample places reveals that apparent instrumental motivations were of little consequence as precipitants in the killings of that year. St. Louis and Detroit were the exceptions in this instance. But even in those two communities, where apparent instrumental motives were stronger than elsewhere, only approximately one-fifth of black male homicides could be tentatively placed in the felony column. It does, however, suggest an earlier break with tradition than that which describes the remaining communities in our sample.

During 1965–1980 a series of intensely felt traumas occurred in the United States in both the social and economic arenas. The successes of the civil rights movement, urban riots, polarization over the Vietnam War, the rise of the Women's Rights Movement, and the subsequent movement to the political right by the body politic brought with them temporary feelings of joy and despair, turmoil and acquiescence, hope and disappointment, all of which intensified the conflict between the "haves" and "have nots." The social turbulence of the times was taking place against the backdrop of economic transition that has been previously addressed.

Changes occurring in the economy led to growing affluence and to a simultaneous loss of economic position in different segments of the work force. These changes cut across ethnic and racial lines, leading to greater interracial inequality as well as intraracial inequality. There is a lack of agreement on how important these changes have been on observed risk levels (Blau and Blau, 1982; Messner, 1982; Sampson, 1985). But various investigators continue to attempt to unravel the impact of these changes on risk, at both an aggregate level (Blau and Golden, 1986) and a subaggregate level (Sampson, 1986). There will be no attempt here to quantitatively test hypotheses specifying the association between some of the suggested change variables and risk. We will simply review, simultaneously, changes in risk and structure in our sample communities as a means of denoting the presence of a trend, a trend we intuitively attribute to the social and economic changes described above.

TEMPORAL SHIFTS IN STRUCTURAL PATTERNS

By the early 1970s, homicide risk levels in many large urban places in the nation had doubled, and, in a few instances, tripled in less than a decade (Barnett et al., 1975). Our sample locations ran the gamut in their experience, although Atlanta, St. Louis, and Detroit were positioned on the high-risk end of the spectrum by that date. Because our immediate concern is structural change in victimization patterns, we will note the structural patterns prevailing at specific intervals during the decade. It was during the first five years of the decade, as a rule, that the most rapid change occurred. Once a trend had been established, it tended to move to its equilibrium position by decade's end.

Measures of Change: A Longitudinal View

There are some shortcomings in using interspersed point data to attempt to establish the development of a trend. Though it is true that we have not used sequential dates throughout the entire period under study, we did evaluate changes on a sequential basis during the period 1970–1975. Sequential observations enable us to observe the extent of fluctuation, on a year-to-year basis, by category of victim-offender killings. But sequential observations do not allow us to specify changes in level of risk by changes in the ratio of victim-offender categories. This can be reliably done only by measuring changes in category of risk in the census years. Therefore, we will assess changes in risk by broad victim-offender categories at the beginning of both the 1970s and the 1980s. Likewise, we will show the variation in the contribution of specific victim-offender relationships in the odd years beginning with 1975. It should be noted, however, that our coverage of all aspects of black victimization is most thorough for the mid-decade year.

Problems in Labeling

Another problem that frequently confronts researchers who attempt to interpret victim-offender data too strictly is one of veracity. That problem has become even more complicated as the categorical relationships take on new meanings. For instance, it has been generally assumed that the relationship between a robbery homicide victim and his/her assailant was that of stranger. But the data are beginning to show that persons other than strangers (e.g., acquaintances) are increasingly taking part in this type of transaction. The nonfelony/felony, primary/secondary, expressive/instrumental dichotomies based on the standard victim-offender typology may fail to convey accurately the precise relationship between victim and offender or the circumstances that motivated the killing. Although aware of these shortcomings, we have chosen to illustrate a move from the more traditional pattern of homicide prevalence to an emerging non-traditional one through the use of a dichotomous victim-offender schema.

The labels "expressive" and "instrumental" will be employed to denote the underlying motive responsible for prompting the lethal strike. Megargee (1981) distinguished between the two by indicating that "expressive" represents an intrinsic motivation, wherein the primary goal is injuring the victim, and "instrumental" represents an extrinsic motivation wherein injury of the victim is incidental to some other primary goal. Megargee also indicates that a number of behaviors designed to enhance one's self image may also fall under the instrumental heading. Nevertheless, we have chosen to assign selected acting-out behavior (i.e., ego enhancing) to the expressive category, along with other behaviors growing out of anger, hostility, or other negative emotional states. In most instances instrumental victimizations are classed as felony murder, whereas expressive killings are generally preceived as acts that are an outgrowth of momentary emotional discord. During the early 1920s, Hoffman (1923), in describing the high incidence of blacks killing blacks in Memphis, Tennessee, was careful to note that these were not criminal murders. At that location and at that time, most black victimizations grew out of angry confrontations or expressive actions. Yet during the more recent era there is growing evidence of an increase in instrumental victimizations, especially in non-southern urban settings (Rushforth et al., 1977; Zimring, 1979; Swersey, 1981; Rose and Deskins, 1980).

The latter trend we will not attempt to document. Combining the categories "family" and "acquaintance" provides us with a rough approximation of the share of total adult male victimizations that evolved from angry confrontations or conflict-motivated homicides (Wilt and Bannon, 1974). These are the homicides that we describe as expressive. "Stranger" and "unknown" relationships most often involve extrinsic motivations and are labeled here as instrumental killings. The majority of stranger homicides tend to constitute robbery homicides (Zimring and Zuehl, 1985; Cook, 1986; Block, 1977), whereas the remainder are generally associated with other crimes of violence. As noted earlier, the growing discrepancy between the assumed motive and the actual motive, based on victim-offender relationships, should strengthen rather than weaken our argument in support of the rise of non-traditional patterns. Nevertheless, there are some puzzling outcomes associated with the dramatic increase in the unknown relationship category toward the end of the decade.

The Structural Pattern Prevailing in 1970

At the beginning of the 1970s in all but one of our sample cities, acquaintances represented the modal relationship (see Table 4–11). In three locations this category accounted for almost three-fifths or more of the violent deaths. Disputes and arguments between persons known to one another but not kin were contributing most to the high observed-risk levels at that date. However, Detroit, by this date, showed the greatest dissimilarity from the other cities because "acquaintances" failed to account for as many as three in ten deaths (or fewer than two-fifths of the total). Detroit showed a strong balance among categories in their contribution to the overall homicide picture. Detroit and St. Louis continued ahead of the rest in the ratio of instrumentally motivated deaths to the total. Thus five years after the period of risk escalation was initiated, only Detroit and St. Louis had advanced substantially along the traditional/non-traditional axis. Although movement was observed for each location, Houston and Pittsburgh remained anchored close to the traditional end of the axis.

TABLE 4–11

The Victim-Offender Relationship and Its Contribution
to the Share of Black Adult Male Homicides—1970
(Percent)

City	Family	Acquaintance	Stranger	Unknown
Atlanta	16.1%	49.3%	18.0%	16.6%
St. Louis	17.5%	42.4%	20.9%	19.2%
Detroit	20.5%	27.9%	26.3%	25.3%
Houston	12.1%	59.1%	15.4%	13.4%
Pittsburgh	29.4%	58.8%	11.8%	——
Los Angeles	8.0%	61.3%	21.8%	8.1%

Source: The FBI Monthly Homicide Reports, 1970.

An Interval of Rapid Structural Change

Between 1970 and 1975, the interval during which risk reached its highest level, our sample locations saw their risk levels moving in concert with the national trend. A year-by-year assessment of our core city sample, in which special attention was directed at the victimization pattern of young adults, reveals some year-to-year variations in annual peaking patterns (see Figure 4–1). Likewise, the patterns of instrumental motivations also vary from place to place, with unknowns dominating this category in St. Louis and Detroit and stranger victimizations relatively more important in Atlanta. Yet there was much fluctuation among categories from year-to-year.

Before we examine trends for the full decade, let us specify just where each community stood at mid-decade as a means of ascertaining speed of movement along the traditional/non-traditional victimization axis (see Table 4–12). Table 4–12 shows that Detroit continued to lead others, and it has advanced farthest from the traditional end of the

FIGURE 4-1

Total and Instrumental Deaths of Young Adult Male Victims: 1975

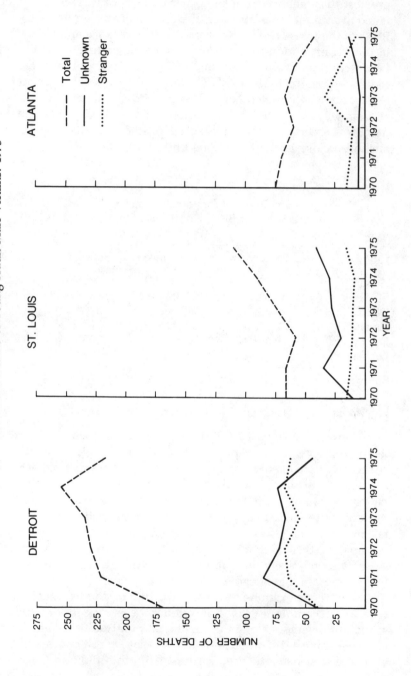

axis. Following closely behind Detroit is Los Angeles, which has moved rapidly from its more traditional location in 1970. The prime questions become, how does one account for the latter's substantially altered structure? Are we simply viewing a random fluctuation that will soon swing back to the equilibrium state? St. Louis, the early take-off leader, maintained essentially the same structure it had shown five years earlier, a condition that now places it in this position on the axis. Atlanta, like St. Louis, demonstrated only limited structural change during the interval and thus was able to retain fourth position. Houston was slower to change, but its structure continued to bear a strong resemblance to that of Atlanta. Pittsburgh maintains the strongest resemblance to its early typically traditional structure.

TABLE 4–12

The Victim-Offender Relationship and
Black Adult Male Homicides Shares—1975
(Percent)

City	Family	Acquaintance	Stranger	Unknown
Atlanta	19.7%	47.0%	10.3%	23.0%
St. Louis	7.6%	53.2%	15.2%	23.9%
Detroit	13.1%	30.2%	30.5%	26.5%
Houston	20.3%	47.6%	18.2%	14.0%
Pittsburgh	25.0%	55.0%	5.0%	15.0%
Los Angeles	15.5%	32.9%	26.0%	25.6%

Source: The FBI Monthly Supplementary Homicide Reports, 1975.

Nationally, risk levels showed signs of decline during the latter half of the decade. It is not obvious, however, how much of that decline is associated with population aging, improvements in the economic position of the population generally, fewer intersexual conflicts growing out of altered family patterns, or the ability of the criminal justice system to remove from the streets a substantial number of persons involved in robbery and the drug business. No doubt each of the above elements contributed in some way to the observed decline, although the effectiveness of individual contributors was likely to depend on the prevalence of specific victim-offender patterns during the interval. It is unclear to what extent an alteration in structure impacts on risk, if indeed it does.

Having set the stage for a demonstration of the risk/structure association, we will now detail how both risk and structure changed over the decade at our sample locations. Moreover, we will demonstrate how the risk-structure association varied among the categories "young adult" and "mature black males." More important, however, is how successful attempts have been to lower risk during the interval among each of the structural groups. Therefore, it is important that we detail the traditional/non-traditional structural changes if it can be shown that risk bears even a modest relationship to structure.

Adult male risk among our sample cities varied greatly between the years 1970 and 1980. A decline in risk was denoted in Atlanta, Houston, and Detroit. In the latter community, however, the change was very modest. The opposite characterized changes in St. Louis and Los Angeles. The aggregate increase in St. Louis was somewhat nominal, but it was already high in the base year. On the other hand, aggregate male risk in Los Angeles was exceeded only by that prevailing in St. Louis. But much more insight into the nature of the circumstances leading to death can be derived by partitioning risk by life-cycle stage and motive (see Table 4–13).

TABLE 4–13

Young Adult/Mature Adult Contribution to Risk by Risk Type
(per 100,000)

	Atlanta		St. Louis		Detroit	
	1970	1980	1970	1980	1970	1980
Young Adult:						
Expressive	181	111	195	128	66	79
Instrumental	89	125	119	130	109	55
Mature Adult:						
Expressive	129	68	115	116	78	93
Instrumental	94	89	83	160	61	76
	Houston		Pittsburgh		Los Angeles	
	1970	1980	1970	1980	1970	1980
Young Adult:						
Expressive	127	69	115	82	94	55
Instrumental	48	35	10	37	29	185
Mature Adult:						
Expressive	92	69	69	33	39	74
Instrumental	40	35	9	23	25	117

Source: FBI Monthly Supplementary Homicide Reports, 1970 and 1980.

Places in which there was evidence of an aggregate increase in risk over the ten years were places in which instrumental risk was substantially elevated. In St. Louis, instrumental risk increased sharply in the mature adult population while registering only modest gains among young adults. Of course, young adults in St. Louis were already subject to high instrumental risk during the initial year. Thus young adults in St. Louis were exposed to high instrumental-risk levels during both time periods, but only during the latter year had instrumental risk come to dominate killings occurring among mature adults. At the same time the so-called street-corner man life-style maintained its stability as an important source of risk among this life-cycle group.

Standing in sharp contrast to the changes described for St. Louis are those occurring in Houston. Expressive risk, which accounted for the vast majority of the risk in the initial time period, experienced a major decline among young adults and a smaller decline among mature adults. Modest declines were observed in the already relatively low levels of instrumental risk among both life-cycle groups. The patterns of interpersonal conflict described by Bullock (1955) more than a generation ago to explain risk in Houston's black community appear to be weakening as a major contributor. Nevertheless, the motivations prevailing at that time continue to be important. For some unspecified reason, instrumental motivations in Houston have been much slower to take hold.

Detroit is characterized by the most inconsistent pattern among our sample locations. It started the decade as the farthest advanced along the traditional/non-traditional axis. Yet there was an apparent slowing of this movement by mid-decade and a seeming reversal in movement by decade's end. The most evident is that associated with a decline in the risk of stranger victimizations, which had been dominated by robbery killings. This decline manifests itself most strongly in the behavior of young adults. A modest increase does occur in expressive victimizations in both life-cycle segments, but these increases are inadequate to produce an upward movement in aggregate risk. These changes cannot be explained easily other than to suggest that risk of victimization is etiologically complex. Nevertheless, the approach we have followed allows us to consider a variety of possibilities in an attempt to unravel the risk, structure, and life-cycle associations.

What is apparent is that in communities experiencing a rapid growth in their share of instrumentally oriented victimizations, a subsequent increase occurs in aggregate male risk. Nevertheless, the Detroit data show that this process is reversible. Likewise, in some locations expressive risk was declining while instrumental risk was increasing, whereas in others, both were declining. In one instance, expressive risk increased and instrumental risk declined concomitantly. Most often, however, an increase in instrumental risk was observed in both life-cycle stages while expressive-motivated behavior declined. Aggregate risk levels at the end of the period related to risk levels prevailing in the base year and the rate and direction of movement of our dichotomous categories over the interval.

A general overview of the risk-structure association reveals that in the nation's larger black communities, a set of forces that favor instrumentally motivated killings exist, especially among young adult males. The strength of these forces varies from one location to another. When the emerging risk behavior is combined with those elements that favor expressive-motivated killings, as was more common in the mature adult population in the initial year, then high aggregate risk levels can be anticipated. Moreover, expressive motivations apparently have begun to wane, especially among young adults. Thus generational differences in one's world view tend to promote differences among segments of the population regarding the appropriate uses of violence. Yet the extent to which these tastes are abetted or thwarted is thought to be related to specific external actions such as increases in unemployment and the effectiveness of the criminal justice system.

Those who have chosen to confine their money-making activity to the irregular economy as a matter of taste run a high risk of instrumental victimization. Similarly, those individuals who are dislocated from the regular economy often encounter strains that heighten the probability of interpersonal conflict with persons to whom they are emotionally bonded, a situation that favors expressive killings. As a case in point, the situation observed in Detroit at the end of the decade leads one to conjecture about the motives supporting the homicide pattern observed there. How much was the downturn in the economy responsible for a return to a substantial upturn in expressive victimizations? Equally puzzling is how one accounts for a reduction in instrumental risk under the same conditions. Unfortunately, there seems to be no simple answers, an indication that this situation bears close scrutiny.

THE URBAN QUARTER CENTURY COMES TO A CLOSE

It was during the early 1960s when evidence that black risk, after a decade of seeming stability, was beginning to edge upward. The takeoff in risk, however, did not occur until the second quinquennium of the decade. Risk levels peaked during the mid-1970s and, after 1975, began a three-year decline. Although there was again evidence of an upturn in the late 1970s, that upturn was short-lived. The aggregate black homicide rate in 1980 was only 79 percent of the observed level at the beginning of the 1970s. During the last five years of the period under review (1980–1984), risk levels declined by another twenty-five percent, and had begun to resemble pre-takeoff levels. It appeared that the urban quarter century would end just as it had started with risk levels that suggested greater civility than that prevailing during the decade of the 1970s. But the observed temporary decline in risk was interrupted during the final year of the period.

Trends in Risk Among Urban Sample

Why the risk pattern observed during the early 1980s was so abruptly breached has not yet been fully explained. Nevertheless, as the curtain closed on the last five years of our review period, the future appeared less bright than had been expected based on the short-term trend. Not all of our sample cities, however, were affected in the same way; some defied the trend by resisting involvement in the latest upturn. Detroit was less fortunate, however, because it showed evidence of once again experiencing elevated risk. On the other hand, Atlanta, Houston, St. Louis, and Los Angeles maintained risk levels that bore a striking resemblance to that prevailing in 1980. Moreover, the cities in our sample appeared to differ from a number of those in which a large share of black Americans reside (see Fig. 4–2). The upturn was sharpest in New York, whereas the most noteable decline was observed in Cleveland. The observed broad variations in risk occurring in the nation's larger black communities in 1985 suggests the need to look more closely at the unique characteristics of individual places.

It is important that we attempt to account for the changes noted above. Yet, given the recency of these changes and the position of individual places in the national urban system, no more than a tentative explanation is likely. In addressing these changes, most attention will be directed to Detroit and Los Angeles. Because Atlanta and Houston were both characterized by moderate risk levels in 1980 and appear to have stabilized at those levels, we have decided to forgo a discussion of their post-1980 trends. Moreover, it appears that a permanent state of elevated risk, such as that observed in St. Louis, and/or an incipient upturn in risk, such as seen in Detroit, are the product of forces that distinguish them from our southern cities. Caution is advised, however; the forces responsible for the observed 1985 risk levels in these places may simply diffuse to other locations over time.

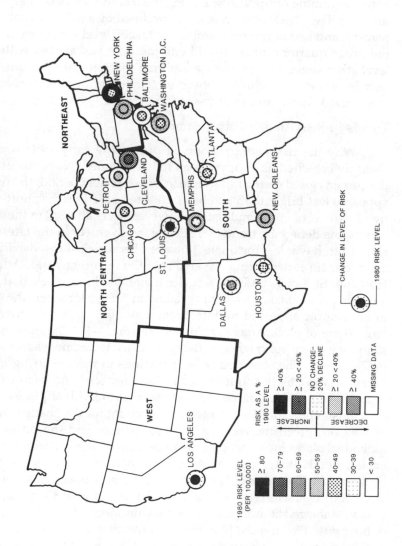

FIGURE 4-2

Estimated Change in Black Homicide Risk in a Large Urban Network: 1980–1985

The cycle of violence that swept through most of the nation's larger black communities during the 1970s appeared to have peaked in many by 1980. But among our six-city sample, both St. Louis and Los Angeles were characterized by higher risk levels at this time than those prevailing a decade earlier. Pittsburgh, on the other hand, seemed to be leading the way toward decline, at least in terms of returning to pre-1960 levels of risk. The 20 percent national decline in black risk that occurred between 1980 and 1985 was not observed uniformly across places, as the estimates shown in Table 4–14 show. As revealed, none of our sample locations registered a decline of the magnitude that characterized the national aggregate. Los Angeles did better than all others but was still characterized by a level of risk that was almost twice as high as that prevailing in 1970. Yet Detroit, which had experienced declining risk during the late 1970s, was experiencing a different risk trajectory—risk was beginning to edge up again. St. Louis and Houston experienced slight elevations, but they, along with Atlanta, appear to have reached a temporary equilibrium. But if the St. Louis condition represents an equilibrium state, it holds serious implications for places with similar characteristics.

TABLE 4–14

An Estimate of Prevailing Risk Levels in the Black Urban Sample—1985

	1980 Risk Level (per 100,000)	1985 Risk Level (per 100,000)	Percent Change	Expected Risk (based on 20 percent aggregate decline)
Atlanta	46	43	−6.5	35
Houston	45	46	+2.5	35
Los Angeles	87	75	−13.7	70
Detroit	59	69	+16.9	47
St. Louis	92	95	+3.2	74

Source: Computed by the authors based on projected population growth between 1980–1985.

The Involvement of Young Adult Males in the Cyclical Upturn

As the urban quarter century came to a close, risk levels clearly remained persistently higher among the non-southern cities in our sample. Of course, this may simply reflect the unique situation of individual places rather than an association with a regional culture, but we come away with an impression that the higher levels of observed risk are an outgrowth of the changing behavior and outlook of young adult males. There is growing evidence of an increasing propensity for young adult black males to be drawn into life-styles in which violence becomes an accepted form of behavior, at least among their peers. Harvey (1986) attributes this to the emergence of a "subculture of exasperation." The exasperation that he describes is associated with the inability of young blacks, especially males, to participate in the mainstream economy. He also emphasizes the psychological consequences associated with this inability. Needless to say, those on the outside looking in are likely to adopt an alternative view. To be sure, however, those places with the highest victimization and offending levels are places wherein a disproportionate share of the prevailing risk is attributable to the behavior of young adult males.

The renewed elevation in risk in Detroit is disproportionately concentrated among young black adults. As a matter of fact, the vast majority of the 100 additional black deaths occurring in the Michigan city in 1985, over and beyond those that occurred in 1980, were those in which the victims were male and under age 30. Detroit experienced a 62 percent increase in risk among the 15–29 year old black males, while registering less than a 17 percent aggregate increase. Yet, young adult males in Detroit were still at lower risk of victimization than were members of this segment of the population in both St. Louis and Los Angeles. The critical issue, however, is what the circumstances are that lead young black adults to occupy such a precarious position in the scheme of things.

Changing Risk Behavior in Detroit

In Detroit, the reasons appear diffuse. The FBI's Supplementary Homicide Report (SHR) fails to demonstrate a substantial change in stranger victimizations during the five-year interval (e.g., the incidence of robbery homicide) but shows a major change in the number of victimizations in which the relationship between the victim and offender was that of acquaintance or unknown. The "unknown" category was the most telling because confrontations among persons who were not necessarily unknown to one another, but for whom the relationship itself was unknown increased in importance. The largest number of individuals in this category were those under age 25, with those aged 15–19 found only slightly less often among the victims than those aged 20–24. Some have attributed the increase in risk among this group to random shootings, to growing disrespect among peers, and the increased involvement of teenagers in the drug distribution system (see

Mieczkowski, 1986). Whatever the reason, risk has moved down the age structure and has captured the attention of citizens in ways that previously went unnoticed. Recently, students in Detroit schools were checked for weapons, classes were curtailed for a day so parents, students, and school officials could discuss the gravity of the situation, and a group of mothers whose teen children were victims of homicide formed an organization to assist in combating the problem. The acronym for that group is SOSAD (Save Our Sons and Daughters).

In Detroit, as well as in other selected northern urban centers, we are witnessing the coming of age of a cohort socialized in an environment where instrumental behavior has become entrenched, and, as a result, gratuitous violent confrontations have become more commonplace. This situation is fueled by the changing demands of the mainstream economy, the lure of the irregular economy (e.g., drug trafficking), the strengthening of secular values, and the growing attractiveness of the street hustler as a role model. Is the Detroit model being exported? What can be done to save a generation of youth?

Street Gangs and Risk Levels in Los Angeles

Over the period of a single decade, Los Angeles has become a dominant center of risk of violent victimization. It began the urban quarter century with risk levels, at least during the takeoff stage, that were unusually low when compared to each of the other sample communities, with the exception of Pittsburgh. Its takeoff lagged behind the others, but, since the late 1970s, risk levels have remained high. The growing problem of gang violence in Los Angeles represents a prime element in the transition from low risk to high risk (see Maxson, Gordon, and Klein, 1985). Yet, the reasons for the emergence and/or the reemergence of gang activity, remains unclear at this time. Street-gang activity in New York during the 1950s supposedly diminshed with the introduction of heroin. Yet, during the 1970s, gang activity was again on the upswing in large urban communities that had ethnically diverse populations. The latest resurgence of gang activity, however, distinguishes itself from earlier activity in that gangs are known to be involved in a variety of criminal enterprises and have in their possession a wide range of weapons, including automatic weapons, which results in their becoming a much greater threat than was earlier the case.

A review of the FBI's Supplementary Homicide Report provides solid evidence of not only the magnitude of the problem, but its structural character as well. Unlike in Detroit, where the modal relationship between victim and offender in 1985 was unknown, in Los Angeles the modal relation was that of persons known to one another—i.e., acquaintances. Yet, at least half of the victims were not involved in a primary relationship with their killer. What becomes readily apparent, especially among young adult black males, are the non-traditional circumstances leading to death among persons with at least a passing familiarity with one another. Two-thirds of those killed under non-traditional circumstances were victims of gang-related behavior, whereas another one-fifth were involved in drug-related transactions. Thus the fact that approximately one-third of all victims among this group are acquaintances of the offenders and approximately one-fifth are unknown to the offender implies that gang-related killings may play a major role in sustaining high homicide risk among young adult males in the Los Angeles black community.

The role of gang-related killings in the Los Angeles black community received heightened attention in 1984, when four members of the family of Kermit Alexander, a former, well-known, California University athlete, were killed (see *Los Angeles Times Magazine*, August 2, 1987). This home invasion by three members of a gang called the Rolling 60's Crips, who had contracted to kill a prospective witness against another member of the gang, led to the death of four innocent persons. The killers went to the wrong address and fired widly at all persons in view. This killing highlights one of the earmarks of gang-related killings, which is the often random nature of the act. The rise of gangs and their growing involvement in drug trafficking is creating havoc in previously quiet middle-class neighborhoods as drive-by shootings become more commonplace. At this writing, the problem in the Los Angeles community has become even more serious as the police conduct massive sweeps through the community as a means of regaining control. In the August 30, 1984, edition of the *Los Angeles Sentinel*, the city's major black newspaper, Paul Ciotte described the situation in the following way:

> Community violence has reached a new high. Within one 16 hour period, there were nine shootings in one specific area of our community. Within a 10-day period there were 16 shootings in the same communities. This might be considered normal but we cannot allow this to continue...But in order to stop these random shootings by gang members and by drug oriented youths, there must be a concerted effort on the part of the community.

SUMMARY

We have attempted to demonstrate in a straightforward manner how the structure of victimization in a sample of large black communities underwent change over a twenty-year period (1965–1985), with the primary emphasis on changes occurring during the decade of the 1970s. This interval was chosen because it was during the first ten years of the period that homicide rates began to rise sharply and reach a peak before beginning to slowly decline in the last half of the period. This also represents an interval in which far-reaching changes were occurring in the national economy. The changes in the economy have led to the adoption of an altered pattern of routine activities (Cohen and Felson, 1979) and subsequently have led to modifications in the value hierarchy (Rokeach, 1973 and Spindler, 1977).

In general, this was a period of great flux during which many Americans enhanced their quality of life, while others struggled to sustain an already marginal position. Black males, in particular, became targets of heightened risk of victimization, because segments of that population were ill-prepared to make a satisfactory transition from an industrial economy to a post-industrial economy. Their failure to adapt apparently led to their participation in the irregular economy and, subsequently, involvement in violent predatory behavior.

The observed risk pattern in our six-city sample, however, bears a strong association with structure of victimization and age-related propensities to engage in high-risk life styles. In those communities in which young blacks had experienced less success in sustaining themselves in the regular economy, non-traditional patterns of victimization were most in evidence. Houston, in which little negative feedback was experienced as an outgrowth of economic transformation, had moved much less slowly away from the traditional end of the structural spectrum than had those communities that experienced much negative feedback. Therefore, the basis of continuing examples of elevated risk appears to be indirectly dependent upon urban growth and the ability of young adult males to find a satisfactory niche for themselves in the growth sector of the economy.

5

Black Females and Lethal Violence

INTRODUCTION

During the last decade more scholars have focused on the role of females in assaultive and nonassaultive crimes and on their role as victims of various types of crimes (Hoffman-Bustamante, 1973: Adler, 1975). No consensus has been reached, however, on either the nature of female criminality or the leadership role women are thought to play in criminal behavior.

Some of the studies conclude that the women's rights movement has resulted in increased female participation in aggressive and violence oriented crimes (Adler, 1975, Ward, Johnson, and Ward, 1969; Austin, 1982). Others conclude that the increase in opportunities for women to work outside the home has provided greater opportunities to commit property and economic offenses. On the other hand, the changes in the legal status of women and their increased feelings of self-confidence will serve to decrease or at least stabilize female participation in violence offenses (Simon, 1976). Scholars differ in opinion, however, about whether the increase of female participation in some offense categories is the effect of equality or the overall effect of the recession during the past decade.

One view is that empirical evidence fails to support a correspondence between increases in female criminality and the rise of the women's rights movement (Steffensmeier, 1978, Weis, 1976; Hartnagel, 1982). A more recently expressed view is that the historical gender gap in crime continues to exist despite the overall increases in crime and the changes in sex roles during the last several decades (Wilson and Herrnstein, 1985). Wilson and Herrnstein see some narrowing of the gender gap, but the sex differences appear to be diminishing more for minor and juvenile offenses than for serious and adult offenses. The debate surrounding the nature of female criminality obviously will continue.

Despite the debate, one much-ignored area is the involvement of females in acts of lethal violence. There have been some studies on female homicide offenders in general (Totman, 1978; Wilbanks, 1983a; 1983b; Weisheit, 1984; Jones, 1980; Mann, 1988); however, the role of black females in homicide has been given far less attention (McClain, 1982a; McClain, 1982b; Mann, 1987). Black females are associated far more often with acts of lethal violence, either as victims or offenders, than their white counterparts. The risk of involvement also has increased as homicide levels have increased in the nation's black communities in general; thus, examining the role of black females in acts of lethal violence is crucial to an understanding of the nature of female involvement in violent acts in general.

The consequences of urban decline and its relationship to homicide, as discussed in earlier chapters, have been on the macro- and medial scale, framed within the context of an ecological explanation of homicide risk. The individual-level behavior of those involved as either victims or offenders of homicide was examined for males in chapter 4; in this chapter we examine the black female's participation both as homicide victim and offender.

Contextual Aspects of the Lives of Urban Black Females

One cannot begin to discuss black females as homicide victims and offenders without first describing the urban environmental context within which these women conduct their daily lives. Over the last several decades American society has witnessed a steady decline in employment opportunities in urban areas. Economics have shifted from a production of goods to the delivery of services, businesses have relocated from the central cities to the suburbs, and industrial centers have shifted from the urban areas of the Northeast and Midwest to the Sunbelt region of the West. These factors, in combination, have reduced the employment opportunities of blacks, both male and female, who reside principally in the abandoned environs of once thriving manufacturing centers. The effect of these lost employment opportunities on the labor-force participation of black females is of particular importance to our contextual picture of life for urban black females.

Since 1972 black female unemployment rates have been twice those for white females, and among black females, unemployment rates decreased with each progressive age group. Thus the highest unemployment rates were among 16–19 year olds, and the lowest were among those 65 and over in 1972 (Jones, 1986). Wallace (1980) pointed out that once black women became unemployed, they often remained so, eventually leaving the work force.

In 1975, 66 percent of the black women who left the unemployed category actually left the labor force and 33 percent found jobs. By comparison, 45 percent of the white women who left unemployment found jobs (Wallace, 1980:45).

Differences in educational levels may be one reason for the difference in new employment opportunities. However, recent figures indicate that in 1980 the median educational level of black females in the population was 12.0 years, only a half year less than white females whose median educational level was 12.5 years. The median years for black and white women in the labor force in 1980 was 12.4 and 12.7, respectively (Jones, 1986:22). What this seems to suggest is that those black females with low levels of education are the ones most likely to leave the labor force. In 1983 only 21 percent of black females with five-to-seven years of schooling were employed, and only 27 percent of black female high school dropouts were employed. Conversely, 82 percent of black females with five or more years of college were employed (Jones, 1986:22). Moreover, in terms of income, in 1980 the average black woman working in periphery industries (i.e., those characterized by low wages, intense labor, low profits, and high competition) earned only 31 percent of the average white male salary and 53 percent of the average black male salary (Gwartney-Gibbs and Taylor, 1986).

The changing character of the black family is another variable that one must consider when developing a picture of the contextual milieu in which urban black females exist, one which also may partially explain why employment opportunities are limited for many black females. By 1984, 44 percent of all black households were headed by females, and, for poor black families, 73 percent were headed by females. Moreover, one out of every two black children lived in poverty, and 74 percent of those children lived in female-headed families (Rodger, 1986). Even when female heads of households are employed they tend to earn less than male heads of households, and black female heads of households earn even less. A majority of black female-headed families, however, exist with no income other than Aid-to-Families-with-Dependent-Children payments and live well below the poverty line (Rodger, 1986:47).

The reasons for the increase in the extent of poverty among black female-headed households are numerous. Some feel that this phenomenon is the result of high rates of divorce, out-of wedlock births among never-married women, especially teenagers, and fertility combined with limited sources of income from employment, child support, and social welfare programs (Rodger, 1986; Darity and Myers, 1984).

The change in the composition of black families may be a consequence of life in urban environments (Furstenberg et al., 1975). Furstenberg et al. suggest that economic conditions of urban areas directly impact black family structures. This is manifest in high levels of black male unemployment, and extremely high infant-mortality rates. A sizable number of female-heads of households are never-married black females, and black women who experience an out-of-wedlock pregnancy are less likely to marry than those who have not (Darity and Myers, 1984). Staple (1987) suggests that one of the principal reasons for this is the lack of a sufficient pool of black males of marriageable age. Although black male births outnumber black female births, there is a shortage of black males over fourteen years of age, which may be attributed to their higher infant-mortality rate and the extremely high mortality rate of young black males from homicide, accidents, suicides, drug overdoses, and war casualties (Staples, 1987). As of 1982, the remaining 46 percent of black males of marriageable age were not in the labor force and thus were not capable of contributing to the support of a family.

One of the factors that supposedly contributes to female labor-force participation is marital status. Generally, never-married (single), divorced, and separated women have higher labor force participation rates than married women. Given the increasing number of black female-headed households, one would expect an increase in the number of never-married black females in the work force. However, in recent years employment rates among black women have not been following this pattern. Rates of unemployment among never-married black women were lower than those for married black women living with a spouse, and rates among divorced black women have fluctuated over time rather than trending upward, as is the case for white divorcees (Jones, 1986).

These data indicate that life for many urban black females is one characterized by limited economic and social opportunities. Employment opportunities are few, and low levels of education may preclude many urban black females from those jobs that are available. The absence of a available pool of employed black males often makes marriage an impossibility, and the number of out-of-wedlock births is on the increase. Many of these new mothers are teenagers whose opportunities for a different life decrease substantially with the birth of the child. Limited employment opportunities, low education levels, children to support, and an unemployed or absent black male mate adds up to a very undesirable picture of life for many black females in urban settings. It is against this backdrop that we examine black females as victims and offenders of lethal violence.

Black Females as Homicide Victims

In 1973 the homicide rate for black males of all age categories was, at minimum, eight times the rate for white males. In some age categories the difference was as much as ten times. The situation was slightly better for black females, but the rates were still considerably higher than those of white females. Black females in all age categories were at least five times more likely to be victims of homicide than their white counterparts (Shin et al., 1977). These trends continued upward until 1975, when the rates began to stabilize or, in some instances, decline.

In recent years researchers have begun to direct their attention to identifying and examining causal determinants that contribute to this disproportionate representation of blacks as homicide victims, but because males are the predominant victims of homicide, little attention has been given to examination and explanation of black female homicide victimization.

Besides the predominance of male victims, perhaps another reason for the lack of research is the tendency of researchers in the field of victimology to be concerned with the evaluation of the victim's responsibility for the offender's act. Victims of certain crimes, homicide and rape, are usually stigmatized because they are viewed as the "losers" in situations that have a game-like quality. Some individuals (e.g., lower-class individuals, racial minorities, women) are held to be more "legitimate" and deserving victims than others (Weiss and Borges, 1973). Thus, the "triple legitimate" victimization status of black females—poor, black, and female—also may account for the absence of research on their role as victims of lethal violence.

Profile of Female Homicide Victims

A byproduct of Wolfgang's 1958 study of homicide patterns in a large northeastern city was the development of a general typology of females who are victims of homicide and the circumstances under which they are murdered (Wolfgang, 1958). The female homicide victim in usually lower class, most often black, and an urban dweller. She is most likely to be murdered by a male rather than another female, and that male is most likely one with whom the victim has a personal relationship, such as a husband or lover. She is also most likely to be murdered in the home during the course of a domestic altercation. Wolfgang, however, did not include information about the behavior patterns or life-styles of the victims prior to the homicide as part of the typology.

This profile will serve as the analytic framework for assessing the data on the characteristics and life-style of black female homicide victims. In an attempt to develop a more complete picture of black females most likely to be homicide victims, we will examine some aspects of behavior patterns and life-styles that Wolfgang excluded. The data utilized in this section are secondary information on homicides which include information on black female homicide victims for 1970 through 1975 in three cities—Houston, Detroit, and Atlanta (N=661). This information was augmented by more detailed data provided by surveying a small number of the next of kin of ten black female victims killed in 1975 in three cities (N=10)—Atlanta, Detroit, and St. Louis.

Three concerns may be raised about these data: the limited character of the aggregate data, the small size of the sample, and the nature of the survey data. Researchers are always confronted with the first problem whenever aggregate data are utilized. The second problem, the small sample size, creates problems because generalization from the sample may be distortions of real population parameters. Finally, the survey data must be viewed with the understanding they they are not self-report data, but data on victims provided by the next of kin, and therefore the data may or may not be completely accurate. (That their loved one died in such a violent manner may bias their recollections toward a more positive picture of the victims.)

SOCIAL AND ENVIRONMENTAL CHARACTERISTICS OF BLACK FEMALE VICTIMS

The analysis contained in this section examines various demographic, behavioral, and environmental characteristics of the victims for the three-city sample, amplified by information from the survey data. The areas examined are: age of victims, educational level, fighting behavior, previous encounters with the law, home life and neighborhood environment as a child, family violence as a child, drinking problems and narcotics history, employment patterns, relationship of victim to her murderer, type of weapon used in the homicide, and circumstances surrounding the homicide.

Age

Is there a particular age range within which black females are more likely to be homicide victims? Shin et al. (1977) found that black females between the ages of 25 and 34 had the highest homicide rate among females in 1972, 28.3 per 100,000. Data on the ages of victims were available for the sample cities as well as for the interviewed subsample. Table 5-1 shows the age distributions of victims for the three cities. The age categories of 20-24 and over-40 had the largest percentage of victims, 19.1 and 26.9 percent respectively. The combined total percentages of the 25-29 and 30-34 categories is 27.7 percent, however, which is congruent with the findings of Shin et al. The age distribution for the survey data appears congruent with the aggregate sample data; most of the victims were in the 25-34 age category.

Educational Level

Wolfgang (1958) found that black female homicide victims are usually lower-class individuals. Assuming a relationship exists between education and economic achievement, are black female homicide victims likely to have low education levels? Data on educational achievement were available only for the survey group. These data indicate that five of the victims had less than a high school education,

TABLE 5-1

Age, Victim-Offender Relationship and Type of Weapon—Black Female Homicide Victims—Detroit, Atlanta, and Houston—1970–1975*

Age	0-4	5-14	15-19	20-24	25-29	30-34	35-39	40 & over	
	4.4%	2.3%	8.5%	19.9%	14.5%	13.2%	10.3%	26.9%	
	(29)	(15)	(56)	(132)	(96)	(87)	(68)	(178)	N=661

Victim-Offender Relationship		*Weapon*	
Family	37.52%	Firearm	63.7%
	(248)		(421)
Acquaintance	28.44%	Knife	17.4%
	(188)		(115)
Stranger	12.71%	Other	18.5%
	(84)		(122)
Unknown	21.33%	Missing data	.4%
	(141)		(3)
	N=661		N=661

* Complete 1970–1975 data available for Houston only. Atlanta data are for 1971–1972 and 1974, and Detroit data are for 1971 through 1974.

Source: Paula D. McClain, "Cause of Death—Homicide: A Research Note on Black Females as Homicide Victims." *Victimology: An International Journal*, 7(1982):pp.204–212.

and five had completed high school with several of these having gone on to college. On this very limited scale, it appears black female homicide victims are just as likely to have the median educational achievement of the overall society as they are to be high school dropouts.

Fighting Behavior

Since the victims lives were taken as the result of acts of lethal violence, did they have a history of physical violence? Once again this information is available only for the sub-sample. These data indicate that only three of the victims had engaged in fights as youths, and the occurrences were infrequent. Seven of the victims had no history of involvement in fights. Additionally, none of the victims had ever sustained injuries as a result of a fight.

Previous Encounters with the Law

Did the victims participate in activities that brought them in contact with law enforcement officials and that might have contributed to an increased probability of being a homicide victim? Wolfgang found that 69.8 percent of black female homicide victims in his study had no previous arrest record, compared to only 38.7 percent of black male homicide victims. Among whites, 86 percent of white female and 67 percent of white male homicide victims had no arrest record (Wolfgang, 1958:175). Needless to say, Wolfgang's 1958 profile describes a population that came of age prior to World War II and thus may not constitute an ideal yardstick for purposes of comparison.

Once again, this information is available only for the survey group, but these data indicate a conformance with Wolfgang's findings. Nine victims had no previous encounters with the law, and one had been arrested on drug-related charges (apparently no conviction or jail sentence was associated with that arrest).

Home Life and Neighborhood Environment as a Child

Were the early home and neighborhood environments of the victims of a violent or stressful nature that contributed to an increased probability of homicide victimization in later years? This does not appear to be the case for the sub-sample. Eight of the victims grew up in homes in which the father was absent. Additionally, eight of the victims apparently had strong and warm relationships with their siblings while growing up, and nine had no problem with parental authority. For the one victim who had a conflict with her parents, the source of the problem was her disobedience.

Nine of the victims were raised in neighborhoods that were stable, working-class environments that their next-of-kin felt were good neighborhoods in which to raise children. Only one of the next of kin described the neighborhood in which the victim was raised as "down-and-out." In view of the overwhelming description of the neighborhoods as a good place to live, it is not surprising that ony one of the next of kin felt the neighborhood in which the victim was raised was directly related to the homicide.

Family Violence as a Child

Did the victims come from homes in which physical violence and parental fighting were commonplace? Five of the victims, according to the next of kin, were raised in homes where the parents did not believe in physically punishing children for misdeeds. Additionally, seven victims were raised in homes where their parents never engaged in serious physical fights. The remaining three grew up in homes where physical fighting was present but resulted in only minor injuries. All of the victims grew up in homes where no one ever used a weapon to injure another member of the family.

Drinking Problems and Narcotics History

Did the victims have particular problems, such as alcohol or drug addiction, that may have increased their probability of becoming victims of homicide? Zahn (1975) found that females involved in the drug culture were more likely to be victims of criminal homicide than females who were not. None of the victims in the sub-sample appear to have been heavily involved with either alcohol or drugs. Nine were described as not regular users of alcohol (did not drink more than once a week) or drugs. In response to whether they felt alcohol and drugs were in any way related to the homicide incident, only one of the next of kin believed they were.

Employment Patterns

Were the victims employed on a regular basis or were they in and out of the work force? At the time of their deaths six victims were unemployed, and four were employed in full- or part-time positions. Of those who were employed, most were working in unskilled jobs. In response to a question concerning the annual earning characteristics of the victim, four victims, according to their next of kin, earned less than $5,000 a year. Two earned less than $10,000 and one earned more than $15,000. Information about the earned income of the remaining three were not available from the next of kin.

Relationship of Victim to Her Murderer

Who are the individuals most likely to murder black females? Wolfgang (1958:208) stated, "We must say that when a man is found murdered we should first look for his acquaintances; when a woman is killed, for her relatives, mainly the husband, and after that her paramour, present or past." Our data do not appear to conform to that generalization which was formulated over three decades ago. According to our interview data, seven victims knew their murderers, and three were killed by individuals they did not know. Three were killed by strangers, three by friends or associates, and four by lovers/relatives.

Data on victims for the three sample cities also do not appear to conform to Wolfgang's findings. They revealed that 34.52 percent were killed by family members, 38.44 percent by acquaintances, 12.71 percent by strangers, and 21.33 percent were killed by unknown assailants (see Table 5-1). Apparently, then, black females are increasingly being murdered by acquaintances.

Type of Weapon

Data on type of weapon used in the homicide were available only for the three sample cities (see Table 5-1). The table shows that 63.7 percent of the victims were murdered by firearms. Knives were the weapons in 17.4 percent of the deaths and other means (i.e., physical strength and other objects) accounted for 18.5 percent of the weapons used.

Circumstances Surrounding the Homicide

Why and how did these individuals become homicide victims? Our data are not adequate to answer this question, but they suggest possible situations leading to their deaths. Descriptive accounts of the circumstances surrounding the homicide incidents in the three-city sample may provide partial insight. As the following selected accounts illustrate, the homicide in which a female is killed by a lover/relative is often the result of a domestic or interpersonal dispute. It should be noted that these data about circumstances are biased by the disproportionate share of victims from Atlanta.

Case 1
The victim and her husband were having an argument over the children going to bed. The husband pulled a shotgun and threatened to kill the victim. The victim told her husband that she was tired of him, and if he was going to kill her, then kill her. The husband shot the victim through the head.

Case 2

The victim and her husband were having marital problems. She returned from a friend's house and went to sleep on the couch. The husband tried to awaken her and eventually began to beat her when it seemed she spurned his romantic advances. She was severely beaten. The victim died from multiple injuries resulting from the assault.

But what about the circumstances of females killed by acquaintances? The situation in which a female is killed by an acquaintance, in the three-city sample, ranged from the killing of one female by a female neighbor in a dispute over a backyard fence, to the killing of a female by another female over a parking space, to the killing of a female in a bar dispute with a male patron.

Summary

The picture of the black female homicide victim that emerges from these limited data is that she was either a young or middle-aged woman. She was just as likely to be a high school graduate as she was to be a drop-out, but was most likely unemployed at the time of her death. She was raised in a relatively stable neighborhood in a home with little physical violence. She most likely did not have a police record or a history of participation in fights and did not have a problem with alcohol or drugs. In all probability she knew her killer, who was just as likely to have been a male with whom she had an affectional relationship as an acquaintance with whom she had only a passive relationship. She was probably murdered with a firearm.

Clearly the most significant finding about the victim-offender relationship is that a shift apparently has occurred from Wolfgang's findings of over three decades ago. This shift is demonstrated in both the aggregate and survey data. Wolfgang found that black females usually are murdered by male lovers or family members, primarily husbands, whereas our data indicate that black females are now just as likely to be murdered by acquaintances as by lovers and family members.

The reason for the erosion of this aspect of Wolfgang's typology may be related to the changing roles of women in American society. Wolfgang hypothesized that males in our culture have a broader social participation network outside the home than do females. As a result, males are more likely to be killed by acquaintances outside the home than are females. This shift in victim-offender relationship may indicate females are beginning to participate more in social interaction outside the home. The development of broader social networks increase the pool of potential homicide offenders and varies the circumstances under the which females are killed.

BLACK FEMALES AS HOMICIDE OFFENDERS

Comtemporary studies on violent crime in general have included attempts to explain patterns of homicide participation among black females. Wolfgang and Ferracuti (1967) also included black females as members of a "subculture of violence." They stated that among certain individuals and groups, a set of rules and norms that differ from those of mainstream culture exist, in which to resort to violence (e.g., domestic quarrels) is an acceptable mode of conduct. Within this context, Wolfgang and Ferracuti said that black women strike out at black men—their most frequent victims—because the women feel inadequately protected by men.

This explanation is interesting, but more empirical evidence would be necessary to validate it. It would be necessary to define the concept of "inadequate protection" and to demonstrate that women, of any color, when inadequately protected, strike out at those whom society deems their protectors. The assertion is, at best, a tenuous one and, at worst, a blatantly sexist one. Either way, it is not an adequate explanation for the involvement of black females in acts of lethal violence (Letcher, 1979). Moreover, Wolfgang was describing a cohort of women socialized in the 1930s and earlier. That women socialized in the 1950s and 1960s, as those in our cohort were, viewed the world quite differently is highly probable.

Adler has described the black female homicide offenders as mainly reactive, meaning that most black women probably commit homicide in self-defense as a reaction to a situation, rather than to initiate the action. If this is true, the problem stems from the perception of the existence of an external threat; more often than not, the threat originates with the black male. Again, there is no consensus on the nature and causes of black female involvement in the behavioral sequence leading to homicide.

A PROFILE OF WOMEN WHO COMMIT HOMICIDE

Wolfgang's 1958 study also resulted in the development of a general typology of females who commit murder and the circumstances under which they kill. The female who murders typically is usually lower-class, black, and an urban dweller. She rarely is a participant in felony murder; thus, her homicide is not likely to be the result of criminal activity. She typically commits homicide alone. If she is black, she most likely uses a knife; if she is white, she most likely uses a pistol. Most likely, her victim is male, probably one with whom she has an intense interpersonal relationship—a legal or common-law husband or a lover.

Wolfgang also found that 79.8 per cent of the females, both black and white, who committed homicide did so in the home, compared to 44.7 per cent of male homicide offenders. Males primarily committed homicide outside the home (55.3 percent). Further analysis indicated that of those homicides committed by females in the home, 73.5 per cent occurred in the home of the female offender. Although not explicitly stated, a direct relationship between the characteristics of the homicide incident and the sex of the offender apparently existed.

This profile has served as the typology of female homicide offenders for the last thirty years and, as a consequence, will have to be utilized as the analytic framework for assessing the roles of black female homicide offenders and for identifying any changes that may be occuring. If subcultural changes, represented by shifts in values and patterns of style, have been as far-reaching as previously stated, we would anticipate varying degrees of movement away from the profile established by Wolfgang. Once again, in an attempt to develop a more complete picture of black female homicide offenders, we will examine aspects of behavior patterns and life-style that were not examined in Wolfgang's work.

The data on black female homicide offenders are, once again, secondary data on black women charged with criminal homicide in 1975. Their victims were included in our six-city sample (N = 119). This information was augmented by more detailed data provided by surveying a small number of black female homicide offenders in the three interview cities (N = 9). No female offender agreed to an interview in St. Louis, so the sub-sample consists of two offenders from Atlanta and seven from Detroit. The black female homicide offenders interviewed ranged in age from 26 to 39.

SOCIAL AND ENVIRONMENTAL CHARACTERISTICS OF BLACK FEMALE OFFENDERS

Several research questions are addressed regarding the characteristics of black females involved in homicide transactions. What were the social and environmental contexts of their lives prior to their arrest for criminal homicide? Second, what is the relationship between these social and environmental variables and behavior patterns that increased the probability of involvement in homicide? In the following discussion we examine several personal, behavioral, and environmental characteristics of the interviewed sub-sample of black female homicide offenders. Included among these characteristics are level of education, fighting behavior, previous encounters with the law, crime and violence in the childhood environment, drinking and/or narcotics problems, employment patterns, and suggested personality type.

Educational Level

Totman (1978), Felthous and Yudowitz (1977), and Bunch et al. (1983) found that female homicide and assaultive offenders tended to have a low level of educatonal achievement. A low level of education also appears to be a characteristic of the interviewed sample of black female homicide offenders. Of that group, 44.4 percent finished high school; 55.6 percent had less than a high school education.

The offenders were asked whether they had career objectives when they were growing up. Over three-fourths indicated they had career objectives, but only a third felt they had accomplished their goals. The open-ended responses provided information about why the offenders felt they did not achieve their objectives. One offender indicated she wanted to be a nurse, but " . . . you had to go to college to do it. At the time I could not afford it, because I had to support my children." Another had a strong desire to be a model but " . . . couldn't afford modelling school."

The fact that over half of the females had less than a high school education was reflected in the types of jobs they held when they were employed—clerical and unskilled manual labor jobs.

Fighting Behavior

Was the commission of an act of lethal violence an isolated experience, or were the offenders familiar with and participants in behavioral sequences that involved violence? The survey questionnaire administered to the offenders contained questions relating to fighting patterns and injuries resulting from fights.

The data indicated that over three-fourths of the offenders (77.8 per cent) had been involved in fights as teens or adults. Additionally, exactly half of the offenders had been injured as the result of a fight, some more than once. The types of injuries varied. One offender received a broken jaw in one fight and was shot in the stomach during another. One woman was struck across the head with the butt of a gun by a male acquaintance, and another had her nose broken. These women, it appears, were participants in a lower-class life-style wherein danger is a constant companion.

Interestingly, when questioned about their role in the fights, identical percentages (42.9 percent) indicated they were either the aggressor or the attacked. The remaining 14.3 percent described their role as that of bystander. Surprisingly, although three-fourths of the offenders engaged in fights, an overwhelming majority (85.7 percent) indicated they did not find it necessary to arm themselves. If most of the attacks occurred among intimates in the home, this response appears logical.

Previous Encounter with the Law

Did the offenders' behavior patterns, such as fighting, involve them with law enforcement officials prior to their arrest for criminal homicide? Some studies have indicated that female homicide offenders had limited experience with crime (Ward et at., 1969). Others, however, have indicated that a majority of females arrested for criminal homicide have prior criminal records, many for assaultive offenses (Cole et al., 1968).

Our data on black female homicide offenders appear to conform to the findings that indicated previous criminal experience. Previous difficulty with the law prior to arrest for criminal homicide had occurred among approximately 62.5 percent of the offenders. The types of offenses for which they previously had been arrested varied from larceny to assault with intent to kill.

Home Environment and Violence in Family

Bourdouris (1971) supported the position that family discord among certain social categories is a contributing factor to the largest category of homicides, homicides by family relations. Were the offenders raised in homes in which a great deal of turmoil, physical violence, sibling criminal activities, and so forth, occurred that may have contributed to their involvement in criminal homicide?

All of the offenders indicated they were raised in homes where their parents believed in physical punishment for misdeeds. The degree of physical punishment varied substantially. A majority defined physical punishment as whippings or spankings. For a few, "physical punishment" meant that they were "beaten with extension cords and rope," and their "heads knocked against the wall." These offenders' experiences extended beyond the bounds of physical punishment into the realm of physical abuse. The physical punishment that these individuals experienced illustrates the continuing linkage of subcultural and cultural patterns that had their origin in the antebellum period and show no apparent sign of weakening.

Slightly less than a third of the offenders had brothers and/or sisters who also had encountered the law. The predominant offense for which this group was charged was murder. One respondent's sister killed her husband and was subsequently incarcerated. The same respondent also had a half-brother who was incarcerated, but she could not recall his offense.

When questioned about which person played the strongest role in developing a set of guidelines for their conduct with others, 66.6 percent of the respondents indicated the person was a family member. Of those guidelines established by family members, 44.4 percent felt the one emphasized most was to "always deal with people honestly." The guideline emphasized most in 33.3 percent of the cases was "never trust others," and 22.3 percent stated that the axiom, "attempt to look out for yourself," was most emphasized.

Such family guidelines conform to the Rokeach (1973) instrumental values of honesty, independence, and responsibility. Instrumental values suggest actions that will assist the individual or group to attain its desired end values. If these women were in any way typical of women socialized in a common social milieu, they placed great importance on being honest in their dealings with others. But they also were well aware that to place too much faith in others could lead to disappointment. Typically, these women were informed very early that it would be necessary to do for themselves to survive in a hostile environment.

Drinking Problems and Narcotics History

Did the offenders have particular problems, such as alcohol abuse or drug addition, that may have contributed to the commission of homicide? Studies have indicated that alcohol and/or drugs are often associated with homicide committed by females (Ward et al., 1969). Only 12.5 percent of the women identified themselves as alcoholics. The remainder indicated moderate alcohol usage. Nevertheless, a majority admitted they were drinking at the time they committed the homicide, but only 20 percent of that group believed that alcohol was related to the homicide. On the surface, this could appear to be a contradiction, but when we specify the time of occurence of death (e.g., weekend), it may simply reflect that moderate drinkers confine their drinking to particular leisure periods.

None of the respondents indicated that they considered themselves addicted to drugs; however, one-third of them had used marijuana, heroin, and/or cocaine. Drugs were not related to the homicide incident in any of the cases. Nevertheless, it appears that some of our sample offenders had broad experience with substances that often are considered stimulants to violence in angry confrontations.

Employment Patterns

Were the offenders employed on a regular basis, or did they engage in an itinerant work pattern? At the time of the homicide incident, 66.7 percent of the offenders were unemployed, and only a third of that group were actively seeking work. Most had been unemployed for over a year. Generally, the occupational categories in which they previously had worked were unskilled labor, domestic, and clerical. Only 44.4 percent of the offenders had ever held a full-time job, and the same percentage felt that their earnings were inadequate to support themselves and/or their families. These were women who therefore could be viewed as vulnerable and prone to adopt life-styles in which risk of violence is heightened.

Personality Type

The categorization of female homicide offenders by personality type has been given limited attention in the literature; however, two decades ago Cole et al (1968) developed six categories of personality types of females who commit criminal homicide. These categories are: (1) masochistic, (2) the overtly hostile violent, (3) the covertly hostile violent, (4) the inadequate, (5) the psychotic, and (6) the amoral.

The *masochistic* female killer usually is a reliable, stable individual, who often is overtly religious, exhibits self-control, and is productively employed outside the home. Although she is considered a stable person, she tends to choose an abusive and unstable mate. She often kills while being beaten or while fearful of being killed herself, using a weapon handy at the time, usually one belonging to the victim.

The *overtly hostile violent* female killer characteristically is emotionally unstable, aggressive, impulsive, and active, with a history of violence. She characteristically will attack her victim with the intention to hurt but not to kill. In contrast, the *covertly hostile violent* female killer is not characterized by aggressive and violent behavior. Her main characteristic is expressing hostility in an environment safe from immediate retaliation. Consequently, she often kills a child.

The *inadequate* killer generally has a low coping ability, a dependence on a dominant lover, husband, or friend, and few commitments beyond the avoidance of stress and the pleasing of the dominant partner. She usually is a participant in the offense but not the primary actor. She is either ordered to kill, helps the dominant person, or kills by accident.

The *psychotic* killer is medically diagnosed as psychotic, usually paranoid schizophrenic, and has committed the murder either after having an indiscriminate urge to kill or during a severe paranoid psychotic episode.

The *amoral* killer shows deliberaton and planning in the homicide, which is committed for economic gain or to remove a person preventing a heterosexual relationship. She has a history of asocial and anti-social behavior.

These data are not sufficient to determine comprehensively the role that personality types play in the involvement of women in violent altercations, but partial answers can be suggested on the basis of background data and responses to selected questions. The survey items that provide us with the greatest insight in this instance are those dealing with jealousy, how they were taught to handle it, and descriptive accounts of the homicide incidents.

Approximately 55.6 percent of the offenders indicated that they considered themselves jealous individuals. When asked what things provoked jealousy, the responses were principally related to the attentions and behaviors of their male intimates. Some examples of the responses were: "When he gives his attention to someone else"; "Someone getting too close to someone or something I like"; "Not using discretion in what you do. Things that you do"; "Things that were made aware to me didn't make me jealous but I felt used."

When questioned whether they were taught to handle jealousy while growing up, 44.4 percent indicated that they had not been taught, and 33.3 percent were taught to handle by striking out or getting even. Only 22.2 percent indicated they were taught to control their emotions. Self-control does not appear to be a value strongly emphasized by the principal transmitters of values to the respondents.

Interestingly, over two-thirds of the women had chosen male intimates who behaved in ways that provoked their jealousy. Most of the incidents involved perceived disrespect by their mates—for example, seeing their mates with other women. Their responses to these jealousy-invoking incidents were verbal abuse and, in a few instances, physical violence: "I hit him with a bottle and she ran"; "I got mad and raised hell"; "Several times I would get angry, cuss him out and physically jump on him."

With the exception of three cases, the victims of the offenders were either male intimates or females who were involved with the offender's male intimates. Of the three exceptions, one killed her child, one was involved in felony-homicide, and one murdered a women over a parking space. The following descriptive account of the circumstances of the homicide incident for the remaining respondents is illustrative of the situations leading to the deaths of male intimates.

Offense: First degree murder
The offender (Aged 21) and the deceased had been living together for two years. During the last month the offender had caught the deceased three times going out with a former girl friend. On one occasion the deceased did not come home all night, and the defendant, in the early morning, had seen his truck parked in front of his former girl friend's house and saw him leaving.
One evening the offender went to the parking lot of the deceased's place of employment and asked him to return to her. (The deceased had left her the previous Monday.) The deceased went into this place of employment, and when the offender saw him coming back across the parking lot, she took a rifle from her car and fired one shot to the head, fatally wounding the deceased.

The combined examination of jealousy indicators, type of victim, and circumstances of the homicide for each respondent allows a reserved and qualified assessment of the personality type of the black female homicide offender. Based on these variables, 66.7 percent of the offenders appeared to be the overtly hostile violent type, 11.1 percent the covertly hostile violent type, 11.1 percent the inadequate type, and 11.1 percent the amoral.

ASPECTS OF THE HOMICIDE INCIDENT

In the following analysis we examine aspects of the homicide incident for the six-city sample amplified by information from the survey data. The aspects of violent crimes to be examined include: whether the women acted alone or with others, who the victims were, where the crimes took place, what weapons were used, and the offender's rationale for the homicide.

Criminal Roles of Black Women

The roles of women in homicide have been defined as conspirator, accessory, partner, and sole perpetrator (Ward et al., 1969), and Wolfgang (1958) found an overwhelming majority of females who commit homicide are sole perpetrators. *Conspirator* is defined as one who instigates or has knowledge of the crime but who does not participate in committing the criminal act itself. The *accessory* is one who plays a secondary role in committing the crime—acting as a lookout, driving a getaway car, carrying weapons, tools or the proceeds of robberies and burglaries. The *partner* is one who participates equally in all aspects of the crime. The final category is the women who acts as the *sole perpetrator* of the crime. Data presented in Table 5–2 indicate that 95 percent of the black female homicide offenders in the six sample

TABLE 5–2

Roles, Relationships to Offenders, Sex and Race, and Location of Offense for Homicide Incidents Involving Black Females in Los Angeles, Houston, St. Louis, Atlanta, Detroit, and Pittsburgh in 1975

	N	%
Roles		
Conspirator	---	---
Accessory	2	1.7
Partner	5	4.2
Sole Perpetrator	112	94.1
	(N=119)	
Relationship		
Husband, C-L husband and lover	58	49.6
Relatives	6	5.1
Acquaintances	40	34.2
Strangers	10	8.5
Children	3	2.5
	(N=117)	
Sex and Race		
Black Male	100	85.5
Black Female	17	14.5
White Male	---	---
White Female	---	---
	(N=117)	
Location of Offense		
Offender's Home	55	47
Other's Home	18	15.4
Bar	3	2.6
Street	34	29
Other	7	6
	(N=117)	

Source: Paula D. McClain, "Black Females and Lethal Violence: Has Time Changed the Circumstances Under Which They Kill? *Omega* 13 (1982–1983):pp. 13–25.

cities for 1975 committed homicide as the sole perpetrator. Only 3.4 percent were partners with another person in the commission of the homicide, and 1.6 percent were accessories.

The female roles of conspirator, accessory, and partner principally refer to homicide committed in the course of a felony (e.g., robbery and burglary). Males, black and white, are overwhelmingly the participants in incidents of felony-murder (Wolfgang, 1958). The role of sole perpetrator for females usually involves homicide committed during non-criminal activity (e.g., domestic quarrels). A descriptive account of the circumstances of the homicide event for the interviewed sub-sample are illustrative of the predominant instance of the black female as sole perpetrator in a homicide.

Case 1—Offense: Second degree murder

The offender (age 33) and the deceased had been living in a commonlaw relationship for four years. One evening they were at a friend's house when a fight took place between the friend and another male present. The offender was attempting to break up the fight when the deceased stepped into the fight pulling a small knife from his pociet and cut the other male on the neck. The man ran from the house stating that he would get the deceased for cutting him. The offender returned home shortly afterwards. At approximately 12:15 a.m. the deceased returned home and demanded that the offender go inside the house and get a shotgun. The offender refused and an argument ensued. The offender went into the house, armed herself with a .38 caliber Colt BSR and came out onto the front porch. The deceased, seeing that the offender was armed, stated, "Bitch, you know if you shoot me, you are going to do some time." At this time the offender shot the gun six times, and two slugs fatally struck the deceased.

The data in Table 5-2, as highlighted by the above illustration, suggest that the role of black females as sole perpetrators of criminal homicide has essentially remained constant over an entire generation.

The second case is illustrative of the few instances when a female is involved in a felony-homicide and her role is that of a secondary actor (i.e., accessory or partner).

Case 2—Offense: First degree murder

The offender (aged 18) and a male companion entered a market. The male companion accosted the deceased with a silver gun and robbed him of about $20 and a pistol. During the holdup the deceased was shot in the chest. The offender stood by in the store and escaped with her male companion.

Relationship of Offender to Victim

In the literature, researchers have indicated that in cases of homicide committed by females, the salience of the sex role is apparent. Unlike male homicide offenders, the victims of females are rarely store-owners, strangers, or other individuals slain in the course of committing a crime. Overwhelmingly, the victims of female homicide offenders are persons with whom the offender had an affectional relationship. Husbands, common-law husbands, or lovers are the dominant victims of female homicide offenders (Wolfgang, 1958; Rasko, 1978; Totman, 1978; Biggers, 1979). Specifically, Wolfgang found that at least 84 percent of the victims of females were family members, principally males. Table 5–2 shows the categories and sex and race of the victims for the sample.

Almost half of the victims (49.5 percent) of female offenders were either husbands, common-law husbands, or lovers. Other relatives, such as mother, father, sister, brother, and so forth, were 5.1 percent of the victims; acquaintances were 34.2 percent of the victims; strangers represented 8.5 percent; and children were the victims in 2.6 percent of the cases. The table also reveals that all the victims were black, that 85.5 percent were males, and that 14.5 percent were females.

The evidence that males with whom the offenders had emotional ties are still the dominant victims is congruent with Wolfgang's early research. The actual percentage, however, appears to have declined appreciably. The major increase in percentage of victims appears to be in the acquaintance category.

Location of Offense

The place where the homicide occurs plays an important role in the circumstances associated with the homicide event. Wolfgang found that because female offenders of both races primarily kill during a domestic quarrel, the principal place of occurrence was the offender's home (Wolfgang, 1958). In his sample, 73.5 percent of homicides committed by females occurred in the home. In contrast, a wide range of circumstances are associated with homicide committed outside the home, such as felony-homicide, barroom altercation, and assault. Consequently, only 12.8 percent of female-perpetrated homicides occurred on the highway, 3.7 percent in bars, and 10.1 percent in other places.

Table 5-2 indicates that 47 percent of the homicides committed by black females in the six cities occurred in the home of the offender. Once again these findings concur with Wolfgang's, but the percentage of occurrences in the offender's home has decreased nearly a third and the percentage occurring in the streets has doubled. Apparently, black females, for whatever reason(s), are committing a little over a third (37.6 percent) of their homicides outside their home (on the street, in bar-rooms, and in other places).

Type of Weapon

Is there a female-specific weapon of choice in the commission of homicide? In 1958, Wolfgang identified the knife, specifically a butcher knife, as the most frequently used weapon by female murderers. Knives were the weapons of 69.9 percent of black females compared to only 17.2 percent who used guns. He theorized that because "a large proportion of female offenders kill as a result of domestic quarrels which fequently occur in kitchens while they are preparing meals, it is not unlikely that females should use cutting and stabbing weapons for the purpose of slaying" (Wolfgang, 1958:87). Black females were four times more likely to use knives than white females. He hypothesized that the reason for the predilection of black females to murder with knives stems from a "cultural tradition among lower-class Negroes" to the carrying of a pocket knife or some other type of cutting or piercing instrument (1958:86).

Subsequent studies indicated a shift in type of weapon from knives to firearms; however, the percentage of usage was relatively equal (Ward et al., 1968; Totman, 1978; Biggers, 1979; and Cole et al., 1968). Our data indicate a dramatic increase in firearms as principal weapons since the Wolfgang data were collected over three decades ago. Firearms were used by 72.6 percent of the sample of black female homicide offenders; 23 percent used knives, 2.7 percent used some physical means (such as a hammer or plastic bag), and 1.7 percent used other physical means, such as an automobile.[1]

Offender's Rationale

What reasons do black females give for committing homicide? The survey questionnaire administered to the offenders contained several questions relating to circumstances leading to the homicide incident and situations that they believed justified killing another person. The predominant answer related to cases of physical abuse and beatings. When asked whether there are other situations in which they feel a person is justified in taking the life of another, an overwhelming majority answered "No!."

When asked to account for the situation that led to the homicide, almost half indicated that an argument had ensued and subsequent anger led to their action. All believed that, in retrospect, there were things they could have done to prevent the homicide. Understanding that the survey sample data are not representative of the population of black female homicide offenders generally, the data nevertheless indicate that the motives and/or rationale for the homicide of the interviewed sub-sample are still somewhat tied to the female sex-role, but not completely. The offenders apparently believed that the only situation in which a female is justified in taking a life is if she is the victim of physical abuse. She had the right to fight back and protect herself. Yet, on the other hand, problems in the interpersonal relationship between the offenders and their male intimates still appear to be the primary circumstances leading to homicide.

SUMMARY

The limited data base and exploratory nature of the analysis presented in this chapter preclude generalizations to the population of black female homicide offenders. Yet the findings may provide information that provides a better understanding of black females who commit murder.

Demographically, indications are that black females who commit criminal homicide are usually individuals with low socioeconomic status, low level of education, and most likely unemployed. There is a high probability that they were raised in a home in which children were physically punished for misdeeds. Behaviorally, the offenders probably had a history of involvements in fights. In some instances the fights were related to the inability to handle jealousy-provoking situations, usually involving their male intimates. In addition to the fighting, they most likely had a criminal record prior to their arrest for criminal homicide. The women likely had been drinking at the time of the incident, and the victims probably were their legal or common-law husbands or lovers. Their modal personality type was probably overtly hostile violent.

Wolfgang's findings of over three decades ago indicated the salience of the sex role in the circumstances and characteristics of homicide committed by females. Females, primarily black females, usually murdered their male intimates with knives during the course of a domestic altercation that occurred in the kitchen while preparing dinner. Our findings, for the most part, indicate the circumstances under which black females commit homicide still are congruent with Wolfgang's findings. However, many changes appear to be taking place.

Although black females still are more likely to kill males with whom they have an emotional relationship, our data indicate that high percentages of them are murdering individuals with whom they had no emotional ties. Likewise, the modal place of occurrence is still the offender's home, but a higher percentage of homicides are being committed by black females outside the home.

No apparent change is observed in the role of black females in the commission of homicide. They still are sole perpetrators. Our data do indicate, however, a complete change in the type of weapon utilized. Females now primarily use firearms rather than knives, which may reflect changes that have occurred not only among females but in the overall society. First, the number of firearms in American society has increased dramatically in the last several years (Bruce-Biggs, 1976). Second, a firearm is considered a "safer" weapon than a knife because attack or defense may be made from a safe distance; thus, females may find that committing homicide with a firearm is safer than using a knife. Third, more females may own guns for defensive as well as offensive purposes or have easy access to them. Fourth, assuming that most or all of the preceding rationale are valid, the possibility still exists that the shift to firearms as principal weapon may indicate females are no longer committing homicides in the traditional female way—while cooking dinner in the kitchen—but are doing so in situations where "kitchen utensils" are not readily available, and firearms, for whatever reasons, are easily accessible. Of course, this also could indicate a change in the site of the incident from one location in the house to another.

Additionally, on the basis of a limited number of interviews, black females apparently believe they are justified in killing a male intimate if they are the object of physical abuse. This position represents a willingness to fight back and protect oneself. Yet, on the other hand, their homicides still appear to be the result of domestic altercations. If the trend indicated by these findings continues for another decade, Wolfgang's theory may no longer serve as an appropriate explanation for black female behavior in lethal acts of violence.

The explanation for what appear to be an eroding of Wolfgang's findings are probably related directly to the changing roles of women in American society. The change in attitudes of and toward women is resulting in women's development of broader social networks outside the home. This also broadens the range of circumstances under which females, specificially black females in this instance, may kill. Therefore, there is a strong possibility that the greater freedom of movement and more aggressive manner of women may effect a change in the character of circumstances of the homicides they commit.

The frustrations and limited opportunities associated with being female, black, and poor create stress that may lead to hostile outbursts (Rose, 1978). Additionally, the statistic that indicates that over 50 percent of black children live in poverty and in homes headed by single black females presents a picture of poor black females as independent operators without the support of a mate. The lower marriage rates among black females under thirty years of age do not bode well for a decline in the number of families headed by single black females; however, they may have a potential dampening effect on husband/wife victimization.

6

Individual Attributes and Risk of Victimization

INTRODUCTION

In the previous chapters, variations in the intensity of aggregate homicide risk in a selected set of the nation's larger black communities were addressed. Much of the attention was focused specifically on variations in risk at the neighborhood scale within those communities. In an effort to explain the observed variation, we chose to emphasize intracommunity differences in the distribution of absolute levels of stress. Stress was employed as a measure of the likelihood of victimization within an ecological context, because we thought stress represented a valid surrogate for resource availability. Likewise, we suggested that stress levels, at least indirectly, reflected economic decisions made at a variety of environmental and/or decision-making scales that impacted individual neighborhoods. Yet, we are well aware that, within specific neighborhoods, selected individuals are at greater risk of victimization than are others. Thus, in this chapter, we will direct our attention to a sample of individuals who were involved in lethal confrontations as a way of assessing the contribution of individual level attributes on risk.

TARGET ATTRIBUTES

A number of individual-level attributes have been identified in the literature as contributors to elevated risk among segments of the population in general, and among blacks in particular. For instance, after longitudinally examining the victimization experience of a sample of black St. Louis males, Robins (1968) took the position that the presence of selected attributes such as truancy and high rates of scholastic failure, could have been utilized to forecast their death. Others are less sanguine regarding the effectiveness of clinicians or behavioral scientists to predict risk based on individual level traits

(Steadman, 1986). Yet, it should be emphasized that Robins (1968) simply demonstrated, based on an ex post facto assessment, that selected traits were found more often than others among males who had become homicide victims at an early age. So, although Steadman (1986) may be technically correct in assuming that the accurate prediction of certain rare events is not yet possible, such as predicting homicide based on the knowledge of the presence or absence of selected traits, that position does not represent a fruitful approach to the problem. Without getting bogged down in current arguments regarding dangerousness, we think there is merit in examining a selected set of individual-level attributes thought to enhance riskiness. Moreover, if effective intervention strategies are to be designed, a thorough knowledge of the prevalence of high-risk attributes is a primary requisite.

In this instance, attention will be focused on a restricted set of individual-level characteristics that are often highlighted by researchers engaged in the study of violent aggression and/or violent crime. The distinction made between these two classes of violent action is that the former generally connotes an association with anger, whereas in the latter, anger may or may not represent an element in triggering violent confrontations. Therefore, the attributes we have chosen should allow us to address a broad range of prospective types of violent confrontation. Documented evidence shows that intense personal anger growing out of disputes between emotionally bonded individuals (Levi, 1981) differs substantially from the violence emanating from crimes of opportunity (Stern, 1979). Yet, some researchers would have us believe that those engaged in a broad band of differentially motivated acts of violence possess a common set of attributes growing out of a subculture of violence or an inherent sociopathy.

The attributes that are most often investigated in association with research on at risk populations can be consolidated into the following groups: a) a propensity for fighting, b) school problems, c) deviant life styles, d) alcohol and drug use (including drug-trafficking), and e) behavioral problems. In order to shed light on how these attributes impact risk among persons in urban black communities, we will examine the characteristics of a sample of victims and offenders drawn from three of our six sample cities. It should be noted however, that we will be generalizing from small numbers, and therefore caution is advised in the interpretation of our conclusions. We will pay special attention to the attributes of our Detroit sample, since in this instance, it will serve as our referent community.

The Survey Sample

The survey data employed were collected during 1978 and 1979 from the next of kin of victims who were fatally assaulted in 1975 and from persons who were charged with committing a fatal act. Unfortunately, we were seldom able to acquire information on matched pairs of victims and offenders. Nevertheless, victims and offenders are often distinguishable on selected dimensions. However, in many situations, the primary distinction simply relates to the luck of the draw. Greater attention will be directed toward victims because our primary emphasis is on victimization rather than offending. Yet, if one is to gain a sound understanding of the homicide act, then it clearly becomes vitally important that we become familiar with the wide variety of transactions between dyads that ultimately lead to death. Thus the information acquired by members of our survey team, utilizing a standard questionnaire developed for the investigation, should enable us to better understand the role of selected traits and the concerns that individual participants brought to the confrontation.

To state that the task of designing, executing, and financing a field investigation of the type conducted in our sample cities is extremely difficult is an understatement. The lengthy survey questionnaire, coupled with sensitivity to some questions that were perceived as threatening, resulted in non-responses on a number of items. This, along with a high refusal rate from the next of kin of victims and with our inability to locate a substantial proportion of prospective respondents, added to our difficulties. In most instances, offenders who agreed to participate in the investigation were incarcerated. Moreover, we were seldom able to interview victim surrogates (i.e., next of kin) and offenders who were involved in the same lethal transaction. Our survey questionnaire was designed primarily to acquire information describing the life history, life-style, and attributes of character of the participants. The questionnaire focused only limited attention on the lethal event. Although more insight may have been achieved if we had been able to draw a much larger number of matched pairs into the interview process, our inability to do that does not seriously detract from our research goal.

Only information from the interview experience that highlights those attributes previously described as fostering elevated risk (that is, fighting, school problems, alcohol and drug use, etc.) will be examined in this chapter. But before we initiate the general discussion, we will review the extent to which these attributes were present or absent among a sample of Detroit victims. A primary goal is to ascertain how they might have influenced the circumstances that led to their deaths. Moreover, we will take a hard look at a set of Detroit matched pairs in which there was evidence of a history of prior fighting behavior, school problems, and drug involvement. These observations should allow us to ascertain the role played by those elements in triggering the fatal blow.

ATTRIBUTES OF DETROIT VICTIMS

Detroit, in many ways, represents the epitome of the historical promised land of American blacks. Its strong manufacturing base, good wages, job protection, and opportunity for workers with limited skills to find a secure niche for themselves was often greater than that existing in other non-southern urban locations. This led, over a forty-year period, to a continuing succession of black migrants entering the city in search of the promise that was detailed by relatives and friends who had entered the same migrant streams in prior years. The magnetic attraction that Detroit held for black southerners is reflected in the magnitude of growth in its black population between 1940 and 1980. In 1940, fewer than 150,000 blacks lived in the city, but forty years later, more than 750,000 blacks would call Detroit home. Unfortunately, large numbers of migrants continued to pour into the city during the waning decades of a healthy manufacturing economy. By 1980, however, black migrant streams had begun to diminish as the harsh reality of the city's economic decline had begun to settle in.

It is against a backdrop of economic deterioration, ethnic competition, changing values, and a loss of social control that escalating violence in Detroit's black community reached its apex in the early 1970s. During that period, Detroit was labeled the "murder capital" of the nation. It became evident as well that the structure of victimization in Detroit was changing, differentiating it from its southern counterparts where vicitmization levels were also high (e.g., Atlanta). Yet, an investigation during the early 1970s continued to focus on traditional patterns of victimization (Wilt and Bannon, 1974). Later investigations, however, directed attention toward an escalation in robbery-homicides (Zimring, 1979), and other felony-motivated acts leading to death (Dietz, 1983). Apparently, a highly differentiated social structure in the city's black community had evolved such that the circumstances provoking confrontation had expanded beyond the narrow range of transactions that supported traditional high-risk levels. In light of these changes, we have chosen to look more closely at the attributes and circumstances of our Detroit victim sample.

The Next-of-Kin View of the Victim as a Person

Table 6-1 details the characteristics of homicide victims from our Detroit sample in 1975. These attributes, as mentioned previously, are assumed to have influenced the circumstances of victimization in some way. Of the thirteen items appearing in the table, all but one—victim-age—were extracted from the questionnaire responses provided by the next of kin of victims, most often mothers. Since most of the respondents were parents, who were themselves migrants from the rural or small-town South, their description of their child's life history undoubtedly reflects a positive bias. Yet, a message that frequently came through was their inability to exert control over their children's lives in an urban setting. Thus, respondents often attributed the lethal event to the character of life in the urban environment. Loss of control was often viewed as one of the penalties that they as parents suffered during their stay in the "promised land." Based on the parent or parent-surrogate descriptions of the victim, we are in a position to examine the commonalties that existed among the victims on selected attributes. The frequency with which selected attributes occur should place us in a better postion to judge which of the selected attributes tend most often to place individuals at risk.

Needless to say, respondents may be reluctant to report information that they find embarrassing or that casts their child in a less-than-positive light. Therefore, interviewee bias may, in some instances, result in a less-than-candid description of selected attributes of individual victims.

Items Selected for Examination

Thirteen items from a 140-item questionnaire have been selected for more intense scrutiny. We assume that analyzing these items will provide additional insight into understanding elevated individual risk (see Table 6-1). Certain traits appear more frequently across the sample revealing the predominance of males, the predominance of persons labeled young adults, the predominance of high school dropouts, the prevalence of unemployed persons, and the prevalence of individuals who were never married among the victims in Detroit in 1975. Thus individuals having this set of traits were at greater risk of victimization than persons having an alternate cluster of traits.

Victim Community Reputations and Life-Styles

Having identified a cluster of traits that seem to place individuals at greater risk, we are still somewhat uncertain what the relationship is between these traits and choice of life-style. The answers provided

TABLE 6-1

Selected Attributes of a Sample of Detroit Victims: 1975

Individual	Victim-Offender Relationship	Community Reputation	Age at Death	Sex	Migrant Status	Employment Status	Prior Assaultive Record	Drinking at Time of Death	Known Drug User	Marital Status	School Problems	Prior Felony Conviction	Educational Status
A	Acquaintance	Religious	26	M	M*	Unempl.	Yes	--	--	Single	Yes	Yes	< 12 yrs.
B	Unknown	Hustler	20	M	NM**	Unempl.	Yes	--	--	Single	No	--	< 12 yrs.
C	Acquaintance	Good Timer	27	F	M	Unempl.	No	No	Yes	Single	No	--	H.S. grad
D	Family	Hustler	24	M	NM	Unempl.	No	--	--	Single	No	--	< 12 yrs.
E	Family	Mature Settled	49	M	M	Employed	No	Yes	Yes	Married	Yes	No	< 12 yrs.
F	Acquaintance	Responsible Family	20	M	M	Unempl.	No	--	--	Single	No	--	< 9 yrs.
G	Unknown	Mature Settled	15	F	NM	Unempl.	No	No	No	Single	No	No	< 12 yrs.
H	Unknown	Responsible Family	16	M	M	Employed	No	No	No	Married	--	No	< 12 yrs.
I	--	Mature Settled	47	M	NM	Employed	No	Yes	No	Single	No	--	H.S. grad
J	Unknown	Hustler	22	M	M	Unempl.	--	--	--	Single	No	--	< 12 yrs.
K	Unknown	--		M	M	Unempl.	No	--	No	Single	No	No	≤ 12 yrs.
L	Unknown	Good Timer	24	M	NM	Unempl.	No	No	No	Single	Yes	Yes	< 12 yrs.

TABLE 6-1 *continued*

Selected Attributes of a Sample of Detroit Victims: 1975

Individual	Victim-Offender Relationship	Community Reputation	Age at Death	Sex	Migrant Status	Employment Status	Prior Assaultive Record	Drinking at Time of Death	Known Drug User	Marital Status	School Problems	Prior Felony Conviction	Educational Status
M	Unknown	Mature Settled	26	F	NM	Employed	No	No	No	Single	No	No	H.S. grad
N	Unknown	Mature Settled	30	M	-	Unempl.	No	No	No	Single	Yes	No	< 9 yrs.
O	Unknown	Good Timer	25	M	M	Unempl.	No	-	-	Single	Yes	-	< 12 yrs.
P	Unknown	Good Timer	29	M	NM	Employed	-	Yes	Yes	Married	No	No	< 12 yrs.
Q	Unknown	Hustler	16	M	NM	Unempl.	No	-	-	Single	No	-	< 9 yrs.
R	Unknown	-	40	M	M	Employed	-	-	-	Married	-	No	-
S	Unknown	Mature Settled	21	M	NM	Employed	No	Yes	No	Single	No	Yes	< 12 yrs.
T	Unknown	Good Timer	22	M	NM	Employed	No	-	-	Single	No	-	< 12 yrs.
U	Unknown	Good Timer	22	M	M	Employed	No	No	No	Single	No	No	H.S. grad
V	Unknown	Mature Settled	22	M	NM	Unempl.	No	No	No	Single	No	No	H.S. grad
X	Family	Religious	21	F	NM	Unempl.	No	No	No	Single	No	No	< 9 yrs.
Y	-	-	52	M	NM	Unempl.	No	No	No	Single	No	No	< 9 yrs.

*migrant
**nonmigrant

by next of kin, although useful, are not unbiased. Therefore, some uncertainty continues regarding the strength of the association of traits and choice of life-style. Nevertheless, we assume that the next of kin suggested community reputations of the victim (e.g., hustler) might provide some indirect evidence of victim life-style and, thus, we have included it among the selected attributes in Table 6–1.

It is not unusual for researchers to develop typologies to explain behaviors. Both the life-styles cited by Hannerz (1971) and the strategic coping styles developed by Mancini (1980) were attempts to demonstrate how inner-city males adapt to their environment. Our typology was developed specifically to address people involved in violent altercations. The reputation categories are: 1) mature settled individual, 2) likes to have a good time, 3) responsible family person, 4) hustler, 5) religious person, and 6) irresponsible. Within our sample, the most frequently designated community reputation was that of the "mature settled individual." But persons identified as "liking to have a good time" were almost as numerous. We interpret the former identity as conformist if employing the Mancini schema, but we are less certain where it fits within the framework of the Hannerz construct. On the other hand, those whom the community perceived as persons "liking to have a good time" no doubt conform, at least minimally, to Hannerz's "swingers" and Mancini's "cool guys."

Persons whose reputations in the community were that of "hustler" turn out to be problematic because whether they were admired or disdained by persons who viewed them in this way is unclear. Mancini would probably label these individuals "con artists" and would suggest that their interests were largely motivated by personal gratification needs. This life-style label was assigned to almost as many individuals as the label "likes to have a good time." Because of the need to be manipulative to succeed in the street world of the hustler, such persons, no doubt, often find themselves in situations that enhance the likelihood that they will be attacked so they will need to be prepared to defend themselves.

The urge to hustle appears to distinguish between individuals along a conformist/nonconformist dimension. Ezekiel (1984), who conducted interviews with a number of persons from a high-stress neighborhood in Detroit in the early 1970s, reported the following remarks of an individual identifying himself as a hustler:

> I mean, there is this little glamour thing to this hustling thing, where it's not with that working-man thing. The working-man has the security and everything, he still works thirty-five or forty

years, retires for about five years he lives on, and then he—kicks off. Well, a hustler, he parties every day, you know. The money's easy the broads are around and, whatever he's doing drinking or using he has fun doing it. (p. 116)

The hustler added, "And then one day, if you hustle long enough, you're going to get busted. You gotta go to jail, you know. I mean this is the price that you are going to pay for it" (Ezekiel, 1984:116). What he does not say is that if you hustle long enough and happen to choose the wrong pick you end up dead at an early age.

Among the community reputations that were said to best describe the victims in this investigation were those that could be interpreted as conformist, at least in terms of local community norms. Yet, on reviewing the coping styles developed by Mancini, as well as the early coping styles manifested by a group of Central Harlem school children (see Silverstein and Krate, 1975), one essential style that showed up among both groups was missing from the identities appearing on our questionnaire. The missing identity was "rebel" or "tough guy." Apparently, this orientation differentiates between those individuals who get caught up in expressive transactions leading to death and those who become involved in instrumental transactions, at least as it relates to the aggressor. (The questionnaire did, however, allow offenders to employ an alternate identity if none of those appearing on the questionnaire represented the image they held of themselves.)

DETROIT CASE REVIEWS

We will now take a somewhat harder look at four cases about which we were able to talk with both representatives of the victim and the offenders. In this instance, we will seek to determine the extent to which the elements that were previously suggested as risk-provoking were present among the participants in the fatal transactions. The similarities and differences among the individual actors will be noted. Finally, the context in which these transactions took place will be described. The information that follows was extracted from police case files.

The cases represent a diverse set of circumstances but because of the small pool from which they have been drawn, they should not be considered as representing the broad array of circumstances that motivate individuals to engage in life threatening confrontations. Needless to say, we fully realize that a growing share of such confrontations are nonvoluntary (e.g., robbery-homicides). Among the cases we have chosen to highlight is one involving sibling conflict, one involving other family conflict, an unknown relationship, and one involving acquaintances. Let us begin the process by reviewing the circumstances and aspects of the life histories of the conflicting parties. In order to be able to keep our account brief, we have devised a standard format that will be utilized in each instance.

Case 1

Victim-Offender Relationship: Sibling

Circumstances

Victim threatened the offender's sister by throwing her to the ground and placing a knife to her neck. The victim was intoxicated and had a record of attacking family members when inebriated. The offender secured a shotgun and confronted the victim. The victim was struck by two rounds from the shotgun and expired a short time later.

Setting

The actions leading up to this tragic event occurred at a party at the home of the offender. Numerous acquaintances and family members had gathered for this occasion. An argument ensued between the two male siblings regarding one's treatment of a sister. The argument led the offender to end the party. The fatal blow was struck on the street as persons were leaving the party.

Victim	*Offender*
Gender: Male	Gender: Male
Age: 24	Age: 25
School Problems: Disliked school, but was enrolled in special program; subsequently dropped out.	School Problems: Occasionally suspended; subsequently dropped out.
Drinking or Using Drugs at time of incident: Yes; victim was thought to be a narcotics addict	Drinking or Using Drugs at time of incident: Yes, intoxicated
Community Reputation: Hustler	Self-Image: Responsible family person
Fighting Propensity: Yes	Fighting Propensity: Nonfighter

The case perhaps involved sibling rivalry, but the triggering mechanism leading to the death of the victim was the victim's own conduct relative to other members of his family. The victim's prior history of assaultive behavior when intoxicated, an implication of narcotics addiction, and a nonreluctance to disrespect female family members no doubt served as a powerful inducement that prompted the offender to take the steps that he did. Yet, by his own admission, had he not been intoxicated, he would not have struck the fatal blow.

Case 2

Victim-Offender Relationship: Stranger

Circumstances

Victim was unknown to the offender. The offender reported he was intoxicated at the time of the incident. The offender and his party had been told to leave a tavern or the police would be called and the offender's threatening behavior would be reported. The offender left, but returned shortly thereafter with a gun and began firing wildly, striking two patrons. One patron was slightly wounded, but another died from a gunshot wound to the chest.

Setting

The fatal blow was struck in a tavern setting. The offender was alleged to have earlier threatened the tavern disc jockey, who had stopped the music after the offender refused to stop smoking. The violent response initiated by the offender reflected an antagonistic response to being asked to leave the tavern as were persons who were close to him. The offender suggests that he would not have visited this particular tavern had he not been intoxicated.

Victim	*Offender*
Gender: Male	Gender: Male
Age: 47	Age: 30
School Problems: none, dropped out	School Problems: suspended frequently
Drinking or Using Drugs at time of incident: No	Drinking or Using Drugs at time of incident: Yes, intoxicated
Community Reputation: Mature settled person	Self-Image: Hustler Responsible family man
	Fighting Propensity: Yes, frequently

The victim was a passive actor in the drama that led to his death. He simply happened to get caught in the cross fire of a confrontation that had earlier occurred between the tavern manager, one of her employees, and the offender. The offender, on the other hand, appeared to be performing before an audience of his peers, under the disinhibiting influence of alcohol. In this instance, it appears that loss of control manifested itself in a challenge to what the offender perceived to represent appropriate behavior in a tavern setting, e.g., smoking. Needless to say, this on stage behavior led to the useless taking of the life of an innocent bystander.

Case 3

Victim-Offender Relationship: Acquaintances

Circumstances

The circumstances under which this incident occurred essentially are blurred. Yet, the act clearly was instrumentally motivated rather than a response

growing out of an angry confrontation. It is suggested from the offenders'
response that the primary motive was robbery. Two offenders were involved,
but the details of the actions leading up to death are sketchy.

Setting

The transaction took place in the apartment of the victim, which was
described by the offender as a dope pad. The victim's next of kin described
him as a successful dope dealer. Because dope houses are often places where
both cash and drugs are stashed, they often are targets of home robberies.

Victim	*Offender*
Gender: Male	Gender: Male
Age: 26	Age: 25
School Problems: Enrolled in program for students with behavioral problems; dropped out	School Problems: Frequent suspension, dropped out
Drinking or Using Drugs at time of incident: Unknown	Drinking or Using Drugs at time of incident: Yes, moderately intoxicated
Community Reputation: Religious person	Self-Image: Responsible family person
Fighting Propensity: Yes, infrequently	Fighting Propensity: Yes, infrequently

The victim and offender were known to one another in this instance but
apparently were not close associates. Since the victim was alleged to be the
operator of a drug house, he was vulnerable to attack—he was believed to have
both cash and drugs in his possession. Cases of this general nature were
growing in frequency in Detroit in the early 1970s. Thus this represents a special
type of robbery-homicide.

Case 4

Victim-Offender Relationship: Family

Circumstances

As in Case 3, the circumstances leading up to the fatal incident are vague.
But the ultimate conflict apparently grew out of an effort by the victim to ward
off a sexual assault. The offender seems to have been infuriated by the victim's
screams. Both the victim and her younger brother, age 7, were strangled, and
the victim also was stabbed by the offender. Why the younger victim was killed
can only be conjectured based on the evidence. The body of the victim was
discovered by her mother, with whom she resided. After the offender was
picked up by the police for questioning, he informed them of the whereabouts
of the second victim.

Setting

The victimization of the female occurred in the basement of her residence. She was bound, gagged, and tied to a support structure. The younger boy was secured similarly in a vacant garage. The offender was a secondary relation of the victim and because of that relationship, was granted access to the home. He was identified as a suspect by the victim' mother because it was known that he had previously attempted to assault another member of the family. The defendant was judged to be sane and he stood trial for the commission of the act.

Victim	*Offender*
Gender: Female	Gender: Male
Age: 21	Age: 20
School Problems: None	School Problems: Fighting; suspension
Drinking or Using Drugs at time of incident: No	Drinking or Using Drugs at time of incident: No
Community Reputation: Mature settled person	Self-Image: Responsible family person
Fighting Propensity: Nonfighter	Fighting Propensity: Yes, frequent fights

This case represents a type that occurs less frequently than the types of homicides in either case #1 or case #2, at least in terms of motivation. Likewise, cases of this type are less predictable based on the character of the actors involved, the circumstances, and the setting. Based on the information available to us, the two victims in this instance apparently became involved in an encounter with a male relative who was primarily motivated to engage in an act of violent aggression as means of achieving sexual gratification. The offender in this instance expressed no remorse for his conduct.

The four cases just described, although providing us with a feel for the circumstances surrounding the fatal act, unfortunately do not allow us to grasp the broad range of circumstances and settings in which acts of lethal violence are unleashed. Nevertheless, they provide some insight regarding the characteristics manifested by the interacting parties and the nature of the interaction. We are simply attempting to detect, in some very general way, how the characteristics or attributes previously identified led persons to become involved in situations that might be described as risk-provoking. Although we found that the attributes we singled out often were possessed by victims or offenders or both, it is still unclear how these traits were responsible for bringing the interacting dyads together and/or how they contribute to the character and intensity of the interactions. We think that the life-style characteristics and/or the images that persons hold of themselves are the keys to understanding the nature of the confrontation and the moves that the individuals are likely to make in the transaction. Therefore, we must reassess briefly our earlier position regarding life-style/self-image orientations before becoming involved in a more extended discussion of how these risky attributes were involved in lethal confrontations occurring in Detroit, St. Louis, and Atlanta. That discussion, however, will focus on the aggregate sample or subsample rather than individual cases.

Tentatively, it appears that the attribute that most often leads individuals to adopt risky life styles is failure to graduate from high school. We fully acknowledge that this attribute may not discriminate between older cohorts in the way we think it distinguishes between the life-style orientations adopted by persons born since 1945, and especially those born since 1960. Yet, without carefully assessing the reasons for leaving school, we may run into a dead end. Based on our review of only four cases, we cannot explain the importance of this attribute on victimization. Although most of these persons had been suspended from school on a number of occasions, most indicated at least a mild dislike for school, which was manifested at times by a failure to achieve success in the school setting or by being strongly attracted to the life on the street. There is a growing body of literature wherein it is suggested that early school failure and/or other evidence of poor student/school fit is a crude indicator of future deviance, criminality, as well as other forms of pathology (for example, see Robins, 1968; Loeber, 1987; Spivack and Marcus, 1987). This point will be pursued again later in the chapter.

The question that we raise now is how important community reputations and/or self-images are on the likelihood of becoming involved in confrontations that might be considered risky. Or, perhaps a better question is, does the view that individuals hold of themselves dictate the appropriate move once a confrontation has been initiated? Thus it appears important for one to grasp a more complete understanding of the circumstances that lead individuals to develop specific images of themselves and how these foster specific life-style preferences. At the same time, one must be able to come to a fuller understanding of how changes in the external environment, at a variety of scales, interact with emerging world views of individuals that seem prone to become involved in confrontations with a high probability of ending in an act of violence. At the moment, however, much of the research interest in this problem leans toward providing genetic evidence that the participants in these confrontations were either flawed or developmentally programmed to engage in such behavior (see example, Wilson and Herrnstein, 1985; Loeber, 1987; Daly and Wilson, 1988). This orientation is appealing in that the individual can be held responsible for the frequency and outcome of these confrontations. Those who support this orientation are not required to grapple with the role of the external environment as a potential contributor to risk.

We are uncertain at this point if the self-image/community-reputation paradigm described previously is adequate to provide the kind of insights that we earlier envisioned. The established categories may be too vague and, as a consequence, lead to excessive variance in interpretation. Nevertheless, the community reputational image appears to provide a better indicator of life-style orientation than does the image offenders hold of themselves. Frequently, offenders demonstrate a segmented image of themselves; for example, they may identify themselves both as hustlers and respectable family persons or some other combination. When offenders describe themselves segmentally, whether the individual is more likely to engage in conforming or nonconforming behavior is unclear. Thus our paradigm, if it is to become more useful, will require additional work. It should be pointed out, however, that the category "hustler" turned out to be the least ambiguous, whereas the image "respectable family person" tends to be the most ambiguous.

Furthermore, a better designation of the role of the individual and/or the moves made by the individual leading up to the fatal act may be better determined by denoting the presence or absence of a prosocial orientation. Each of the offenders surveyed was asked to respond to a twelve-item questionnaire that used a semantic differential construct designed to ascertain a prosocial versus anti-social outlook. Thus, for offenders, we were able to combine some additional information to that describing self-image. A careful review of these two sets of information suggests, for instance, that hustlers with prosocial views are likely to be involved in a different category of conflict and respond differently to the outcome than do hustlers whose views are strongly anti-social. Although life-style and world views tend to be related, persons also could exhibit similar life-style and self-images while manifesting dissimilar outlooks. This quality possibly exerts the strongest influence on the role and/or actions one takes in lethal confrontations.

Analysis of the alterations in the structure of victimization that have evolved during the period under review reveals that the number of individuals manifesting an anti-social orientation may have increased. Dietz (1983) suggests, for instance, that selected persons who kill for profit (e.g., contract killers) develop a killer identity. More specifically, she stated, "when actors hold violent self-images, they are able to interpret situations in ways that permit them to justify the use of violence" (Dietz, 1983:24). Whether the justification for engaging in offensive acts of violence is an outgrowth of a genetic or developmental predisposition, as some researchers suggest (Daly and Wilson, 1988), or whether it can be attributed to a process of socialization, as suggested by others (Brummit, 1978), the image that the actors hold of themselves clearly influence their world views—a situation that ultimately influences the nature of the confrontation as well as its likely outcome.

AN AGGREGATE ASSESSMENT OF HIGH RISK ATTRIBUTES: INTERCOMMUNITY VARIATIONS

We will now look at how the previously identified set of individual-level attributes manifest themselves in acts of lethal violence involving a sample of victims and offenders. This effort will, in some instances, allow us to distinguish among individual black communities in terms of the relative importance of individual dimensions on the propensity for provoking acts of lethal violence. We will turn our attention first to fighting behavior. Until recently, most black homicides were the product of angry confrontations initiated by verbal disputes that escalated into a physical fight. In the process of fighting, one or both of the combatants would resort to the use of a weapon in an effort to bring the conflict to closure. The tendency and willingness to engage in fighting behavior represents an important element in establishing the general likelihood that members of this population will be placed at higher risk for victimization. Frequently, the critical elements that determine whether confrontations of this type will end in death is the intensity of emotional discord, the presence of others, and the nature of the available weapon. Pittman and Handy (1964), remarking on the behavior of a sample of black St. Louis residents, noted that an essential difference between events described as homicides and aggravated assaults was whether or not the combatants possessed a gun or a knife. Nevertheless, one should keep in mind that a growing number of confrontations leading to death do so outside of the context of traditional fighting behavior.

FIGHTING BEHAVIOR

In those environments in which fighting is supported as an approved method of resolving interpersonal conflict, the problem of escalating aggression becomes a more serious one—one that could lead to death. The general conclusion, however, is that support for fighting is more commonplace in low-income communities than elsewhere; consequently, homicides also are more prevalent in these communities. Hostile outbursts that lead to fighting are triggered by a wide variety of stimuli. Often in high-risk environments the initial stimulus is described as trivial by persons whose values and status are not those of the environments they are describing. Fighting behavior of a sample of both homicide offenders and victims will be examined to detect the existence of similarities and differences between them.

In attempting to understand fighting behavior, we must be able to identify the usual role of victims and offenders in fights. Toch (1969) concluded that employment of violence might derive from individual needs, motivated both by internal and external stimuli. These needs are thought to originate from the individual's inclination either to bolster self-esteem or to defend one's reputation against possible doubt. Toch (1969:135) identified these two motivational types as self-preserving strategies. But he also pointed out that a second class of stimulus to violence exists, which he described as follows: "our second grouping of categories may be described as comprising persons who see themselves (and their own needs) as being the only fact of social relevance" (1969:136). According to Toch, this includes persons who engage in bullying, exploiting others, self-indulgence, and releasing emotional tensions. The self-centered motivations associated with this group are thought to be growing in importance and are emerging as a crucial element in altering the victimization structure. Stern (1979) labeled this type of behavior "gratuitous violence." Acts associated with this second group have been described in the following way: "violence has nothing to do with you personally; it is provoked by your accidental presence" (Stern, 1979:150).

Fighting is basically a physical display employed in the release of aggressive feelings. Aggression, however, is not always expressed in a physical way, nor are all displays of aggression manifested in active behavior. But fighting is a readily observed expression of aggressive behavior, even if it is not the most important. Fighting is thought to represent uncontrolled aggression and is more commonplace among persons who are of low social status. Nevertheless, even persons who might normally be expected to exhibit aggressive behavior have learned to inhibit the behavior vis-á-vis the source of anger. Thus aggressive behavior in the form of fighting is often suppressed or inflicted upon a safe target if the penalty for this acting-out behavior is feared to be excessive. Needless to say, some maintain only limited control over feelings of aggression and are inclined to fight when their anger threshold has been reached regardless of possible penalties.

Fighting is simply an index of the extent to which one is able to bring or keep feelings of aggression under control. The extent to which uncontrolled aggression ends in the death of a participant in a fight is often a function of the joint anger level, the strength of the desire to punish, and the weapons used. Minimal anger and desire to punish might be offset by the use of an extremely lethal weapon.

Crain and Weisman (1972) argued that blacks have a greater problem of treating pent-up hostility than do whites, and that because of the position of the two groups in society, they have developed different styles of handling aggression. Using fighting behavior as an index, they also concluded that blacks have greater difficultly in bringing their aggression under control than do whites. Employing a survey questionnaire, they reported that 28 percent of the black respondents indicated they had been in a fight, whereas only 19 percent of white respondents indicated they had been involved in this kind of activity (Crain and Weisman, 1972:35).

Persons who are less likely to recall anger are thought to be better able to inhibit aggression. This led Crain and Weisman to conclude that regional differences existed in the ability to display anger, which led northern-born blacks to report they had engaged in fights more often than did southern-born men. The problem, though, is one of being able to express anger and subsequently to handle anger in non-maladaptive ways.

Because fighting behavior involves two or more participants, it is important that we understand the role of each. Unfortunately, this is somewhat difficult to do without talking with persons who observed the fight. However, the modal role of each participant in a fight can be determined. Employment of the labels "victim" and "offender" is known to obscure the participant's role in fights leading to death. Luckenbill (1977:179) stated in this regard that they "are heuristic labels that neither emerge in the transaction nor are an artifact of the battle." Nevertheless, on closer examination, significant differences might be found that characterize the modal fighting role of persons who, in the final analysis, are identified as victims and offenders.

OFFENDER FIGHTING BEHAVIOR

Because offenders have been accused and often indicted for committing an act of lethal violence, one might assume that they were persons who had in the past frequently displayed an inability to control their aggression by engaging in fights. So, as a means of determining what the prior fighting experience of our offender respondents had been, they were asked to indicate with what frequency they had been involved in fights, both as youths and as adults. More than four-fifths of all offenders reported they had been involved in fights during their lives; only one-sixth of this population indicated a lack of prior fighting experience.

The offenders' fighting behaviors stand in contrast to the third-party report of fighting behavior of victims. Only 47 percent of the victims were reported to have ever engaged in a fight. Both offenders and victims are reported to have exhibited a higher likelihood of engaging in fights than were those persons identified in the Crain and Weisman (1972) survey. The implication is that both groups had difficulty managing their aggression, but that the problem was much more severe among offenders than among victims.

Although offenders, as a group, were not strangers to fighting, their role in fights was, however, unclear. In attempting to shed light on the usual role of offenders, we were basically concerned with whether the offender was the aggressor or the attacked. In some instances, offenders reported that they played neither of these roles, but simply happened to be bystanders or engaged in some other uncertain role. More than two-fifths of the offenders reported they were usually the person attacked in fights in which they were involved. Thirty-five percent identified themselves as aggressors. Almost one-fifth described their role in a less precise fashion.

Those persons whose role in fights was most often that of the attacker clearly had a more serious problem with control of aggression than persons who most often were the attacked. It appears advisable then to attempt to ascertain what attributes distinguish these two groups.

Role in Fights and Frequency of Fighting

Fighting frequency and fighting role are means of ascertaining any unique characteristic possessed by individuals who have difficulty inhibiting feelings of uncontrolled aggression. We also are concerned about the attributes of persons who are often singled out as targets of aggression.

As was previously noted, most offenders reported that their usual role in fights was the result of being the target of someone else's aggression. More than one-half of the persons who indicated they had most often been attacked were persons who had a background that included only limited fighting. The percentage of those who were attacked declines continuously as frequency of fighting increases. Only 12 percent of those who identified themselves as frequent fighters were persons whom we included among those who were targets of others seeking to release feelings of aggression. Perhaps the "whipping boy syndrome" was at work here, but it does open up some interesting possibilities.

Aggressors were more likely to be persons who frequently engaged in fighting. Yet, among those persons indicating they were infrequent participants in fights, 43 percent identified themselves as aggressors. The relationship between frequency of fighting and one's fighting role is less clear among aggressors than among targets of aggression.

Offender Self-Image and Role in Fights

Among the six self-image categories previously identified, the major distinctions usually occurred between the dichotomous image of hustler/nonhustler. The nonhustler category was dominated by persons who identifed themselves as responsible family persons. Among the two categories that most persons tended to identify with— responsible family persons and hustlers—the ratio of aggressors to target of aggression was quite similar.

Role uncertainty was the major difference that distinguished between these two groups. Almost one-fifth of the responsible family persons described their role as that of bystander or one of being drawn into an ongoing conflict. Hustlers, on the other hand, were more precise in specifying their role, and they were almost equally as likely to be targets of aggression as they were to be the aggressor. Responsible family persons were much more likely to say they were the aggressors than were hustlers. Hustlers, however, far more often reported they owned a gun at the time of the incident than did nonhustlers, which presumably indicated their willingness to engage in aggressive behavior. This might imply that self-identified hustlers were more bent upon inflicting serious injury when they became embroiled in the release of aggression than were persons with other self-images.

Parent Support for Fighting

Fighting was a procedure for resolving conflict among persons in our offender sample. Whether this behavior is an outgrowth of children imitating behavior learned in the home or elsewhere as an appropriate means of resolving conflict is not clear. Serious quarrels within the family were not uncommon events in the households from which offenders were drawn, leading one to assume that occasional violent outbursts among family members served as models for resolving a variety of interpersonal conflicts. Although slightly more than one-half of the offenders reported that serious quarrels were not uncommon in their parents' homes, parents did not normally condone their children fighting. In fact, more than four-fifths stated that their parents generally were not supportive of fighting. Some indicated, however, that if they were attacked, parents urged them to defend themselves. Likewise, some parents suggested that if their children had been wronged by others, fighting represented an approved form of conduct. The responses of our offender sample implied that both imitative and sociocultural learning were associated with information transmitted by parent to child, in both indirect and direct ways, regarding the appropriateness of fighting as a conflict-resolving effort. Thus, parental support for fighting apparently was limited to a narrowly defined set of circumstances based on subcultural norms.

One other dimension associated with parenting is sometimes held to influence a child's acceptance of externally directed aggression. The extent to which physical punishment is inflicted upon children for the commission of unapproved social acts is sometimes viewed as tacit support for the use of violence in interpersonal relationships. Some psychologists not only support this notion but also indicate that the child's response to punishment might vary as a function of which parent inflicts it. How important these acts are in the present context is unclear, but parental support for punishing children physically for unapproved social behavior is extensive. Support for physical punishment occurred in more than 80 percent of offender households. The mother usually undertook the task of inflicting physical punishment.

Difference in Fighting Propensity among Sample Cities

The individual's usual role in fights and fighting frequency differs from community to community, although the greatest discrepancy exists in the fighting role. Persons who had not engaged in fighting either as an adult or adolescent ranged from 12.5 percent in Detroit to 20 percent in St. Louis. Numerous fights (26.7 percent) were characteristic only in St. Louis. Limited fighting occurred more often in Atlanta (61.6 percent) and occurred with the same frequency among St. Louis and Detroit offenders (47 percent).

The offender's fighting role, however, appears to be unique in each city. Aggressors and targets of aggression occur with the same frequency (42 percent) in Detroit, but in Atlanta, almost three-fifths of the offenders report their usual fighting role as that of the attacked. Seldom did Atlanta offenders report their role as that of the aggressor.

In St. Louis the offender fighting role was more uncertain. St. Louis offenders report they were neither the aggressor nor the target of aggression in most fights in which they were involved. They imply they simply got caught up in the action in which they were not one of the principal actors. One might expect this situation to prevail more often in gang-related fights.

Our Detroit offenders, however, principally viewed themselves as aggressors or targets of aggression. One's life-style and correspondent situational difficulties are likely to dictate one's fighting role. Self-image does indeed lead to very distinctive fighting roles, with hustlers more often perceiving themselves as targets of someone else's aggression and responsible family persons more frequently acting in the role of aggressor.

FIGHTING BEHAVIOR OF VICTIMS

Do victims as a group differ from offenders in their fighting experiences? This question will be tentatively explored on the basis of our next-of-kin responses, but the strength of our findings is weak as a result of the small size of the sample. Even though the findings are tentative, we expect them to point in the direction of behavior that might be thought characteristic of the population they represent.

It was indicated earlier that victims were reported to have fought less often than offenders. This might imply that victims basically differ on some significant dimension related to the release of aggression. On the other hand, victims might have found themselves in situations that differed from those of offenders. Luckenbill (1977) suggested one should review the role played by each member of the dyad in the homicide transaction as a means of determining who should appropriately be labeled victim and offender. To do this, he describes the series of events leading up to the act of death.

Do Victims and Offenders Differ in Response to Gestures of Aggression?

The question that emerges from the specified series of events is whether victims and offenders, as a rule, tend to respond differently to the opening act of the transaction. If there are differences in their response to the opening act, who is better able to withdraw from the transaction before it escalates to the point of no return? Other researchers have pointed out that the victim frequently initiates the transaction leading to death. Wolfgang (1958) described those homicidal outcomes in which the victim initiates the transaction by an extreme show of physical force or weapon display as victim-precipitated homicides. He also indicated they are most likely to take place among persons engaged in a primary relationship, in which emotional responses are readily intensified.

The lesson to be learned is that those persons inclined to strike out against others in a fit of rage often end up as the victims in the homicide. This would imply that these are persons with limited impulse control, for whom the provocation is thought not to warrant the kind of aggressive display shown by the victim. Wolfgang contended that black males are more likely to display manifestations that lead to their demise than are other race-sex groups. The extent to which victims precipitated their own demise is not clear. No doubt some victims initiated a show of force that ultimately led to their death. Victim-precipitated homicides are most likely to occur in situations in which the emotional bond within the dyad is strong and in settings in which saving face is an important contributor to the escalation of aggressive behavior.

If self-defense can be employed as a surrogate for victim-precipitated homicides, only 14.1 percent of those persons from the offender sample viewed the transaction from that perspective. Hustlers, persons aged 25–29, and persons who responded that the victim was someone liked by them were most likely to indicate that the situation that led to the death was self-defense. It is not known at what point in the transaction the offender perceived the need to defend himself or herself vigorously against violent attack. Thus we are unable to validate the position of the offenders who indicate that their defensive acts were provoked by the behavior of the victims.

Frequency of Fighting

Victims were less inclined to be fighters than were offenders. Only 55.6 percent of the victims, whose fighting behavior was reported by next of kin, were recalled as having fought during their youth. Of those who did fight, the modal frequency of fighting was "now and then." This can be construed to mean that this set of victims had a relatively high threshold of aggression. Few were identified as frequent fighters; twice that number indicated they seldom engaged in fights. Thus the threshold of aggressive response was deemed very high among that 44 percent of the victims who never fought, high for the group who seldom fought, intermediate for those who fought now and then, and low for frequent fighters. Because frequent fighters were so few, the victims whose frequency of fighting might be described as intermediate represented the pool most likely to display aggressive behavior.

Adult Fighting Behavior

After victims reached adulthood their fighting behavior diminished. In fact, almost 70 percent of the victims were reported not to have engaged in fights as adults. Most victims who continued to fight as adults were persons whose adult personalities were described as either outgoing and friendly or cautious and reserved. Persons manifesting these personality traits were most likely to fight with friends; persons who fought with spouses were described as hostile and aggressive. Personality differences among victims tended to establish the target of aggression. Because of the gregariousness of the youthful victim, he or she was more likely to have been reported as having engaged in fights than had the more retiring types. When persons with non-outgoing personalities became adults, they were more likely to have fights than when they were youths. The targets of their aggressive energy also were likely to differ from those of their more gregarious peers.

Similar differences were noted between personality characteristics of victims and prior difficulty with the law. But seldom did fighting lead to this problem. When there was evidence that fighting led to difficulty with the law, the hostile-aggressive personality was disproportionately represented, and persons with that personality type more often had difficulty with the law as a result of drug violations or commission of a felony. The hostile-aggressive personality in this sense seems to be in accordance with the earlier identified anti-social orientation that described selected self-image types.

Fighting and Prior Difficulty with the Law

In the matter of victim difficulty with the law, a strong association with youthful fighting behavior exists. Victims who were characterized as intermediate-frequency fighters were more likely to have encountered problems with the law than had any other fighter group, including nonfighters. Intermediate-level fighters were most often arrested for public drunkenness and robbery. Ninety percent of those persons reported to have seldom fought never encounterd difficulty with the law. On the contrary, 87.5 percent of those identified as intermediate-frequency fighters did report difficulty with the law. Pulkkimen (1987) recently described persons who fit our intermediate-frequency fighters in terms of prior contact with the law as persons who manifest offensive aggressive behavior. Persons possessing these characteristics are likely to be those charged with the commissions of felony homicide.

Persons identified as intermediate-frequency fighters apparently had limited impulse control and a tendency to engage in troublesome behavior. These persons were disproportionately out of work at time of death (70.6 percent), were more likely to have been suspended from school (55.6 percent), and were more apt to be concerned with improving their personal appearance (31.3 percent). These individuals were strongly self-centered and manifested little respect for institutional norms of behavior.

JEALOUSY AS A TRIGGERING MECHANISM IN THE ACT OF HOMICIDE

The threatened loss of emotional support and the corresponding possibility of the transfer of that support to another leads the threatened individual to experience feelings of jealousy. Jealousy is most often an emotion that grows out of interpersonal relations involving intimacy. Moreover, it is conditioned by cultural expectations, and response to jealousy can range from mild feelings of being hurt to feelings of outrage that are sometimes accompanied by acts of violence.

The possibility of jealousy leading to acting-out behavior is thought most likely to occur among those populations who engage in life-styles characterized by intimate involvement with multiple sexual partners. Not all such behavior is associated with conflict between sexual partners; but the response to feelings of jealousy generally is more intense in that context. The economic marginality of most of our offenders should be expected to prompt some to engage in behavior in which signs of jealousy would be evident. The nature of these responses is likely to be conditioned by the personality of the respondent, cultural expectations, and the specific setting in which the triggering act occurs.

Jealousy and Male Honor

Family violence is often related to undercurrents of jealousy. Much of the behavior associated with jealousy is explained in terms of male honor. Daly and Wilson (1988) suggest that the role of male sexual jealousy may be underestimated as a motive in homicide violence. Halleck, in discussing family violence, described the jealousy-provoking situation as follows: "The most common situation related to violence in families is that in which a loved one threatens to leave or arouses feelings of possessiveness and jealousy by showing interest in another partner" (1978:54). Curtis (1975) seemed to see this turn of events as inevitable among black ghetto residents. He wrote that, "the economic marginality of street-corner men commonly results in quick-changing and undefined relationships with women," and added that, "As a result, there is considerable disagreement and distrust about sexual unfaithfulness" (Curtis, 1975:50). Both Halleck and Curtis described triggering mechanisms that include feelings of jealousy, but these feelings are undergirded by a code of conduct based on the need to protect male honor.

The male honor code is said to be based upon a double standard of sexual morality wherein men are permitted to engage in sex with a number of women, whereas women are expected to engage in sex with a single marital partner (Martin, 1978:184). The extent to which these attitude and behavioral styles are manifested among our offender population likely influenced the potential for jealousy-provoking acts of violence leading to death.

Because jealousy is an essential ingredient in about 10 percent of all homicides in the nation, respondents were questioned regarding their perception of themselves as jealous persons. More than two-thirds of the respondents rejected the idea that they could be considered jealous persons. Of the respondents who identified themselves as jealous persons, 40 percent were aged thirty or older. In this instance it is uncertain whether the determining factor is age, or if jealousy among your.g offenders is manifest in the emergence of personalities less senitive to traditional stimuli. Among attributes of offenders cross-tabulated with "Are you a jealous person?", only one was significant: jealousy was found to be strongly associated with marital status.

In our sample, no "never married" respondents considered themselves to be jealous. The largest percentage of persons indicating that they were jealous were those describing their marital status as separated. On the other hand, a large percentage of those describing themselves as not jealous were persons involved in common-law marriages. Single persons and those involved in common-law marriages indicated that they were not likely to lose control as a result of jealous emotion. But for some persons involved in civil unions and whose marriages had been dissolved or temporarily disrupted, jealousy could present a problem, depending upon the circumstances.

Jealousy-Provoking Behavior

Because the feeling of jealousy frequently leads to a temporary loss of impulse control, it is recognized as a potential triggering mechanism for the commission of acts of violence. Because the most intense arousal of jealous feelings is associated with conflict between the sexes, potential for intersex homicide is heightened. Suspicion of spouse's infidelity, lovers' arguments, and conflicts between members of the same sex for the affection of a member of the opposite sex all represent situations in which jealousy might trigger homicide.

Jealousy was a factor in a relatively small percentage of the total homicides in which the offender from our sample cities were involved. For example, in Atlanta 15.4 percent of the offenders implicated jealousy as an element in the transaction, and only 10 percent of the Detroit offenders cited jealousy as a critical factor. It was more frequently the basis for homicides in St. Louis (20.0 percent) than elsewhere. Of the total reported violent transactions, 10–20 percent were undergirded by jealousy-inducing stimuli.

DRUG AND ALCOHOL USE AND ITS ASSOCIATION WITH VIOLENCE

Violent acting-out behavior often is associated with the consumption of mood-altering substances. Some researchers contend that selected substances play a primary role in triggering the transaction that ultimately leads to death. When inhibitions are released by drugs and coupled with other negative personal attributes associated with drugs, the stage is set for initiating transactions that become threatening and later escalate into physical confrontation. The extent to which black subjects use these substances is likely to influence risk of victimization.

Alcohol is the substance most often implicated in such confrontations. A study undertaken during the 1970s by the Medical Examiner's Office in New York City indicated that approximately one-half of the violent deaths in that city were associated with alcohol use (Haberman and Baden, 1978).

Wolfgang (1958), in his Philadelphia study, also demonstrated that more than one-half of both victims and offenders had been drinking at the time of the incident. He found the percentage to be even higher for black males. The association between alcohol consumption and homicide is strong, but the blood alcohol content of the participants in the act is seldom specified in the evidence. Although blood alcohol levels for blacks and others involved in homicides were recently reported in a ten-year evaluation of homicide in Los Angeles (Goodman et al., 1986), it is difficult to assess the precise role of alcohol in the homicidal outcome. Yet it is evident that the consumption of alcohol prompts individuals to alter their usual behavior and thereby heightens the prospect for violent conflict.

The association between drugs and violent death is more tentative than that between alcohol and violent death. For one thing, the array of drugs used and their impact upon behavior is more diverse, making generalization more difficult. Some drugs have been found to produce an effect that spurs individuals to engage in bizarre behavior, including extremely violent behavior. Powers and Kutash (1978:317) reminded researchers that in attempting to assess the role of drugs on aggressive behavior, the following factors should be taken into consideration: drug type, pre-morbid personality, dosage, expectations, and environment.

It also should be kept in mind that many persons are multiple substance users, ingesting alcohol in combination with a variety of drugs. But the profile of victms of violence who were known drug and alcohol abusers indicates some important distinctions. Haberman and Baden found in their post-mortem analysis of a sample of substance abusers that black alcohol abusers were older (over thirty), and drug users were younger (under thirty). They also indicated alcohol abusers were much more likely to be southern migrants, whereas drug abusers usually were persons who had grown up in the city. Thus the choice of a mood-altering substance appears to be in part related to both age and sociocultural origins.

One final point should be made regarding the general relationship between drugs and violence. Much of the violence associated with drugs is only indirectly associated with drug consumption. Violence seems to be more often associated with acts designed to ensure access to drugs than to drug consumption and its effect upon behavior (Nurco et al., 1985). Powers and Kutash, in describing the influence of heroin on violence, had this to say: ''The direct effect of the drug, however, is to reduce aggression rather than increase it'' (1978:330). Nevertheless, the user's ire might be raised if he is unable to secure drugs, leading him to assault persons believed to be responsible for denying him drugs. The behavior associated with participation in the drug culture rather than the taking of drugs more often heightens risk of victimization. This is made extremely clear when viewing the situation in New York City. There narcotics abusers are most often killed in disputes or actions directly associated with narcotics. According to Haberman and Baden (1978:88–90), narcotics abusers are most often killed by friends or acquaintances (47 percent), and guns were the most frequently used weapons. Yet these deaths could generally be attributed to participation in the drug culture rather than to the influence of drugs on criminal behavior.

The Use of Alcohol by Offenders

The use of mood-altering substances among our offender population was widespread, and the use of alcohol on a regular basis was characteristic of more than 70 percent of the offender sample. But alcohol use is prevalent in the black community nationally, just as it is in the larger community. The central issue is the extent to which a population's use of alcohol results in a permanent or temporary impairment of the faculties of a significant segment of the population. Persons who find day-to-day survival most difficult are more likely to use alcohol to alter the perception of their harsh realities, leading us to assume that alcohol consumption would be more intense in high stress areas than in low stress areas.

Alcohol consumption reaches its apex on weekends. Bourne sees this problem as follows: "Drinking among the Black urban poor is strongly identified as a weekend phenomenon geared to alleviating the stresses of the previous week" (1976:41). Using alcohol to cope with a difficult life is thought to be widespread among the black urban poor; therefore, excess alcohol consumption should not be an unexpected attribute among persons in our offender and victim samples. Although most offenders acknowledged that they were regular consumers of alcohol, only 16.4 percent were identified as problem drinkers. Victims were less often reported to be regular users of alcohol (42.3 percent). As was indicated earlier, older participants are more likely to be problem drinkers whereas younger persons often show a preference for marijuana—although multiple substance abuse was shown to be widespread.

Some evidence indicates a migrant/non-migrant disparity in an expressed preference for marijuana among offenders. Non-migrants were more than twice as likely to use marijuana regularly than were migrants. There was no appreciable difference between these two groups in excessive hard liquor consumption. Non-migrants were more likely to be addicted to drugs; migrants were much more likely to be alcoholics. Marijuana use generally was more widespread among offenders than was excessive use of hard liquor; this might simply represent a property of age. Only a small percentage of this population identified themselves as either alcoholics (7.4 percent) or addicts (14 percent).

Among both offenders and victims in our sample, problem drinkers are a small percentage of the total. Yet we find that alcohol frequently is implicated as playing a central role in the homicidal act, with almost one-fourth of victim deaths said to be alcohol-related. Almost one-half of the offenders reported that alcohol was directly related to the incident. The amount of alcohol consumed by either group is thought to determine when alcohol was involved in the incident. Powers and Kutash (1978) indicated, however, that the relationship between aggression and alcohol consumption tends to be curvilinear, and that persons whose blood alcohol content shows a medium level of consumption are likely to be most aggressive.

Unfortunately, we are unable to specify the amount of alcohol consumed by participants in the lethal struggles. According to Haberman and Baden (1978), the amount of alcohol required to raise the blood alcohol content to an aggression-provoking level in the average person would be more than five highballs, 1.6 pints of ordinary wine, or ten beers. Yet they indicate loss of inhibition and critical judgment is reached at somewhat lower levels of blood alcohol content. Of the offenders in our sample, more reported that they were mildly intoxicated than in any other single state of alcohol influence—probably indicating blood-alcohol content sufficient to produce some impairment in judgment and inhibition relaxation.

The data describing victim drinking behavior do not allow us to identify a group of persons who could be classified as alcoholics. Nevertheless, drinking was a frequent characteristic of this population. Most persons who fought frequently were regular users of alcohol. It is uncertain how victims differed from offenders on most drinking-related attributes, other than that they were less often regular drinkers. To this extent, one would assume that victims' use of alcohol was less frequently implicated in their deaths than that alcohol usage was a catalyst that promoted offenders to behave in a violent fashion.

The Role of Drugs in Homicidal Behavior

The role of drugs as a variable in homicidal behavior is less clear cut than that of alcohol, partially because of the more diffuse reactions engendered by individual drugs and the greater difficulty of detecting the level of ingestion in the victim's body. Some drugs act as stimulants; others act as depressants. Heroin, a narcotic, is the drug most often associated with homicide, although it is far from being the most widely used.

Heroin is described as a depressant and therefore should not be expected to act as a triggering mechanism for aggression. But because heroin was the preferred drug of persons engaged in hustling at the time of the survey, the circumstances in which such individuals found themselves provided a context in which an aggressive display might be thought necessary. Powers and Kutash (1978:331) stated, "The surest way to identify heroin users in a slum is to observe the way people walk. The heroin user walks with a fast, purposeful stride, as if he is late for an important appointment." Rapid movement is said to be associated with the means of securing heroin and the selection of a sanctuary in which it can be used.

Death might occur in any number of settings associated with the acquisition of resources needed to secure drugs or with disputes growing out of conflicts between users and/or suppliers. Haberman and Baden (1978) classified motives associated with deaths as an outgrowth of narcotics abuse as (a) disputes, (b) crime-related, and (c) narcotics-related. The first category is attributed to the risks inherent in the drug culture; the second category implies that the presence of narcotics in the body was in some way related to death; while the third is associated with the trafficking of narcotics. The largest percentage of drug-related deaths are associated with the first category, disputes, that takes place among acquaintances. The elevation of acquaintance deaths among young black males may indeed be tied to the motive frequently identified by the police as drug-related, which has grown in importance over time. The recent entry of crack cocaine in the market place and the rise of crack cocaine distribution systems dominated by anti-social gangs have increased the risk of gratuitous (unnecessary) violence.

Pathologists Monforte and Spitz's (1975) assessment of the evidence of narcotics use in a sample of Detroit victims emphasized the frequency of drug-related deaths. They found that 43 percent of the victims in 1973 could be described as users, but that only 11 percent of the deaths were described by police as narcotics-related. They therefore thought that the actual role of narcotics in Detroit victimizations was underestimated. Moreover, they contended that if deaths associated with narcotics trafficking were included in the definition, the role of narcotics in Detroit victimizations would be shown to be much more substantial. The police department in New York City has already adopted a broader definition of drug-related homicides. Heffernan et al. (1984), based on their New York studies, define drug-related homicides as those "where persons are killed as a direct result of business in the distribution of illegal drugs" (p.4).

Thus the role of drugs in homicide deaths has become more complex, and some analysts suggest that simply to confine one's attention to evidence of victim's use will result in underestimating the role of drugs in catalyzing risk levels. In a recent nine-city survey of drug-related deaths, drug use in association with homicide was found to be prevalent in Chicago (15.6 percent), Philadelphia (36.2 percent), and Washington, D.C. (28.0 percent) (Gottschalk, 1979). Narcotics are clearly the most important drug group implicated in behavior leading to homicide, but one must concur with Powers and Kutash that both the personality and the environment should be investigated in order to unravel the homicide and drug connection. Yet, neither victims nor offenders in our sample indicated widespread contact with the drug culture.

Drug Use and Self-Image or Community Reputation

Both victims and offenders showed a differential propensity for drug use on the basis of community reputation and self-image. Among victims, persons identified as hustlers had the most extensive contact with the drug culture (44.4 percent). Victims described as persons who liked to have a good time were slightly more prone to be drug users than were mature, settled individuals or family persons. Almost one-fifth of the group that liked to have a good time were drug users, whereas one-tenth or fewer of the mature, settled individuals and family persons had contact with the drug culture. Drug choice also differed among victims; heroin and methadone were preferred by hustlers, and heroin and cocaine were the choices of persons who liked to have a good time. Marijuana use was not distinguishable by reputational type.

Among our offender sample, hustlers preferred heroin and hallucinogens; persons who viewed themselves as irresponsible preferred heroin; religious persons used hallucinogens; and responsible family persons were hooked on amphetamines. It should be remembered, however, that these descriptions are based on extremely small values and could prove misleading. Yet intuitively, they provide an expected response on the basis of what is known about the life-style of persons we have described.

Father Absence and Drug Use

Father absence is the one attribute that best distinguishes drug users among our victim sample. With the exception of cocaine, all drugs were used more extensively by father-absent victims than by all other victims. It is unclear to what this pattern might be attributed. Attempts to identify a unique drug-user personality have met with mixed results. The influence of father presence or father absence on the child's emerging personality also remains an area of limited exploration. Robins et al. (1971), however, contends that anti-social fathers (which includes father absence) contributed to anti-social personality traits in a sample of black St. Louis school boys.

Offender Self-Image and the Use of Mood-Altering Substances

Among offenders the propensity toward dependence on, or at least regular use of, mood-altering substances seems to be best distinguished by their self-image. This is particularly true among heroin users, who were heavily represented in the group identifying themselves as hustlers. Hustlers were most likely to report that they were heavy consumers of the drug; responsible family persons were most likely to report that they never used it. Among these two major self-image groups, there were no reported differences in the limited use of heroin. These two self-image groups also clearly maintained a different pattern of relationships with their adult peers. Hustlers were more likely to report that their relationships with adult peers were hostile or cautious, whereas responsible family persons were likely to report them to be cautious or friendly.

Both alcohol and drugs were used by a sizable segment of both the victim and offender samples. Alcohol use, as was expected, was more commonplace among both groups. More than 70 percent of the offenders were consumers of hard liquor, although most were persons who consumed only limited amounts. Fewer than two-fifths of the victims, however, were regualr users of alcohol. Like alcohol use, drug use occurred more frequently among offenders than among victims. Among the offender group, one-half used marijuana, almost one-third used cocaine, and more than one-quarter used heroin. On the other hand, less than one-fifth of the victims used drugs, with marijuana and heroin being those most frequently used. The question that now emerges is whether there was a difference in alcohol and drug usage by city.

Differences in Substance Abuse by City

Alcohol was implicated as being related to the homicide incident in 52.2 percent of the Atlanta cases. The victims were, by community reputation, persons who liked to have good time (43.5 percent) and mature, settled persons (30.6 percent). Alcohol was seldom implicated in Detroit (13.6 percent) and even less so in St. Louis (11.1 percent). Drugs were said to be related to the victim's death in 42.9 percent of the Detroit sample and in 30.0 percent of the Atlanta sample. Only in St. Louis were drugs seldom related to the vicitm's death. But in that city almost one-half of the victims were identified as mature, settled persons, persons whom we would assume to be only weakly attracted to drugs. On the other hand, this implies that the St. Louis victims in our sample, who were described by the next of kin, are not necessarily representative of victims from that city.

Hustlers were more frequently found among Detroit victims, which may account for the higher percentage of deaths in which drugs were thought to be involved. Unfortunately, we are not certain what the drug linkage is in those deaths thought to be drug-related. The connection might relate to drug ingestion, to problems associated with drug acquisition and distribution, or to some combination of the two.

Almost two-fifths of the offenders were reported to be drinking at the time of the homicide, a value considerably below that found in a number of other studies. The median percentage of drinking at the time of the incident, based on a number of studies, is reported to be 54 percent (Goodwin, 1973:151). Most offenders in our sample indicated that they were mildly intoxicated at the time of the homicide. The extent of alcoholism was previously examined among our offenders and was found to characterize only a limited number. But Goodwin said that homicide "is associated with drinking much more than it is with alcoholism," and added that, "Alcoholism is rarely diagnosed in homicide offenders" (Goodwin, 1973:154).

In our three-city sample, there were observable differences in the frequency with which offenders reported they were drinking at the time of the incident. It occurred most frequently in Detroit, where 39 percent were imbibing. Lower drinking frequencies were reported in Atlanta (32.8 percent) and St. Louis (30.8 percent). In both Detroit and St. Louis, fewer than 10 percent reported they were drunk. Moreover, no Atlanta offender reported being drunk. The modal category of self-reported level of intoxication was that of mildly intoxicated. Almost 30 percent reported this level of intoxication in Altanta, whereas only 15 percent reported this level in St. Louis and Detroit where a similar share of the offenders perceived themselves to be more severely intoxicated.

Among offenders, drug use at the time of the incident was less than one-half that of alcohol use. Likewise, it is less clear what role drugs might have played in triggering the homicide. Drug use by offenders was much more frequent in Atlanta and St. Louis than in Detroit. Only 11.9 percent of the Detroit offenders were said to be using drugs at the time of the incident, whereas 27.3 percent and 30.5 percent were using drugs in Atlanta and St. Louis.

BLACK PSYCHOPATHOLOGY AND HOSTILE RESPONSES

It is easy to ignore the potential for pathology among blacks when hostile responses are viewed almost exclusively from the perspective of assigning importance to the immediate stimuli believed to have acted as a triggering mechanism. Overemphasis on the subculture of violence discourages a view that would incorporate elements of both micro and macro environmental contributions to behavior. Bonime (1976:7), addressing aspects of the larger culture, suggested that "Ours is an angry culture." He indicated that persons who are confined to environments where blocked opportunities and social inequities prevail are likely to become highly hostile. A sense of anger becomes a part of one's identity, but not without pathological consequences. He further pointed out that most persons, "growing up in an angry milieu experience their individuality as participants—either attackers or defenders—within angry forces" (Bonime, 1976:9). The pathological consequences of this anger most often are ignored.

The Relationship between Culture and Psychopathology

The relationship between culture and psychopathology is a complex one (Dressler and Badger, 1985; Adebimpe, 1984), but evidence of their interrelatedness is clear. Value shifts promote a disruption in socially acceptable behaviors and corresponding attitudes toward those who adopt the new behaviors. Conflict often arises between parents and children over conduct growing out of value shifts. The counter-pressures associated with conformity can produce inner turmoil leading to neurotic or psychotic reactions. These problems are more seriously aggravated when the social milieu of residence promotes extreme deviations in base line behavior during a single generation. Value changes among blacks have tended to emphasize the desirability of a prosperous life. Moreover, the conduct associated with this value shift frequently is thought to lead to deviant behavior and conduct that might be thought of as anti-social. Selected persons who are unsuccessful in attaining the goals designed by their value systems might well develop traits that fall within the psychiatric spectrum.

How Important is Psychological Impairment
in Promoting Lethal Violence?

The question of psychological impairment was previously raised as a critical variable that might also act to increase the risk of victimization in certain kinds of interaction. This issue generally receives less attention because of the lack of precision associated with describing mental states that qualify as psychologically impaired states. Any defense for conduct abhorred by the general public is likely to receive only limited sanction. Thus the problem of the mental state or psychological attributes of the interacting parties seldom is an issue when the case involves a low-income or minority defendant. Nevertheless, it is imperative that we begin to attempt to learn what the role of the mental makeup is of persons inclined to engage in aggressive behavior that results in the death of an attacker or defender.

By the term "psychological impairment" we refer to any psychological state that would lead to a loss of the level of impulse control considered appropriate for the circumstances. To do this, one must be able to distinguish conduct that is culturally induced from that which is psychologically induced. Because this is not a simple task, it is much easier to rely upon cultural explanations to account for these behaviors as long as the victims and offenders are disproportionately members of low-income minority groups.

Psychological impairment as an element in the outcome leading to violent death is given only minimum attention unless there is gross evidence of severe mental disturbance or if the potential exists to employ it as a legal defense on behalf of the accused. In the latter instance impairment is employed to excuse behavior and to ensure the defendant will be only minimally punished—or possibly not punished at all—for his/her role in the fatal altercation. For this reason, elements of the criminal justice system seem reluctant to pursue the contribution of impairment to the fatal act. A cultural explanation of the act provides the system greater leverage in seeing that the defendant is adequately punished for his or her misdeed. Thus the central issue here is not that of insanity or incompetency to stand trial, but simply the determination whether some character flaw might have been involved in influencing one or more participants to behave in specific ways leading to the death of another.

SCHOOLING, SCHOOL BEHAVIOR AND RISK

Level of educational attainment in American society is positively correlated with social status. To succeed in American society, it is generally assumed that some minimal level of educational attainment will have to be satisfied. The required threshold level has continued to shift upward as the demands of society become more complex, with the median level of educational attainment today standing at more than twelve years and continuing to rise. For those who have difficulty negotiating the American educational system, at least in reaching some socially determined critical level, the promise of a productive future is seldom bright. This positon is buttressed by evidence that those who drop out of high school prior to graduation are at higher risk of becoming involved in criminal and other deviant acts (Thornberry et at., 1985; Farrington et al., 1986). Moreover, the belief that one's future is in large measure associated with schooling has led to much emphasis not only on educational accomplishment but also on attending the right school.

The median level of black educational attainment continues to lag behind that of whites, though it increased significantly with the previous generation and continues to rise. Black parents historically have assumed that education was the key that would enable their children to enjoy a more productive life than they themselves had known. Although that attitude still lingers among the parental genera- tion, it does not appear to assume the same level of importance among the student generation. Nevertheless, most still contend that success in the educational system is vital if one's life chances are to be improved.

The reverse of the above position tends to imply that a lack of success in the educational system relegates one to a menial position in the labor force, at best, or participation in the shadow economy, at worst. Because of the central role asssigned to schooling in this country, the experience of both victims and offenders within that system might provide clues to better enable us to understand the sequence of events that led to death.

Educational Experiences of Victims

There is evidence of generational improvements in the level of educational attainment between victims and their parents. The greatest improvements were apparent among St. Louis victims. This is interpreted to mean that a disproportionate share of migrant parents in the Detroit sample had completed fewer years of formal education than St. Louis parents (who were less often migrants). The movement to the city enabled some victims to expand the educational gap between themselves and their parents. Without a significant improvement in the generational difference in education between parent and child, the mobility status of the child is likely to be impeded.

Victims displayed a greater affinity for education than was true of offenders. This was evidenced by the higher percentage of persons graduating from high school. For some reason Detroit victims were less likely to be high school graduates than were those in either St. Louis or Atlanta. Detroit victims also liked school less than persons from the other cities did. Approximately 25 percent of the Detroit vic- tims indicated a dislike for school. Evidence of alienation from school is said to be strongly predictive of the likelihood of dropping out (Ekstrom, 1986).

The strongest positive attitudes about school were displayed by St. Louis victims. In fact, school was positively viewed by most victims as a place to socialize with friends; other aspects of school were seldom taken as seriously as the social function the school satisfied. St. Louis victims did indicate a liking for their teachers, which was on par with their expressed positive view of school as a social meeting place.

School Retention and Extracurricular Activities

The school's retention power was similar in each city. Approximately three-fifths of the victims attended school during their teen years. Those who quit school did so for a variety of reasons that varied substantially from city to city. In Atlanta more than 20 percent of the victims quit school to take jobs, possibly indicating that a larger share of these persons came from low-income families. In St. Louis, quitting to take a job and quitting because school was boring were tied in importance. Most persons who quit school in Detroit did so because they found school boring (29.2 percent). Competing interest, as was the case with the offenders, was much in evidence among victims as well.

Participation in the extracurricular activities of the school is no guarantee that students will stay in school through the completion of high school. Students were less active in extracurricular activities in St. Louis and Atlanta than in Detroit, but the inverse of the pattern was observed in retention. Athletic activity most often attracted students in all cities, but it was disproportionately appealing in Detroit. This pattern may well have been associated with sex of victimization. The level of victim and offender participation in extracurricular activities were quite similar in each city, with Detroit victims and offenders being drawn into these activities much more extensively than others.

Because athletic programs appeared more often than did other activities or programs, we sought to examine the extent to which participants had been rewarded. It is generally assumed that if an activity is sufficiently rewarding, individuals are likely to develop positive views toward the provider of the activity. In this instance one woud expect that persons rewarded for participating in school activities would develop favorable attitudes toward school. If the school did not serve as a source of valuable rewards, the participants would be required to seek positive identities for themselves in other arenas.

Though a majority of victims participated in extracurricular activities, particularly athletics, it was found that few of them excelled in these activities. Possibly upon discovering they were unable to excel in organized sports, the victims' weak interest in school diminished further, leading them to withdraw from school. Only in Detroit did more than one-half of all victims participating in athletics excel in those programs. In the other two cities, those who excelled numbered from close to one-third to almost two-fifths.

Scholastic Performance and School Retention

Victims viewed school to be more important as a place to meet friends than as a place to gain knowledge. Nevertheless, some students develop positive self-images partially on the basis of scholastic performance. As a group, victims were reported to be fair to good in their scholastic performance. Grades in school appear a more powerful index of retention than participation in school social life. Good and very good students were much less likely to quit school prior to graduation than were students characteristized by mediocre and poor scholastic performance. In fact, students exhibiting poor scholastic performance were most likely to quit because they found it boring. The largest percentage of victims to quit school for that reason were in Detroit, and secondarily in St. Louis. Atlanta victims were most likely to quit school to take a job or because they were in difficulty with the law.

Some victims had been enrolled in special school programs because they had been recognized early on as possessing traits that would require attention or their progress in the regular school program would be slowed. Special programs had not been utiltized by any Atlanta victims. This might mean that such programs were not available when these persons attended school, or that it was not thought they required special assistance. About 25 percent of Detroit and St. Louis victims had been enrolled in programs for slow learners and persons with behavioral problems. But victims enrolled in special programs in St. Louis were primarily persons with learning difficulties. Next of kin from St. Louis viewed these programs as minimally beneficial. Yet almost one-half of the Detroit next of kin thought they were advantageous.

Victim Suspensions

Most victims, like most offenders, failed to complete high school but one difference that seems to distinguish victims from offenders was the absence of the need to suspend them from school for behavior perceived to be in conflict with school goals and values. It is not clear whether this fact indicates that victims tended to adapt better to the school environment or if it is a bias associated with third-party reporting. If third-party bias is not responsible for this difference, it appears that victims apparently engaged in disruptive or maladaptive acts less frequently than did offenders.

Suspensions among victims were confined to those attending school in St. Louis and Detroit. In Detroit nearly 30 percent of the victims had been suspended, and 25 per cent of St. Louis victims had been. The most frequent reasons given for victims having been suspended were, in order of importance, fighting, conflicts with teachers, and problems associated with truancy. The pattern of infractions leading to the temporary dismissal from school is quite similar among both victims and offenders. It is uncertain, however, if any linkages exist between the dismissal behavior and behavior that might have been implicated in the death of the victim.

None of the victims in Atlanta was reported as having been suspended. This could indicate either a difference between school policies and administrative styles in northern and southern school systems, or differences partially associated with a regional ethos which defines both appropriate school conduct and guidelines for handling it (e.g., corporal punishment in lieu of suspensions). We are without hard evidence to corroborate the underlying causes for these differences. But we can tentatively conclude that victims less often engage in those behaviors that lead to school suspensions than do offenders. A school in which the environment lacks warmth is not likely to engender favorable attitudes. Teacher attitudes, however, might be directly related to existing conflicts between the values carried by teachers and those that prevail in the environment in which the school is located. "Friendly" was the modal characteristic employed by most of our respondents in all three cities to describe teachers. Many viewed the victims' teachers as disinterested in their welfare, a response given by almost one-fifth of the next of kin. But even when teachers appeared to be less than friendly, students perceived them as willing to help.

Educational Attainment in the Offender Sample

The experience of homicide offenders with the educational system is highly varied and strongly influenced by the age of the offender and the environment in which schooling took place. Twenty-five percent of the total offenders sample completed high school, a level that must be considered low in terms of today's norms. The highest percentage of high school completions occurred among our Detroit offenders, with almost one-third reporting they were high school graduates. In Atlanta and St. Louis 15.4 and 13.3 percent, respectively, reported earning a high school diploma. Thus, the mean level of high school completion is strongly influenced by the large number of offenders in our sample from Detroit.

Most offenders reported that they had dropped out of high school between ninth and eleventh grades. Only in Atlanta was the modal level of educational attainment less than nine years. But the offender age structure is more varied in Atlanta than in the other two cities. The mean age of Atlanta offenders is forty-two; mean ages in both Detroit and St. Louis are age twenty-nine. For some reason, only a small percentage of the offender group continued high school beyond the eleventh grade. At some point in their middle adolescent years either dissatisfaction with school or the pull of the external environment prompted them to withdraw.

Attitudes toward School

The attitude of the offenders toward school was mixed, but in each city, a weak majority indicated favorable attitudes. In Detroit, where the majority was smallest, 52.5 percent expressed a favorable attitude. The Atlanta and St. Louis respondents showed an even more favorable response to school, with 61.5 and 60 percent, respectively, viewing school as a positive experience. A variety of positions were expressed by those persons holding unfavorable attitudes toward school. For instance, they talked about qualities of the school itself including teaching methods, regimentation, and confinement, as well as attitudes relating to the race of teachers. Other responses illustrated the presence of parental conflict, feelings of personal inadequacy, competing interests, and peer influence. In Detroit, competing interests and peer influence explanations seemed to predominate. For example, one respondent from that city expressed his position in the following way: "Caught up in two different rhythms: wanted to do something fast and slick."

Competing interests apparently play a major role in student attitudes toward school. For those at ease in the school setting and who find a place for themselves in the school's social life, one would expect favorable responses relating to school. But for others for whom school seems to offer very little, the development of unfavorable attitudes—as well as subsequent withdrawal prior to graduation—is to be expected.

Student Discipline Patterns among Offenders

A growing issue in urban education has to do with student discipline. In many school districts increasing evidence shows that teachers are unable to discipline students, and this lack of control makes teaching difficult. An effective learning environment can hardly exist in schools where chaos abounds.

One means of handling the disciplinary problem is through the use of suspensions or expulsions. Suspensions, in particular, have become a primary tactic in attempting to rid schools, at least temporarily,

of students who are viewed as disruptive or who have exhibited difficulty in conforming to school regulations. This tactic has been
employed with great frequency in inner-city schools, where the greatest
incongruence between school values and student values exists. An
attempt was made to determine which members of the offender sample
were thought to be conformist or nonconformist in terms of school
values. To do this, a review of the disciplinary history of each individual
was undertaken to ascertain who had been suspended or expelled from
school, how many times the individual had been suspended, and for
what acts.

Suspensions had been given to a majority of respondents in
Detroit and St. Louis schools, but to only a small minority of the
respondents from Atlanta. Sixty-five percent of the Detroit respondents
and 72 percent of the St. Louis respondents had been suspended one
or more times. Only 15 percent of Atlanta offenders reported they had
ever been suspended. But it should be recalled that Atlanta offenders
are older and thus were often in school during an earlier period in
which student conformity was a less serious problem. Likewise, fewer
Atlanta students were still in school when they reached late
adolescence.

Multiple suspensions were the established pattern in the northern
environment. In Detroit more than one-fifth of the respondents had
been suspended five or more times. The frequency of suspensions for
individual students was lower in St. Louis, but the proportion of
persons suspended exceeded that which characterized either of the
other two cities. Suspensions themselves, though a general indicator
of school-student value conflict, are not as instructive in pointing up
deviant behavior as is information identifying the violation for which
the suspension was made.

Suspensions or expulsions were practiced against a variety of
behaviors held to be in conflict with school norms. It is not known how
important an offender's history of deviance (e.g., previous suspensions), prior record of negative behavior, and so forth, affected the
decision to remove the student from school temporarily. But in our
two northern school systems the offender sample was found to
frequently engage in behavior considered inappropriate in a school
setting.

Fighting was the act for which most of the suspensions were
ordered, with almost half of all suspensions for that reason. In fact,
it was the single most important reason for suspending students in
Detroit. Moreover, fighting was the sole reason cited for suspensions
in Atlanta, but because so few students were suspended, it is difficult

to evaluate the implications of this behavior. One would generally be inclined to assume that other forms of conduct considered inappropriate in a school setting were less evident in Atlanta. Nevertheless, fighting was less important in accounting for suspensions in St. Louis than in the other two cities. Inappropriate conduct, which often took the form of teacher disrespect, use of profanity, and poor self-control, accounted for more than one-half of all the St. Louis suspensions. Thus incivility directed at authority figures rather than conflict with one's peers was in evidence at northern schools at an earlier date than in the southern school system.

Truancy was also observed to be an important factor associated with suspensions in Detroit and St. Louis, but it was seldom mentioned as a factor leading to student suspensions in Atlanta. Truancy is thought to be a good gauge of the existence of competing interest and is sometimes used as an indicator of the probability that one will fail to complete high school. The truancy level was somewhat higher among the St. Louis sample than among the Detroit group.

Participation in Extracurricular Programs

One would expect school extracurricular programs to serve to promote positive attitudes toward school. Moreover, the variety of such activities present in big city schools should provide satisfactory outlets for the many talents and interests normally found in diverse student populations. With this in mind, a comparison of the participation level in extracurricular activities of our sample offenders was undertaken for each city. More than one-half of all respondents reported they participated in extracurricular school activities. Almost two-thirds of the Detroit respondents stated that they took part in these social activities, whereas only 53 percent of the Atlanta and St. Louis respondents were found to be participants. It is unknown if the higher level of participation in school programs was in any way responsible for the larger percentage of students completing high school.

Most of the respondents who identified the extracurricular activity in which they were involved indicated a sports activity. Many took part in a number of events, but in most instances, their second activity was also sports-related. Most were attracted to what are perceived to represent the more masculine-oriented activities. This might simply indicate a difference in outlook based upon self-image. Nevertheless, it would be of interest to determine if those who participated in school social life differed in their relationship to the victim from those who were unable to find a place for themselves among school-based social activities.

SUMMARY

Variations in risk from one city to another and within individual places are associated directly with a set of individual attributes that influence vulnerability. We chose to highlight a selected set of these attributes that we think make a major contribution toward an understanding of individual level risk; that is, we expected the extent to which frequency of fighting, frequency of school failure, frequency of school suspension, and intensity of drug use exposes such individuals to high risk of victimization and offending. Our treatment of these individual contributors to risk was based on data drawn from a survey of a small number of offenders and the next of kin of victims. The questionnaire employed in this instance enabled us to elicit the same kind of information describing the attributes of both actors in the lethal drama. While the size of the sample does not enable us to make broad generalizations, it does provide us with insight that could not be derived based solely on aggregate data. Therefore, we conclude that these data exhibit a more substantial contribution to an understanding of the problem than the simple reliance on one kind of ecological analysis or another.

The position we take is that individuals who exhibit the traits that expose them to elevated risk can most likely be detected at an early age. A limited review of the school history data does much to provide support for this position. Thus early detection of extremely aggressive individuals, individuals with learning and/or emotional disorders, and individuals who display little interest in school represents one approach to aid in reducing future vulnerability. It has been demonstated that persons possessing these traits are prime targets of school dropout. Moreover, school dropouts exhibit a greater likelihood of engaging in criminal activity during the early post-dropout interval (Thornberry et al., 1985). Early detection problems should thus begin in the schools.

Every effort should be made to identify the most appropriate environment-individual mix to assist individual students in overcoming deficits that will influence their later life chances. Yet such programs must be innovative and professionally developed and managed if they are to be made workable. Likewise, every effort should be made to include family and neighborhood groups in such efforts.

7

Weapons, Homicide, and Criminal Deterrence

INTRODUCTION

One of the overriding questions that emerges from this study is, how do we reduce the likelihood of occurrence of acts of lethal violence? Clearly, as we have demonstrated, numerous factors impact this phenomenon. However, we would be guilty of an oversight if we failed to address the contributing role of weapons in the recent upturn in lethal violence. American gun manufacturers produce approximately four million long guns (rifles and shotguns) and two million handguns annually (Wright et al., 1982). The number of privately owned guns was recently estimated to be more than 140 million (Bruce-Briggs, 1976). What role do handguns play in lethal violence? If one were to control the availability of weapons, would this impact the number of homicides committed? We are aware, however, that a rational weapons policy will have to embrace a broader range of guns than simply handguns, as the growing use of other automatic weapons in drug-related killings attest. As recently demonstrated, several jurisdictions in California have passed legislation banning the sale and ownership of AK47s and other automatic weapons.

Another aspect of homicide risk reduction that will be explored is the nature and pattern of deterrent strategies employed by the criminal justice system. Specifically we will be concerned with the sentences meted out to offenders appearing before the courts. Are the sentences of such a nature that they would deter others from committing the same crime? In this chapter we will focus exclusively on the question of the role hand-guns play in elevating homicide risk and on the issue of sentencing patterns of both black males and black females convicted of homicide.

THE ROLE OF WEAPONS ON RISK

The weapons available to would-be assailants vary in terms of effectiveness, the amount of energy expended and the reciprocal danger the assailant believes himself/herself to be in. From a diverse battery of items that could possibly fill the bill, individuals generally choose what they perceive to be the most effective tool for the task at hand. There is little question that the combination of weapons of greater lethality, coupled with easier access, has altered the weapons mix employed in American homicides.

The Handgun Phenomenon

The most notable change in choice of weapon is the demonstrated preference for handguns on the part of those persons who become involved in assaultive behavior leading to death. As recently as 1959, only 12.6 percent of U.S. households reported owning handguns, but by 1977, the figure had risen to 20.5 percent (Wright et al., 1982). During that interval, a domestic arms race was under way as the number of guns owned by the American population more than doubled. This situation, however, could be attributed partially to some households acquiring multiple weapons.

The domestic arms race has not been lost on the nation's larger black communities, where a dual demand is generated among those who have chosen criminal life-styles and those who wish to protect themselves and their belongings from criminal attack. This pattern of demand has had the effect of elevating the prevalence of handgun use in fatal attacks in black communities and, at the same time, increasing the risk of victimization (Farley, 1980; Baker, 1985). In 1975, blacks were killed with handguns nationally at a rate of approximately 26 per 100,000, whereas in 1960, the handgun death rate was only 11.3 per 100,000 (Shin, 1980). But the question remains, how important has the easy availability of firearms been on intensifying black risk?

Ideology and Gun Availability

There is a lack of consensus regarding efforts to restrict availability and/or handgun supply. Some analysts assume the position that any policy that denies the citizen the right to bear arms must be resisted at all cost. At the other extreme are the proponents of a total ban on handgun sales. Kates (1986) argues that the unrealistic position advocated by those who wanted to ban handgun sales led to the 1986 legislative victory favoring citizens rights to bear arms. Instead of being a policy favoring more regulation of firearms, the 1986 law seemed to favor less regulation.

How, then, are unsuccessful attempts to regulate gun availability likely to impact risk? Such a question is not easy to answer without a thorough knowledge of the structure of the market for handguns and specific kinds of outlets upon which individual user groups basically depend. It is well known that persons seeking weapons for use in the commission of a felony are far less dependent upon legitimate outlets than those who seek to acquire handguns to satisfy some legitimate need (Cook, 1982).

Likewise, a gun policy aimed at lowering risk generally may fail to satisfy that goal by failing to take into account the diverse aspects of risk. Luckenbill (1984) suggested that gun control laws may be expected to impact positively on instrumental behavior, but may have only a modest effect, at best, on expressive behavior, or what he termed "character coercion." Yet, Rossman et al. (1980) discovered that the Massachusetts' Bartley-Fox Law had a larger deterrent effect on assaultive homicides than on felony killings in Boston during the first year following its passage. Some ambiguity seems to exist in how gun regulatory policies might be expected to impact risk.

Gun Attitudes and the Black Community

Efforts to regulate the availability of handguns are seldom addressed at the level of the black community. Many of the national surveys have so few black respondents that it is not possible to generalize to the larger black community. In 1982, however, the National Opinion Research Center (NORC) over-sampled blacks, yielding a sample of 510 black respondents. On the question of whether or not a police permit should be required before an individual could purchase a gun, 79.8 percent of the black respondents favored the requirement, and 20.2 percent were opposed. To get a more accurate reading of black attitudes on the issue, at least in one location, McClain (1982–1983) surveyed a group of households from high- and low-risk neighborhoods in Detroit. The perceptions of those respondents seemed to have been sharpened as a result of widespread experience as victims of a violent attack and/or having had their homes burglarized. Therefore, in neighborhoods in which violent crime has become commonplace, the demand for guns to protect one's home and property apparently has intensified. Yet, in spite of the demand, a majority of residents favored some form of gun regulation.

Handgun Deaths in the Core-City Sample

During the period 1970–1975, the years in which risk was escalating, handgun deaths among our core-city sample varied as a percentage of total deaths. In 1970, nationally, handgun deaths accounted for approximately 50 percent of the total, with other gun deaths accounting for another 15 percent. At the same time, firearms were implicated in 71 percent of black victimizations nationally. Yet, the extent to which handguns turned out to be the preferred weapons varied among places within our core-city sample (see Table 7–1). From Table 7–1, it is clear that handguns were relatively more important in 1970 as weapons of death than they were nationally.

TABLE 7–1

Changes in the Prevalence of Black
Handgun Deaths in Core-City Sample
1970–1975

City	Total Victimization		Handgun Deaths (%)		Total Gun Deaths (%)	
	1970	1975	1970	1975	1970	1975
Atlanta	184	150	69.0	69.3	80.4	78.6
St. Louis	234	203	67.5	68.5	79.9	75.4
Detroit	408	517	60.5	58.6	77.5	76.2

Source: Computed from FBI Monthly Homicide Reports, 1970 and 1975.
Note: The 1970 Atlanta row information actually represents death occuring in 1971.

Handguns remained the staple weapon of choice in Atlanta, showed a nominal increase in St. Louis, and a modest decrease in Detroit. But, in no instance did dependence on handguns diminish substantially. Handguns, by implication, seem to be the most sought after weapon of destruction regardless on one's motivation. However, the demand for handguns is likely to vary as a function of level of perceived fear and the extent of local involvement in felony-related activity. Moreover, one should not discount the role of region on gun-owning traditions, which are likely to influence base ownership rates independent of other factors.

Victim Characteristics and the Differential Likelihood of Gun Victimization

Although aggregate data describing the extent to which handguns are involved in black-on-black killings are interesting, it is more important that we know the conditions under which handguns are most likely to be employed. Several traits tend to distinguish higher probability situations from lower probability ones. The sex of the victim clearly affects the likelihood that a handgun will represent the preferred weapon. Black males stand a much greater chance of becoming handgun victims than do black females. For instance, in 1970, 45 percent of the black female victims in St. Louis were killed with handguns, and in Detroit, 33 percent of the black female victims were killed with handguns. For males, the respective frequency was 70.6 percent and 65.5 percent. No doubt the circumstances leading to death differentiates on the basis of sex and, subsequently, influences the choice of the weapon employed. Howard (1986:87) asserted that because most female deaths are an outgrowth of domestic discord, "husbands and wives appear to shoot each other much less often than homicide offenders overall."

Older black males also appear to be at lower risk of handgun victimization than do younger black males, which reflects, in part, age-graded differences in motivation. Younger males are somewhat more likely to be victims of instrumentally motivated actions, and expressive motivations continue to account for a much larger share of older male confrontations. Among older males, guns other than handguns and knives still make a rather substantial contribution to death. In Detroit, in both 1970 and 1975, these weapons were employed in approximately one-third of mature male deaths. Other guns were also an important tool in killing young adult males, but knives were far less the choice among young adult males. Perhaps the southern tradition of knife carrying had not disappeared among older black males.

One final point on the pattern of weapon selectivity is directed toward the victimization structure. The increasing share of homicide victimizations motivated by instrumental concerns is believed to influence weapon preference. This preference most often is a handgun. More specifically, Cook (1981) indicated that the choice is more often a handgun with a barrel length of less than three inches. This weapon type is both concealable and intimidating while allowing the perpetrator to overcome, in specific instances, his own physical disadvantages. Data from Detroit (1972) reveal that black males killed during felony-related transactions were killed with handguns in more than three-quarters of the cases. On the contrary, handguns were employed in slightly fewer than 60 percent of the cases in nonfelony transactions. Clearly the structure of victimization is directly associated with the weapon selected by assailants in most lethal confrontations.

A Policy of Interdiction: The Case of the Saturday Night Special

It is assumed by some observers of handgun violence that the problem of excessive victimization in the nation's black communities can be reduced by a policy of interdiction. The most often recommended policy is one that would outlaw the sale and distribution of

Race, Place, and Risk

the so-called Saturday Night Special, a cheap, poorly constructed, low caliber, short-barreled handgun thought to represent the weapon of choice of young street criminals. Cook (1981) is of the opinion that the ambiguity surrounding the definition of what constitutes such a weapon will make it extremely difficult to formulate a policy outlawing it. Furthermore, there exists some doubt that this indeed is the weapon of choice of those who engage in instrumental lethal attacks. A review based on 1970 St. Louis gun victimizations by victim-offender relationships lends some support to the previous statement (see Table 7–2). The caliber of weapons that are displayed in Table 7–2 are those most frequently chosen by assailants. A diffuse array of other weapons, including other calibered guns, constitute the total weapon battery. From the perspective of handgun preference, the calibers identified in Table 7–2 constitute the standard package, although the picture might be somewhat distorted by the large percentage of unknown gun types associated with instrumental killings. Assuming this does not constitute a seriously biasing factor, offenders show a clear preference for the larger calibered weapon. Though this preference is clear across three of the four types of relationships, it is seemingly strongest among perpetrators of instrumental killings. This finding is similar to that observed earlier by Zimring (1968), although in that instance, preference for the smaller caliber weapon was somewhat stronger. Nevertheless, attempts designed simply to deny access to the so-called Saturday Night Special are possibly misguided if the weapons most often employed in lethal confrontations include calibers of .32 and above.

TABLE 7–2

Weapon Caliber and Black Victim-Offender Relationship:
St. Louis—1970

Caliber	Acquaintance	Family	Stranger	Unknown	Total
.22	14	6	7	1	28
.25	10	3		2	15
.32	14	5	5	2	26
.38	19	6	23	7	55

Source: The FBI Monthly Homicide Reports for St. Louis, 1970.

Growing Handgun Demand and an Appropriate Gun Policy

No simple straightforward way to curb access to the growing handgun supply appears to exist. Some jurisdictions, sensitive to growth in handgun demand, have attempted to limit access through specific licensing procedures or outlawing the sale and distribution of such weapons. Nevertheless, the likelihood of a community adopting measures to outlaw the sale of guns appears extremely minimal. The opposition to attempts to impose stringent regulations grows out of widely hailed legitimate uses for firearms ownership, including the presumed constitutional right to bear arms. Furthermore, efforts of this type are directed at legitimate distributors of firearms, who may not constitute the primary outlet for firearms used in lethal confrontations. This, then, raises the question of how effective such regulations can be expected to be if only a modest share of the handguns involved in fatal confrontations are secured through legitimate outlets.

The market for handguns is diverse, ranging from collectors, who make purchases of high-priced, exotic weapons for display purposes only, to those who wish simply to acquire a working weapon suitable for use during the commission of a street crime. Given the nature and diversity of demand for handguns in the nation's larger black communities, one would suspect that the outlets from which such weapons can be secured would vary greatly from place to place. Based on the response received from those offenders in our core-city sample, the firearms used in the lethal conflict were derived from a number of sources. The largest share were secured through street transactions (37 percent), followed by licensed gun outlets (23 percent). The remaining guns (19 percent) were secured from diverse sources. It must be remembered, however, that our respondent sample was small and, thus, does not warrant generalization. It does, however, provide insight into the diversity of sources available to persons in high-risk environments. Likewise, it raises some questions by implication regarding the kind of handgun policy that might be most effective in reducing risk.

In those places where risk elevation is attributed primarily to instrumental motivation, no doubt some type of interdiction policy is warranted. Two of the more touted examples of an interdiction policy aimed at curbing street crime are Michigan's Felony Firearm Statute (1977) and Massachusetts' Bartley-Fox Law (1975). Michigan's law added a flat two years onto the sentence of persons convicted of using a gun during the commission of a felony. Massachusetts' law, too, was characterized by the requirement of a mandatory minimum sentence; the mandatory add-on was one year. The Massachusetts' law, however, covers the illegal carrying of handguns, a matter overlooked by the Michigan law. Evaluation of the effectiveness of these two pieces of legislation in curbing crimes of violence produced different results. Rossman et al. (1980) contended that the Massachusetts' law has had a positive impact on curbing violent crime in Boston, but Loftin et al. (1983) are less sanguine about the effectiveness of the Michigan law in curbing violent crime in Detroit. Based on several time-series analyses comparing gun/non-gun use in the commission of violent crimes, they rejected the position that the Michigan gun law made a difference. Both research groups were careful to point out that specific actors in the criminal justice system can behave in ways which thwart the intentions of the law.

What are the Prospects for a Workable Gun Policy?

Based on continuing legislative support favoring nonregulation, serious effort to intervene in the sale and distribution of handguns clearly will not come through regulation. If we correctly interpret regulation to mean a restricted supply, then it is unlikely that this can be considered a viable option in efforts to reduce risk. As a case in point, the public health service acknowledges the seriousness of risk in the nation's black communities but also indicates that it will not address the gun availability issue as a potential deterrent (Meredith, 1984). If firearms availability is assumed to increase the level of risk, the problem will have to be pursued outside the context of regulation—if the issue is to be addressed at all. Otherwise, we may be forced to adopt the position recently stated by Barnett (1982) that Americans are "learning to live with homicide." No doubt, this reality prompts some legislators to support enhanced punishment when firearms are employed during the commission of a crime. However, these laws apparently are aimed only at violent felony offenders, a group that constitutes only one element—though a substantial one—in the risk on the instrumental side. Failing this, black communities are likely to become, if they have not already, armed camps where the good guys and bad guys lie in wait for each other.

If the above scenario were to become commonplace, governing bodies may be required to rethink their licensing policies to bring them more in line with reality. Rose and Deskins (1980) argued the time has arrived for permits to be allocated on the basis of intended weapon use. Base on intended use, a set of guidelines could be structured that specify how the weapon should be maintained, stored, and displayed. Further, specific training in gun use and safety might be required for a specific user group. We envision the designation of selected environments as high-risk environments and the subsequent issuance of defensive gun permits to residents of those districts who might qualify. Permits would continue to be off-limits to proscribed individuals (e.g., minors, felons, and the mentally unstable).

Many problems are associated with this tongue-in-cheek recommendation, but, obviously, as the situation becomes more acute, such recommendations may not be entirely unrealistic. To ignore the problem in high-risk environments simply is to grant the advantage to the felon and/or simply to assume the threat of lengthy sentences will convince the would be assailant to cease and desist. We are well aware that such a recommendation is likely to offend those who support unrestricted access to firearms, as well as those who wish to have firearms sales totally regulated. But advocates of neither of these polar positions are likely to be residents of high-risk environments.

There is little question that the proliferation of handguns in urban environments during the previous twenty years has contributed substantially to observed levels of risk, but we are not so naive as to suggest this is the central problem. The central problem is the emergence of values that support the use of violence in nonconflict-motivated settings in particular, and under other circumstances in general. The problem of values is more complex and, in some instance, seems intractable. Nevertheless, the killings continue and, until epidemic-like conditions become more pervasive, our society is likely to be slow in devising effective intervention strategies.

During the summer of 1986, in Detroit, gun assaults reached a new high, and the number of homicides was again on the rise, showing a close resemblance to the pattern that existed more than a decade earlier (*New York Times*, September 14, 1986), when both frequency of victimization and risk reached its peak. As long as killings in high-risk environments constitute what Zimring, Eigen, and O'Malley (1976) have described as wholesale deaths, the motivation to consider policies appropriate to the setting is likely to be weak. But when assailants from high risk environments expand their range and begin to launch gratuitous attacks onto targets that include higher-status persons, then the likelihood of seriously reconsidering the effectiveness of current deterrent strategies will be favored.

Guns are indeed simply tools that may be employed to satisfy a variety of objectives. But to assume they do not lend themselves to uses that are in conflict with normative values is to apply a condition of passive neutrality to them that is undeserved. The continuing fight between groups who assume polar positions on the issue of gun availability makes the problem more difficult to resolve. Meanwhile, risk in specific settings remains high, and the number of life-years lost continues to escalate. Perhaps one assumes that the lives that are lost are trivial, a position enunciated by Bruce-Biggs (1976), who contended that the situation is simply one of criminals killing criminals. Even if he were correct, by implication, we are deciding to whom we should deny treatment and are thereby contributing to a shortening of average life expectancy.

For those who have given up on the rehabilitation model as an effective tool against future criminality, the posture assumed via existing gun policy represents a least-cost-incapacitation strategy. We say this because data suggest that offenders who engage in instrumental victimization, and whose life-styles lead them to be described as career criminals, show a high probability that they, too, will ultimately become victims. At this point, we can say simply that handgun policies, in terms of both regulatory mechanisms and deterrent strategies, should be given a close examination in those communities where risk has reached absolutely unacceptable levels.

SENTENCING PRACTICES: DO THEY ACT AS A DETERRENT?

It is also appropriate that we devote some attention to the issue of deterrence if we are serious about reducing risk. Nevertheless, we have chosen to focus our discussion on a rather narrow aspect of the issue. Most of the following discussion will be directed at detecting how effectively individuals who perpetrate acts of lethal violence are processed through the criminal justice system. The discussion will be based largely on observations that describe system functioning in our core-city samples. The principal deterrent to be addressed here is that of sentencing practices and the extent to which they vary across jurisdictions. But before a sentence can be meted out, a host of preliminary steps and/or decisions necessarily have to be made. Thus we will describe how cases flow through the system and the extent to which they arrive at the point at which a decision is made regarding what is believed to represent appropriate punishment.

We will be concerned not only with sentencing practices in general, but how they vary by victim-offender relationship, circumstances, prior criminal history, gender, and weapon employed. If sentencing practices serve as a deterrent to violent behavior, we would expect jurisdictions that mete out lengthy sentences to deter individuals who are from a common environment from engaging in that behavior in the future, at least in terms of frequency of occurrence. However, our probe will not be exhaustive and will suffer as a result.

The Post-Homicide Chain of Events

To determine how well the criminal justice system functions, it is necessary to examine the actions taken by representatives of the system at a number of defined points in the processing chain. The initial link in the chain focuses upon the work of the police.[1]

Upon receipt of an emergency call of the discovery of a body or a violent altercation, uniformed police are dispatched to the scene. If it appears to be a suspicious death or the injuries to the victim are such that the victim will probably die, the uniformed supervisor calls in the homicide detectives. (Homicide bureaus are free-standing units, often function out of police headquarters, and operate citywide). The uniform supervisor secures the scene, and if the victim has been moved or transported to the hospital, the supervisor, along with the first uniformed officers to arrive at the scene, detail the exact position of the body and note anything that may have been disturbed by the emergency medical team. The uniform officers then begin to talk to and take the names of witnesses, and gather preliminary information to pass on to the homicide squad.

Upon arrival, the homicide squad takes control of the scene and the investigation. In some jurisdictions, a lieutenant or a sergeant will assume control over the scene assigning detectives to various tasks. For instance, one detective will be in charge of processing the scene for evidence, one or two will interview witnesses, and one may remove and interview the suspect, if he/she is still at the scene. With few exceptions, homicide detectives process the scene whether the suspect is known or not. Their primary concern is to insure that at the time of the trial they have not jeopardized the prosecution of the case by not thoroughly investigating it.

The investigation and processing of the scene consists of a number of areas and activities, including fingerprints, footprints, condition of the body, angle of the wound, relationship between victim and offender, whether or not the victim was armed, shell casings, bullet holes, search of victim's and suspect's residence, and the interviewing of witnesses. Information is gathered on the past behaviors of the victim, as well as the suspect, if known. For instance, if the homicide appears to be domestic, neighbors are questioned about family problems and police reports of past-reported problems in the household are pulled. This often is done via radio to the particular precinct or the homicide detectives request that the regular patrol officers or walking-beat officers be dispatched to the scene to provide additional information.

The scene is crucial because it essentially functions as a "witness" to the event. Evidence gathered from the scene provides evidence for prosecution and helps determine whether the event was a homicide, accidental death, self-defense, or suicide. In many instances, evidence gathered at the scene determines whether a suspect is or is not charged with a crime. For instance, if the suspect claims that the victim attacked him/her and appears to have been beaten, the pattern and extent of the bruises help to confirm or disprove the suspect's assertion. If there are no witnesses and the scene yields no clues, there is a break in the process and there are no arrests.

Such a break in the process often proves to be only temporary, however. The detectives continue their investigation and, more often than not, a suspect or suspects are arrested. In 1975, suspects were apprehended in 86 percent, 85 percent and 83 percent of the cases in St. Louis, Detroit, and Atlanta, respectively. Clearly, most of the suspects are arrested and booked on one charge or another. The decision made at this juncture will determine if the suspect will proceed to the next decision point—the indictment.

Case Dispositions

Among our sample cases drawn from Atlanta, St. Louis, and Detroit, wide variations in case dispositions were observed at the time of booking. At that juncture, the prosecution renders a decision to prosecute or not prosecute. Case dismissals appear to evolve out of a determination that the perpetrator did not act improperly in taking the life of another based on behavior attributed to the victim just prior to the fatal blow. Dismissals were rendered in 27 percent of the Atlanta cases, 55 percent of the St. Louis cases, and 29 percent of the Detroit cases. In each of the above instances, the action taken by the perpetrator was deemed justifiable and/or excusable. St. Louis stands out among the group as a location in which victims were frequently engaged in behavior that led to their death. Such decisions generally are associated with killings growing out of attempted felonies and occasionally are associated with family homicides in which an abusive husband is killed by a fearful wife in self-defense. The remaining suspects were thought to be culpable, and their cases were remanded to the grand jury for review.

The action of the grand jury will determine which of the remaining cases will go to trial. If the investigative work of the police and prosecutor's office demonstrates probable cause, the case will be remanded for trial. Prior to taking the case to the grand jury, the prosecutor and the attorney for the defendant may negotiate a lesser plea. Thus a suspect initially charged with "Murder II" may have that charge downgraded to "Manslaughter" if the evidence necessary to support the original charge is weak. If, after hearing the evidence against the suspect, the grand jury is unconvinced of its adequacy to support probable cause, a "no bill" will be handed down and the suspect will be released from custody and/or the charge will be dismissed. The common practice in many states is to seal the court records so that accumulated evidence cannot be used against the suspect at some later date.

In Atlanta, only 10 percent of the 1975 sample cases were "no billed," and in Detroit, only 12.3 percent of the sample cases fell into this category. But in St. Louis, 21.8 percent of the cases fell into this category. The differences in case composition among places led to the greater percentage of "no bills" in St. Louis than elsewhere. In locations in which instrumental motives are widespread, there is a greater likelihood that grand juries will fail to indict. In such instances, the available evidence may be inadequate to support the charge. Therefore, many prosecutorial units have adopted career-criminal or frequent-offender programs designed to amass the necessary evidence to assure that a true bill will be endorsed by the grand jury. The objective of these units is to reduce "leakage" in the system at this stage and to build strong cases against those individuals who are known to police to be violent predators.

The Trial Stage

For those individuals who view punishment as the prime goal of the justice system, the effectiveness of the system most often is assessed at the next stage in the process—the trial stage. Needless to say, for those who place incapacitation and/or deterrence as equal to or on a higher plane than retribution, the actions that are taken at earlier stages may be considered equally important. However, this is, indeed, a critical juncture in the process, because the decision to remove or not remove the suspect from society is rendered at this stage. Not only will a determination be made to remove or not remove, but of equal importance, the length of time that the convicted felon will be required to spend away from the streets is determined.

Arguments regarding appropriate sentence lengths abound. Persons whose motivations are fueled by concern for retributive justice support lengthy sentences and oppose indeterminate ones. On the other hand, those who favor incapacitation strategies view sentence length from the perspective of the number of crimes that will go uncommitted as a result of imprisonment. Supporters of this position advocate sentence lengths that best correspond to the time remaining in criminal careers. Thus their position is dominated by concern with efficiency and the protection of society from persons who have been loosely identified as dangerous (Moore et al., 1984). Our primary concern, however, is the message sent back to the community of origin in terms of sanctioning behavior.

Severity of punishment often is said to vary as a function of race, gender, age, employment status, and relationship between victim and offender, as well as to whether an individual was convicted by a jury or a judge alone (Uhlman and Walker, 1980). In our study, how race affected sentencing severity is less obvious because victims and offenders were same-race individuals. Yet, race may continue to be a factor when appropriate sentence lengths are established for crimes in which one racial group seems to represent a disproportionate share of arrestees (e.g. robbery). Furthermore, researchers have reported that blacks historically have received minor sentences for the commission of homicide when both the victim and offender were same-race individuals. Nevertheless, broad differences in mean sentence length for homicide can be detected from one urban location to another. Jacob and Eisenstein (1975–76), employing 1972–1973 data, showed that the mean sentence was 13 years in Baltimore, 10.75 years in Chicago, and 7.3 years in Detroit. We are not in a position to comment directly on the role of race in the sentencing decision.

The sample cases drawn from our primary sample cities likewise demonstrate considerable variation among places in the extent to which cases reached the trial level and, ultimately, in sentence length. In Atlanta, two-thirds of the cases reached trial stage; somewhat fewer, 58 percent, reached this stage in Detroit; but only 29 percent of the St. Louis cases advanced that far. Obviously, a different set of forces distinguished St. Louis from the two other locations.

If deterrence is a function of certainty and severity of incarceration, as some assume (Silberman, 1976), then the deterrent effect of criminal justice system action should show substantial differences among our sample communities. Intuitively, we would expect a weak deterrent effect in St. Louis and a stronger deterrent effect in Detroit, holding type of homicide constant. It is more difficult to state an expectation regarding deterrence in Atlanta given the high percentage of intimate conflict motivated homicides among the total. Nevertheless, our data on Atlanta clearly demonstrate a higher probability of arrest, somewhat greater probability of conviction, and longer sentence lengths if convicted than occurs in other cities. Therefore, on the surface at least, it would appear the deterrent effect would be greatest in Atlanta, if we could for the moment ignore the structural differences that distinguish between sample places. In St. Louis, a weak signal is sent back to the community because the probability of arrest and conviction both are low. Those who are convicted, however, are punished at a level characteristic of the national level. At the national level, Lunde (1976) observed that the mean sentence length for murder in the first degree was 10.5 years (time actually served), murder in the second degree was 5.0 years, manslaughter was 3.5 years.

Differences from one place to another in the manner of offense-labeling create problems in attempts to identify supposed deterrent effects. For instance, the Atlanta courts fail to distinguish between "Murder I" and "Murder II," whereas, for St. Louis and Detroit, these represent standard charges. At the other end of the offense-seriousness scale, a number of variants are revealed. In Detroit, the charge "careless or reckless use of a weapon" is employed. Presumably, this corresponds to the charge of "involuntary manslaughter" in Atlanta and St. Louis. Thus differences in labeling add to the confusion in attempting to understand the sentencing patterns and practices of individual jurisdictions.

Moreover, the ability to determine the severity of punishment is compromised by variations in reliance on probation as an appropriate punishment. In Detroit, probation was awarded more frequently than in St. Louis and Atlanta. Although, by 1975, there was evidence of lessening reliance on this mechanism than had been observed in the two previous years. On the other hand, in Atlanta, offenders in similar kinds of cases often were given truncated sentences, which lessens the severity of punishment associated with the usual sentence for such crimes. Sentence reduction in St. Louis seems to occur less often, although minor fluctuation on either side of the usual sentence could be observed. Another difficulty in making comparisons among the sample on the dimension of sentence length is the practice in Detroit of employing indeterminate sentence lengths.

THE CRIMINAL JUSTICE SYSTEM:
THE CHARGE STRUCTURE AND SENTENCE LENGTH

Some analysts take the position that violence leading to death among blacks often is related to poor impulse control (Heilbrun et al., 1978; Brearley, 1932). Support for this position seems to be based on blacks' prior status of oppression. The assumption is that, although the act was not premeditated, the intent to kill did in fact exist. Bailey (1976), in a review of state-level homicide convictions, illustrated that non-whites who were sentenced to prison for committing homicide were most likely to be convicted of murder in the second degree and manslaughter, but not murder in the first degree. Yet, the defendant's intention cannot always be deduced from the charge, given that the prosecutor may accept a negotiated plea that results in a lesser charge being lodged.

In pleading guilty to a lesser charge, the defendant accepts the judge's decision on the matter of punishment severity, although in some jurisdictions, a new trial is frequently requested when the punishment is more severe than the defendant anticipated. In many instances, heavy caseloads and the desire to process cases swiftly result in a negotiated plea (Zatz and Hagan, 1985). Such cases have been described as "wholesale cases" (Zimring, 1976). Reviewing the complexity of motivations currently prevailing, however, would lead one to suggest that poor impulse control is just one among many contributors influencing one person to take the life of another, a position that is reflected in the changing structure of victimization.

One of the central questions then becomes, does the nature of the charge against most black defendants conform to the traditionally held view of black impulsiveness and the proclivity of an oppressed people to strike out against one another under circumstances usually associated with loss of honor? If so, to what extent does the criminal justice system view such behavior as trivial and, as a consequence, display a greater willingness to mete out lenient treatment through negotiable pleas? Do such pleas, in fact, reflect these traditionally held views, or do they simply reflect conditions in the environment that make the task of prosecutors difficult? Obviously, these are questions to which we are unable to provide definitive answers. Nevertheless, we will review the charge structure and the subsequent pattern of punishment to gain an intuitive feel for how the system works.

Short-term sentences might be expected to serve as an indicator of the predominance of traditionally held views. Lundsgaarde (1977), upon observing the action of the criminal justice system in Houston, hypothesized that the more intimate the relationship between victim and offender, the less severe the charge and subsequent penalty. He indicated that grand juries are most often made up of persons whose level of educational attainment and income are considerably higher than the corresponding levels of those persons upon whom they are asked to render a decision. This, he believed, leads to the tendency to view violent acts between "primary individuals" (intimate) as less offensive than when such acts involve strangers (public). If Lundgaarde's observations are valid, then these differences should be reflected in the pattern of punishment occurring in our core-city sample.

City Charge Patterns

In all three cities, the charge of manslaughter is the charge against which most defendants have their cases adjudicated. Were it not the case that the charges have been altered in many instances, one could assume that the intention to kill on the part of black defendants is an infrequent occurrence, which would thereby provide support for the impulsiveness argument. Under such conditions, extreme anger prompted by some action of the victim is assumed to lead one to engage in intemperate behavior. We suggest, however, that reality is far more complex than such a position would suggest. The charge frequency shown in Table 7–3 provides some support for our position. Nevertheless, the charge structure does not provide direct evidence of the severity with which individual acts of violence are viewed. Yet, we would expect charge and punishment to be positively associated.

TABLE 7–3

The Black Homicide Charge Pattern in the Core City Sample—1975
(Variations in Homicide Charges by City)

City	Murder I	Murder II	Manslaughter	Other
Detroit	16%	30%	41%	13%
St. Louis	10%	40%	50%	
Atlanta	25%		75%	

Source: Derived from individual city court records.

The more serious charge of murder occurred with greater frequency in St. Louis, although a similar charge frequency could be observed in Detroit. On the basis of the structure of victimization, the existing charges appear to conform generally to what might be expected. The greater frequency of killings among intimates in Atlanta results in proportionally fewer charges of murder. The charge pattern prevailing among our sample of convicted defendants leads us to assume minimal punishment in Atlanta and maximum punishment in St. Louis. All things being equal, Detroit would be expected to show a greater similarity to St. Louis in its punishment pattern than it would to Atlanta. Yet as we pointed out previously, all things are not equal. Both the punishment tradition and the proclivities of individual judges bear upon the actual punishment ordered.

Family Homicide and Criminal Justice Behavior

The most intimate personal relationships involving homicide are thought to be those involving members of the same family, especially spouses. The killing of one family member by another accounts for a significant share of all homicides in Atlanta and must also be considered an important share in Detroit. The manner in which the court treats family homicide varies greatly between cities. The overwhelming majority of all family homicide defendants in St. Louis had their case dismissed by the grand jury, and in Atlanta, 44 percent were dismissed, but in Detroit, only 17 percent were dismissed.

In St. Louis, most family homicides by implication are thought to occur as a result of some action for which a lethal reponse was not totally inappropriate. A similar but somewhat less frequent implication was observed in Atlanta. Why Detroit differs from the other two cities is not readily apparent but might possibly be related to the relationship among family members (i.e., father-son, wife-husband, and so forth). The relationship that distinguishes Detroit from its peers is the smaller percentage of spouse homicides. In Detroit, dismissals appear to be more commonplace when the defendant is the wife. In Atlanta, however, that generalization does not hold. Nevertheless, this observation raises the possibility of a gender bias in both case dispositions and sentencing practices. This matter will be accorded a more detailed treatment in a later section.

For those family members charged and convicted of taking the life of another, the charge of murder is more commonplace in Atlanta than elsewhere. No family related defendant was convicted of murder in St. Louis. In both Atlanta and Detroit, manslaughter is the modal charge in family-related homicides, although its lead over murder in Atlanta is minimal. Family homicide appears to be viewed as a rather serious act in both Atlanta and Detroit. Yet, 25 percent of the Detroit defendants were given probation, whereas only 10 percent were granted probation in Atlanta. Only in St. Louis was the offender seldom punished in family homicides. But family homicide occurred less frequently in St. Louis than in the others.

THE CRIMINAL JUSTICE VIEW OF
FATAL ALTERCATIONS INVOLVING ACQUAINTANCES

Homicides in most cities are an outgrowth of an altercation between unrelated but acquainted persons, usually during periods of leisure. These acquaintance homicides constitute the modal group of our sample cities. Because most conflict-motivated homicides occur among persons who occupy the lowest rung on the socioeconomic ladder, the lethal confrontation often is attributed to life-style patterns that are assumed to be characteristic of the group. To the extent that these assumptions are correct, one would seldom expect the defendant to be charged with murder and/or to be severely punished for taking the life of an acquaintance.

Among our 1975 sample cases, acquaintance killings constituted 79 percent of the St. Louis victimizations and 43 percent of the Atlanta cases, but only 36 percent of Detroit cases. If indeed these are considered trivial cases, the mean severity of punishment score should be lowest in St. Louis, where such cases so clearly dominated the homicide mix of variables. In St. Louis, the grand jury only chose to indict 55 percent of the acquaintance-related cases that came before it. This suggests either that these cases were not viewed as constituting a serious threat to the welfare of the state or that, in almost one-half of the instances, the victim was perceived as provoking the action leading to death. There are other possibilities as well, but most often, these are associated with insufficient evidence. Fewer than one-fifth of all defendants accused of killing an acquaintance in St. Louis were convicted of the charge. In Detroit and Atlanta, one-third and one-half of the defendants, respectively, who were known to their victims were convicted of willfully taking the life of another.

From the foregoing description of the treatment of defendants charged with killing a person known to them, we conclude that the criminal justice system viewed these deaths with varying degrees of seriousness. Because most such cases are heard by a judge rather than a jury, the role of the judge is extremely important in meting out punishment. Apparently, acquaintance homicides are viewed as extremely trivial in St. Louis, moderately trivial in Detroit, but only minimally trivial in Atlanta.

The previous assessment could be seriously biased because it is based totally on the proportion of defendants charged with willfully taking the life of another. We will now review the charge structure by victim-offender relationship (see Table 7–4) in our core-sample cities.

Variations in Charge Structure by City

To assure ourselves that 1975 depicted a representative year, at least for St. Louis and Detroit, the charge pattern in the two previous years was reviewed. Data on Detroit reveal that the share of manslaughter charges remained basically stable over the three-year period, but other charges showed a greater fluctuation. For instance, the second degree murder charge accounted for only 15 percent of all charges in 1973 but only seven percent of the charges in 1974. We do not know if these fluctuations reflect changes in judicial attitudes or if they were, indeed, legitimate changes in the circumstances surrounding death. By 1975, the two charges of murder constituted a larger percentage than was true in the two prior years.

TABLE 7-4

Black Victimization Structure and the Pattern of Charges
Lodged against Defendants among Core Sample Cities—1975

Court Jurisdiction	Court Charges				
	Murder I	Murder II	Manslaughter	Other	Total
Detroit					
Family		11%	23%	2%	36%
Acquaintance	8%	20%	17%	4%	49%
Stranger	6%		6%	2%	14%
TOTAL	14%	31%	46%	8%	
	Murder I		Manslaughter		Total
Atlanta					
Family	17%		21%		38%
Acquaintance	17%		38%		55%
Stranger					
TOTAL	34%		59%		
	Murder I	Murder II	Manslaughter		Total
St. Louis					
Family			10%		10%
Acquaintance	10%	20%	50%		80%
Stranger		10%			10%
TOTAL	10%	30%	60%		

Source: Information derived from court files in individual cities. The data
describes the treatment of a sample of offenders charged with committing a homicide during 1975.

Percentages in St. Louis, too, showed some fluctuation, but the
basic pattern remained intact. In 1973 and 1974, manslaughter constituted 64 percent and 82 percent respectively, of the charges on which
persons were convicted. The small size of the sample of convicted
persons in St. Louis might lead to uncertainty regarding the pattern
of convictions characterizing the universe. In neither of those years
was there a single person in the St. Louis sample convicted of first-
degree murder.

The Prevailing Sentence Patterns

Sentencing practices, like those involving charges, demonstrate
variations among cities as well. Detroit, among our sample cities, is
the only one to employ minimum sentences. Because of this, it became

necessary to derive a mean based on the midpoint of the sentence range. Unlike Jacob and Eisenstein (1975–1976), we have not derived a single value as an index of severity of punishment, but we have derived mean sentence lengths based on the charge for which the defendant was convicted. In each city, persons convicted of first degree murder received a life sentence. These sentences were not employed in establishing mean length. In fact, we used only the sentences of persons convicted of murder in the second degree and of manslaughter to derive mean length, which created a problem because Atlanta does not distinguish between first and second degree murder. For that city, only manslaughter convictions are employed in establishing mean length.

Since manslaughter convictions are most numerous in all jurisdictions, they probably provide the most effective index for establishing harshness of punishment. We previously indicated that most manslaughter charges were a result of negotiated pleas and that a judge, rather than a jury, weighed the evidence. Thus we have an opportunity to view how seriously judges think black individuals should be punished for taking the life of a family member or of an acquaintance. For those convicted of murder in the second degree, it will only be possible to compare sentencing patterns in Detroit and St. Louis.

For the charge of manslaughter, the mean sentence length given by judges in Detroit and St. Louis was quite disparate: 8.8 and 2.4 years, respectively. The small number of cases in St. Louis, however, probably distorts the true mean. In Atlanta, the mean sentence length was 12.8 years. Thus the sentencing pattern on the charge of manslaughter does show wide variation, at least during a single year. In terms of sentence length, the pattern that evolved from our sample shows remarkable similarity to that described by Jacob and Eisenstein (1975–1976). Atlanta judges, like those in Baltimore, tend to mete out more severe punishment.

Of course, the sentence given seldom is the sentence served. In discussing Philadelphia's minimum sentence, Zimring et al. (1976) pointed out that seldom do defendants serve time greatly in excess of the minimum. As mentioned previously, only Detroit among our sample imposes a minimum sentence. The mean minimum for manslaughter in that city was approximately six years. If the pattern described by Zimring et al. (1976) for Philadelphia bears much similarity to the Detroit pattern, manslaughter defendants would seldom serve more than five years.

In St. Louis, for which we have data describing the current release status of our sample of persons convicted for manslaughter in 1975, all but one have now been released. The mean time served for committing manslaughter was 3.1 years, whereas the mean sentence for manslaughter was 2.4 years. If parole decisions in Detroit are much like those in St. Louis, most persons convicted of manslaughter in 1975 will have served their time.

Because manslaughter convicts in Atlanta were given sentences that averaged four years longer, they are not as likely to have satisfied some acceptable minimum period of confinement. But some evidence indicates that sentence length and time served by defendants from Atlanta is likely to be more incongruent than one would expect. By 1978, almost one-third of the individuals in Atlanta who were convicted of manslaughter had already been placed on parole. Of those receiving parole, four-fifths were female defendants.

On the matter of second degree murder, St. Louis officials were slightly more punitive than those in Detroit. The mean sentences were 12.7 years and 10.9 years, respectively. Judges in these two cities apparently differ in the way they view manslaughter and murder in the second degree. In St. Louis, manslaughter seems to be viewed much more trivially, but in the case of second-degree murder, much greater congruence is exhibited as to what represents appropriate punishment. Furthermore, in the case of St. Louis, both certainty of punishment and severity of punishment are minimal, especially if the charge can be negotiated down to manslaughter. But when one is able to get a conviction on the more serious charge of second-degree murder, the discrepancy in length of sentences in St. Louis and Detroit is greatly reduced. Judicial behavior, however, requires closer scrutiny if we are to determine how manslaughter cases that have been negotiated differ from those that have not.

GENDER AS A FACTOR IN CONVICTIONS AND SENTENCING

Evidence presented in chapter five indicates that an erosion of Wolfgang's (1958) findings concerning the characteristics and circumstances of homicides committed by females has occurred. His findings indicated the salience of the sex role in the circumstances and characteristics of female-perpetrated homicides. Females, particularly black females, usually murdered their male intimates with knives during the course of a domestic altercation that occurred in the kitchen while the female was preparing dinner. Our findings, for the most part, indicate that many aspects of the more recent homicides committed by black females are congruent with Wolfgang's findings; however, many changes appear to be taking place.

For instance, although black females still are more likely to kill males with whom they have an emotional relationship, our data indicate that higher percentages of them murder individuals with whom they had no emotional ties. Likewise, the modal place of occurrence still is in the offender's home, but a higher percentage of black females are committing homicides outside the home as well. No change is apparent in the role of black females in the commission of homicide; they still are sole perpetrators. Our data do indicate, however, a complete change in the type of weapon used. Females, like males, now primarily use firearms in the commission of homicides rather than knives.

The data show, demographically and socially, that black females who commit criminal homicides are most often persons of low socioeconomic status, who have low education levels, and who are most likely unemployed. They most likely were raised in a home where children were physically punished for misdeeds. Behaviorally, offenders were more likely to previously have been involved in fights than were victims. As adults, fighting was frequently related to their inability to handle jealousy-provoking situations that usually involved their male intimates. In addition to having fighting experience, female offenders in our sample likely had prior encounters with the law. Female offenders also were highly likely to have been drinking at the time of the incident. Thus female offenders involved in fatal altercations were most often participants in lower-class life-styles and/or engaged in unstable domestic situations. Yet, they exhibit a much lower rate of offending than males possessing similar characteristics.

These findings raise questions regarding how males and females involved in similar acts of violence are treated by the criminal justice system. What happens to these women once they are arrested for homicide? Is there a gender lag when females are involved in instrumental victimizations?

Women and the Criminal Justice System

Researchers in the area of women and the criminal justice system have presented evidence that women are treated differently than men. There is much disagreement, however, on the nature of and direction of the treatment. One view is that female offenders are dealt with more harshly because they exhibit behavior patterns that do not conform to norms and values society has about the personality and role of women (Chesney-Lind, 1973; Temin, 1973; Simon, 1975). One author emphasized that judges "are more likely to throw the book at the female, because they believe there is a greater discrepancy between her behavior and the behavior expected of women than there is between the behavior expected of men" (Simon, 1975:52).

The other view is that women receive gentler treatment from the criminal justice system than men. This differential treatment is purported to stem from assumptions on the part of criminal justice personnel that women are in need of protection (Nagel and Weitzman, 1971; Moulds, 1978). One researcher has suggested that the actions taken by criminal justice personnel reflect the assumption that women are different from men in ways that dictate more protective treatment of women (Moulds, 1978). The same researcher also found that females of all races received less harsh treatment than did their male counterparts. Non-white females, however, received slightly harsher treatment than white females, and non-white males received harsher treatment than white males (Spohn et al., 1987).

Consensus apparently does not exist about whether racial discrimination is a factor in the sentencing of black defendants of both sexes by the criminal justice system. Gibson (1978) found that, in the aggregate, the sentences imposed by judges in his study did not appear to discriminate against blacks. He added, however, that this result was largely an outgrowth of the fact that anti-black judges were balanced by pro-black judges in his sample. Consequently, he concluded that the results support an individual, rather than institutional, interpretation of discrimination. Yet Jacob and Eisenstein (1975–1976) found that the length of sentence seems to be much more the result of the seriousness of the original charge before negotiations than of the identity of the judge or race of the defendant. A number of other studies support their conclusion. These studies show little or no association between race and sentencing patterns; however, several indicate that blacks and Hispanics are more likely to be prosecuted and imprisoned than whites (Burke and Turk, 1975; Chiricos and Waldo, 1975; Bernstein et al., 1977; Perry, 1977; Cohen and Kluegel, 1978; Hagan, 1974).

On the other hand, other researchers have reached the opposite conclusion and are supportive of the position that racial discrimination still is a variable that influences the criminal justice system's treatment of blacks; thus, blacks receive harsher sentences than whites for similar offenses (Bullock, 1961; Thornberry, 1973; Wolfgang and Reidel, 1973; Chiricos et al., 1972; Swigert and Farrell, 1977; Unnever et al., 1980; Zatz, 1987; Unnever and Hembroff, 1988). Moreover, Smith (1987) and Radelet (1981) suggested that the race of the victim, more so than the race of the offender, impacts sentencing in homicide cases. But our primary interest in this instance is the purported differential treatment accorded black males and black females.

Sentencing Patterns of Black Females and Males

Our data are not adequate to determine empirically whether black females are treated more or less harshly than black males by the criminal justice system. Yet, based on observations from Detroit and Atlanta, black female homicide offenders may be treated differently than black male homicide offenders by the criminal justice systems. In cases involving black female offenders that were processed in Detroit and Atlanta in 1975 (N=32), indictments were not produced in 40.5 percent of the cases. In a similar percentage of cases, the women were either convicted of or pled guilty to voluntary or involuntary manslaughter. Another 6 percent were convicted of lesser charges such as "reckless use of firearms" and "assault with intent to commit murder," and a similar percentage were acquitted. Seldom were women charged and/or convicted of first or second degree murder (see Table 7–5).

TABLE 7–5

Disposition of Cases of Black Male and Female
Homicide Offenders in Atlanta and Detroit
1975

	Male	Female
No Indictment/Charges Filed	25.3%	40.5%
	(23)	(18)
Convictions/Pleas of Guilt Manslaughter	29.6%	43.85%
	(27)	(14)
Convictions/Pleas of Guilt Murder	23.1%	3.24%
	(21)	(1)
Convictions for lesser charges	––	6.38%
		(2)
Cases closed/death of defendant	6.6%	––
	(6)	
Acquittals	––	6.4%
		(2)
No data on disposition of case	5.5%	––
	(5)	
	(N=91)	(N=32)

Source: Compiled from Atlanta and Detroit court records.

A comparison of the black female data with data on the disposition of cases of black male homicide offenders (N = 91) in the same year and same cities reveals some very striking differences. Black males are more likely to be indicted for homicide than are their female counterparts. No indictments were issued in 25.3 percent of the cases. Convictions or guilty pleas for manslaughter were obtained in 29.6 percent of the cases, whereas only 23.1 percent either entered guilty pleas or were convicted of either first or second degree murder. Acquittals resulted in 9.9 percent of the cases, and 6.6 percent were closed because of the death of the defendant. No data were available on the disposition of 5.5 percent of the cases.

Examination of the sentences of black females (N = 15) and males (N = 48) for murder and manslaughter should highlight the seeming discrepancies in sentences for the same crimes (see Table 7–6). Among black males who either pleaded guilty to or were convicted of first degree murder, fewer than half, 42.8 percent, received life sentences. A majority, 52.4 percent, received sentences ranging from 2–20 years (combined categories of 4–20 and 2–15 years), and a small percentage, 4.8 percent, received probation. Only one black female was convicted or pleaded guilty to first or second degree murder, and she was sentenced to life in prison.

TABLE 7–6

Sentences for Black Females and Black Males Convicted of
Homicide or Manslaughter in Detroit and Atlanta
1975

	Murder		Manslaughter	
	Male	Female	Male	Female
Life	42.8%(9)	100%(1)	——	——
4–20 Years	23.8%(5)	——	11.1%(3)	——
2–15 Years	28.6%(6)	——	59.3%(16)	50.0%(7)
Probation	4.8%(1)	——	11.1%(3)	35.7%(5)
No Data	——	——	18.5%(5)	14.28%(2)
	N = 21	N = 1	N = 27	N = 14

Source: Compiled from Atlanta and Detroit court records.

Men also received harsher sentences for voluntary and involuntary manslaughter. Almost three-fourths, 70.4 percent, of the black males received straight sentences ranging from 2 to 20 years (again, combined categories); yet, only 50 percent of the females received straight prison sentences ranging from 2 to 15 years. No female received a sentence beyond 15 years. More than a third of the women, 35.7 percent, were granted probation, whereas only 11.1 percent of the males received probation. In Detroit and Atlanta, female offenders have been treated more leniently than their male counterparts. Extenuating circumstances undoubtedly were associated with these decisions. One such factor appears to be related to the sex of the victim. Unlike males, females most often kill persons of the opposite sex.

These data appear to indicate that black females arrested for homicide, for whatever reasons, are not treated as harshly by the criminal justice system, at least in Detroit and Atlanta, as black males arrested for the same offense are. Black males were almost twice as likely to be indicted for homicide as black females were. Black females were more frequently charged and convicted of manslaughter than black males were—who were more likely to be charged with murder.

There are probably a number of additional explanations for what appear to be discrepancies in the indictment/conviction rates and the subsequent sentences of black female and male homicide offenders. One possible explanation for the high proportion of non-indictment among females is the circumstances of the homicide. If, for instance, a sizable number of females kill in self-defense (e.g., an abusive husband/lover), it would logically follow that the non-indictment rate would be high. Males are more often involved in felony-related deaths, which logically would produce a higher indictment rate.

Regarding convictions, it is possible that women, for whatever reason, may have been offered plea-bargains at a rate greater than that of their male counterparts. If so, plea-bargaining would greatly reduce a higher proportion of convictions for and pleas of guilty to first and second degree murder for males. A third possible reason for the greater proportion of murder convictions for males may have to do with state law regarding certain crimes. For instance, Michigan state law mandates an automatic life sentence for conviction of first degree murder; consequently, prosecutors may be more inclined to prosecute males for first degree murder than females, and may be less inclined to impose life sentences of females.

A Neglected Area

The previous comments amply demonstrate how little we know about the factors that contribute to differences in the way in which the criminal justice system treats assailants who kill same-race individuals. We have failed to address many of the issues thought to impact treatment. Perhaps the most important issue not addressed here is that of prior criminal record (Zatz, 1985). The data available to us about this were not comparable, thus a decision was made to forgo that discussion. It should be pointed out, however, that unless one is prepared to judge the quality of each prior contact with the law, one could arrive at highly misleading conclusions regarding prior criminality based simply on frequency of convictions. Individuals in lower-class life-styles have frequent contacts with the law that are nonfelony-related and, on face value, hardly serve as indicators of criminality.

SUMMARY

In this chapter we have discussed the role of weapons on homicide in high-risk environments and the deterrent action associated with criminal justice system behavior. More specifically, we directed our attention to the issue of handgun availability, the need for an effective gun policy, and the indirect impact of certainty and severity of punishment as a deterrent. The latter issues were addressed simply in a descriptive manner to heighten sensitivity to the implication that these are variables and/or issues that play an important role as contributors to local clusters of high risk.

In the latter part of the chapter, we examined aspects of deterrence, principally sentencing patterns. Clearly, a number of veto points exist in the criminal justice systems in our sample cities. Numerous factors combine to impact whether an indictment is issued, the severity of the charge filed, whether a case goes to trial or is plea bargained, and, if ultimately convicted, how severe a sentence is given. Moreover, the relationship of the victim to offender also appears to impact sentencing patterns across cities. Much additional work is required in this area if we are more fully to comprehend the link between weapons availability, deterrence, and high risk environments.

8

What Does the Future Hold?

As a research topic, interest in homicide has grown enormously over the last decade. This increased interest in part parallels changes in levels of risk and the public's subsequent response to growing fears of violent victimization. Our understanding of homicide as a multi-dimensional, complex phenomenon is essentially derived from and informed by the results of both recent and established research. Nevertheless, research isolating the ethnic population at greatest risk of victimization—black Americans—is still meager. Researchers have been urged to fill that void by a growing number of activist policy advocates and behavioral scientists (Comer, 1985; Poussaint, 1984, Hawkins, 1985), who have become keenly aware of the absence of the continuing research required to address the problem.

The present investigation represents one attempt to address selected aspects of environmental contributions to homicide risk in a sample of the nation's larger black communities. It is in those communities that risk has reached the most unacceptable levels, a mean of 56 per 100,000 in 1980. But seldom does homicide research, which is ecologically oriented, address the problem of risk at the sub-city scale. Moreover, we have not focused our attention on a single year, but have chosen a spatial-temporal approach that is more process-oriented than pattern-oriented. By attempting to look at the problem more broadly, although targeting a single ethnic population for review, we might be criticized for not placing greater emphasis on individual attributes thought to represent contributors to risk. In defense of our position we strongly support an initial excursion into an uncharted research arena at a very general level of specificity, a situation which should indirectly promote more detailed segmented investigations of homicide risk in black America in the future.

Although most of the data employed in this principally descriptive analysis was drawn from microecological units and observations of individual level attributes and behaviors of persons involved in the lethal transaction, we were nonetheless equally concerned with the impact of exogenous forces on levels and structure of risk. We are very aware that research in this area is moving in the opposite direction, with growing emphasis being placed on endogenous contributors (Wilson and Herrnstein, 1985; Daly and Wilson, 1988). An improved understanding of constitutional contributors to violent behavior undoubtedly will enhance our ability to formulate policies designed to alter that behavior. Nevertheless, it seems equally important that we understand the operation of selected macroscale forces—economic change that alters the context within which these behaviors occur. Therefore, we have chosen an approach that permits us to focus our attention on the role played by macroscale forces on microscale behavior. We are not assuming that individual behavior is hopelessly dictated by external forces; we simply are suggesting that if how individuals possessing a given set of traits are likely to respond to their external world is not understood, it is unlikely that policies, other than those associated with punishment can be formulated to ameliorate risk.

BLACK RISK AND THE TRANSFORMATION OF THE URBAN ECONOMY

Since 1965, American cities have experienced a major transformation as the economy changed from industrial to post-industrial. The economic transformation has proceeded at varying rates, but it's impact was felt most acutely in metropolitan areas within the American manufacturing belt. Moreover, the larger central cities within the manufacturing belt initially manifested evidence of escalating risk (Hoch, 1974). Our contention is that the observed changes in the structure of the urban economy set the stage for a takeoff in risk that was anchored in selected high-risk environments in the nation's larger ghettos.

At this level of generalization one can temporarily overlook the role of individual attributes on risk and, instead, simply acknowledge that a growing share of the resident population will be ill-prepared to make an easy adjustment to the economic changes under way. The difficulties associated with the adjustment process basically are an outgrowth of inadequate basic skills, a decline in intermediate wage jobs, a sluggish economy, the availablity of surplus labor as an outgrowth of the baby boom after World War II, and socialization for participation in a mass-consumption society. The socialization variable can be attributed to the growing influence of television on consumer habits and material values. Moreover, within ethnic communities a pattern of territorial segmentation exists that is based on socioeconomic status, a condition that promotes differential vulnerability to risk.

We have attempted to draw attention to the manner in which large black communities have responded to the economic and social changes occurring within them. As high-paying, low-skilled jobs transfer from the city to the suburbs and/or selected non-metropolitan locations, and as replacement employment opportunities demand greater skill, substantial numbers of workers and prospective workers find themselves in limbo. Sternlieb and Hughes (1983:456) characterized the situation confronting these individuals and state, ''From the viewpoint of the poor, the city of goods production, the large-scale relatively unskilled employment, has become the city of redistribution—of transfer payments and welfare. For the elite there is a city—far from new, but increasingly vigorous—of information processing and economic facilitation, of consumption rather than production.'' One notable response to this turn of events has been the increase in the level of homogenization in these communities. There is growing evidence that individuals with the skills required for participation in the changing enconomy are inclined to abandon those neighborhoods that appear most threatening in terms of predatory attacks and/or status denial. The outcome of this strategy often is a congestion of households in the least-desired residential neighborhoods composed of individuals who demonstrate a willingness to prey upon others as a survival strategy.

This is the context in which the growth of the irregular economy must be understood, as well as the attendant risk associated with its growth. One of the primary negative externalities associated with the spread of post-industrialism is a heightened risk of violent victimization. The elevation of risk is manifested most often in those sub-areas of the city in which exclusion from participation in the new economy is most evident, especially if the excluded individuals represent first-time labor force entrants. Therefore, unless a larger share of inner-city youth is diverted into productive outlets and away from deviant and/or marginal life-styles, risk of victimization is unlikely to be substantially lowered.

THE CULTURAL PENDULUM IN AN AGE OF MEDIA ADVANCES

In association with these described economic changes, a series of far-sweeping cultural changes have occurred within the same temporal span. A rather extensive discussion of these changes was undertaken earlier, so we will simply highlight their contribution to risk here. Prior to the onset of this most recent developmental period, poor blacks and other minorities were more-or-less isolated from the American mainstream. But this began to change as access to television accelerated. It is now estimated that 98 percent of U.S. households own at least one television set (Stroman, 1984). Likewise, television-viewing represents one of the five ranking leisure activities of all blacks, regardless of class (Stamps and Stamps, 1985), and is, therefore, thought to exert a major impact on that group's world view. Researchers also have suggested that black children, who are known to be ardent televison viewers, often fail to distinguish between the reality projected by television and actuality (Stroman, 1984). Other researchers go a step further, however, and contend that television violence promotes actual violence and/or sanctions violence among viewers. The evidence at this point appears to be rather inconclusive as other researchers challenge this finding (Howitt and Dembo, 1974). But the direct influence of television on violent behavior is not the central issue in this instance, but the ability of this medium to distort reality and to influence values in a way that has had unanticipated negative consequences.

Television may best be described as providing a window through which mainstream America may be viewed. Such a window previously did not exist for many Americans. The perspective provided by television has fostered a convergence of values and the promotion of greater commonality across diverse groups within the population. For instance, in addressing the association between youth culture and the media, in this instance radio, Altheide (1979:245) stated, "ironically, the life situations of ghetto culture were made respectable for middle-class youth emphasizing emotions, absurdity and futility." He then added, "while such themes were undoubtedly good descriptions of the day-to-day consciousness and problems of many black Americans, they came to unwittingly promote similar definitions among youth." In a similar vein, Levine (1984) bemoaned the impact of mid-1960s post-industrialism in promoting far-reaching sociocultural changes in middle-class adolescents. He suggested that the trend in American music did much to undermine traditional values. Moreover, from a psychiatric perspective he concluded:

> No one can suggest that socioeconomic privation and the bitter frustration that it breeds are responsible when the more affluent teenagers of the middle class turn to vandalism, theft, and drug use, engage in self-impairing sexual activity and run away (Levine 1984:159).

Though in these two examples the researchers addressed themselves to the impact of non-visual media on middle-class behavior, a logical assumption is that the more powerful visual medium, television, is even more potent in selling selected aspects of mainstream values to the poor.

As the television industry has grown and matured, its impact on the lives of millions of Americans has become more pervasive, and we contend it has contributed indirectly to the risk of violent victimization. Poor youth seem to have quickly adopted, via television, those behaviors they find attractive, even though the gap separating myth from reality is not easily breached. On the negative side of the equation, Meyrowitz (1985) highlights two products of television's influence that we think are very important in this context. The first is its diminishing effect on age-graded behavior leading to blurring of distinctions between adult roles and non-adult roles. The other is the absence of distinction between frontstage and backstage behavior, such that acts earlier thought to represent private behavior are increasingly conducted in public, at least via the media. The cultural road map in America has undergone far-reaching changes over the past generation, and technological media advances have facilitated the speed at which these changes have occurred. Yet the fact that television does not constitute an anonymous force must not be overlooked, and therefore, television alone should not be seen as a "whipping boy" by those who choose to highlight the negative externalities associated with its development.

THE LINKAGE BETWEEN CULTURE–
ECONOMIC CHANGE AND RISK

The economic and subsequent cultural changes previously documented are thought to have impacted the structure of victimization, thereby altering patterns of risk. We contend that blacks residing in large manufacturing-belt cities prior to 1940 were still strongly bound by aspects of southern culture, even though Nielson (1977) reported that a unique northern ethos was already evolving. Most violent altercations during this earlier period were basically associated with individuals engaged in a primary relationship. The appropriate conduct for terminating disputes in such relationships was largely situationally determined, but cultural rules undergirded the appropriateness of the response in each given situation. Moreover, these rules had passed through several generations without major modification. Thus the impact of the southern regional culture of violence, even among blacks no longer living in the region, was thought to have dictated the structure of victimization through much of the pre-World War II period.

Following World War II, southern migration to northern urban centers continued to escalate, but at the same time, a large base population of northern origin was in the process of formation. In this situation one would anticipate a weakening of selected elements of the traditional culture and the adoption of values prevalent in the environment of socialization. Migrants from the rural South in some locations were introduced to fears they had not previously encountered in their earlier home communities—fear of street assaults. According to Schultz (1962), this led selected individuals to carry handguns as a protective tool to be employed in warding off a possible attack, at least in St. Louis. Rainwater (1966), whose views also are informed by his St. Louis experience, said the following concerning the role of external danger:

> The most obvious human source of danger has to do with violence directed by others against oneself and one's possessions. Lower class people are concerned with being assaulted, being damaged, being drawn into fights, being beaten, being raped. In public housing projects in particular, it is always possible for juveniles to throw or drop things from windows which can hurt or kill, and if this pattern takes hold it is a constant source of potential danger. Similarly, people may rob anywhere—apartment, laundry room, corridor (p. 28).

The conditions he mentioned probably motivated Rainwater to title his essay "Fear and the House-as-Haven in the Lower Class." Threats in the external environment are ever-present, but especially so in those environments in which a sizable segment of the population view themselves as dispossessed and/or whose access to the good life is severely constrained.

The above-mentioned examples are brought to the reader's attention as a means of illustrating the contribution of environmental and temporal dimensions on the socialization process. Values and life-style practices vary through space and over time and subsequently account for difference in the modal pattern of victimization. These two sets of influences operate in tandem and ultimately influence the magnitude of victimization, as well as the character of victimization.

Academics continue to debate the merits of cultural-versus-structural contributors to risk, the structuralist argument generally prevailing (Sampson, 1985). More recently, however, the culturalist orientation is finding qualified renewed support (Messner, 1982: Huff-Corzine et al., 1986). Blau, an ardent structuralist, recently acknowledged the possibility of the existence of a unique southern contribution to risk in the nation's larger metropolitan areas. He specifically concluded "that the idea that there is a Southern subculture cannot be dismissed out of hand" (Blau and Golden, 1986:23). None of these findings, however, assist us in understanding structural variations, although the finding by Sampson (1985) that demonstrated a significant negative contribution of southern location on urban adult non-white robbery rates may serve as indirect evidence of the strength that location has on the structure. By extension, we logically assume that this also applies to robbery-homicide.

In Chapters 2 and 3 we attempted to demonstrate the nature of the culture/structure of victimization linkage. Several generational cohorts are present in large non-southern cities, each having encountered varying social experiences in a range of environments. The complexity of those group's experiences, in terms of time spent in varying environments, should serve to distinguish initially between the prevailing structure in southern and non-southern urban environments, as well as within individual non-southern neighborhoods. Therefore, the very general concept of the existence of a subculture of violence is inadequate to explain levels of risk known to be undergirded by etiological differences based paritally on location.

Location is simply a surrogate for a stage in the economy's developmental sequence and the manner in which identifiable subpopulations adapt to changing sets of circumstances. Thus we have chosen to label the subculture that originated in the South, largely involving primary relationships, as a *subculture of defensive violence*. Yet we find that in the latter third of the twentieth century, young adult blacks have been exposed to a substantially different set of environmental pressures and have subsequently adopted alternative world views. One of these alternative world views, initally manifested in manufacturing-belt cities, has now begun to diffuse across the landscape at varying speeds. This more recent view has fueled the evolution of yet another subculture in which resort to violence is commonplace. We have chosen to label this more recently evolved subculture the *subculture of materialistic aggression*. This subculture has reached its apex in Harlem, where drug-related homicides have taken on increasing importance (Tardiff and Gross, 1986). In most locations, robbery-homicide tends to be the circumstance in which materialistic aggression is modally manifested, but there is growing evidence that as this subculture approaches maturity, it expresses itself in a growing variety of ways.

THE QUESTION OF RISK FUTURES

Black Americans have had a lengthy experience with acts of fatal violence since blacks arrived on these shores. To some extent we detailed that experience earlier. The key issue, however, is whether violent death is likely to continue as a major type of black death in the future. The answer to this question is likely to depend on the time horizon one employs to address the issue—the near future or the distant future. Those academics who describe themselves as "Futurist" are likely to choose the distant future as the appropriate time horizon and proceed to provide the reader with a series of alternate scenarios describing the likely extent to which violent victimization will constitute a prominent feature in the cause of death hierarchy in the year 2020 or 2040. It might be demonstrated, given an extended time horizon, that ethnic identities would have disappeared and/or that violence, as it is currently defined, would no longer represent a meaningful concept. Let us emphasize, however, that the time horizon of greatest interest to us is one of more immediacy. Our interests are more narrowly circumscribed and are confined to the probability of violent victimization among persons already born. Therefore, when we mention risk futures, we basically have in mind the quality of life available to all Americans between now and the year 2000.

As we have demonstrated throughout this book, the primary target of violent victimization has been black males and, secondarily, black females. Among this group it was shown that the age of victimization and offending has moved down the age continuum over time. This leads us to conclude that future levels of risk will most likely be influenced by the emerging status of individuals born since 1970. The extent to which these individuals successfully negotiate the economy will undoubtedly play a critical role in risk abatement, but certainly not the only one. Needless to say, those persons born during the base year of interest are already poised to enter young adulthood, and by the end of the century, they will have passed through the riskiest stage in the life-cycle.

To what extent can we expect the mean level of risk among young adult black populations in the year 2000 to differ from levels prevailing in 1985 or 1975, or 1965, the year of takeoff in risk? It was noted earlier that by 1978, a substantial decline in risk among this population segment was already evident, although the decline was very modest in mid-western manufacturing-belt cities. But since that time, risk has fluctuated, reaching an all-time high in 1980 (Rosenberg and Mercy, 1986) before beginning to fall again. We are uncertain if the annual fluctuations observed are an outgrowth of the changing economies in individual urban places or simply the wide swings associated with rare events.

Those settings assumed to represent prime targets for the elevation in national aggregate levels of risk must continue to be monitored closely. The primary units of observation should be metropolitan areas in which the central cities are experiencing major decline, as well as growing metropolitan areas currently attracting large new immigrant populations whose labor force involvement is likely to be confined to the labor market floor. In both instances, the presence of a large black population is a given. The prospect for heightened risk of victimization is more likely to be borne out in these settings. The risk trajectory in the 1970s for changes occurring in Los Angeles and St. Louis provides support for this argument. Thus heightened victimization is a possibility in the nation's black communities under both conditions of general economic growth and decline. Yet the ingredients promoting risk may differ substantially under these alternate conditions.

IS THE LOWERING OF BLACK RISK A REALISTIC POSSIBILITY?

Efforts are currently under way to alter the risk futures of those for whom risk has been traditionally high. Many researchers have recognized that the homicide rates prevalent in most of the nation's larger black communities   transcend those prevailing in the riskier developing nations. For instance, in reporting 1974 levels of risk in selected countries around the world (focusing upon a period that corresponds to the U.S. peak), Wolfgang (1986) demonstrated the validity of the previous point. In selected large urban communities in the United States with sizable black populations, homicide rates were substantially higher than those prevailing in Colombia (22.3 per 100,000), Mexico (22.0 per 100,000), and Thailand (19.3 per 100,000). Undoubtedly, this kind of information has prompted the U.S. Health Service to begin to devote particular attention to the problem. A recent statement by Rosenberg and Mercy (1986:393) demonstrated widening public support. On this issue, they said, "The epidemiologic analysis of homicide has as its ultimate goal the development of programs which will contribute to reducing the burden of homicide in our society."

Current efforts that are under way to lower risk are somewhat diffuse, but that should be expected when one considers the multifaceted character of the problem. For some researchers, the problem is viewed as essentially a crime problem, whereas others take a more expansive view of its dimensions. Nevertheless, the problem clearly should be addressed at a number of levels—neighborhood, community, national—as a means of increasing the likelihood of a successful solution. By a successful solution, we mean bringing risk levels within some predetermined level of acceptability. To do less than this would suggest current levels are acceptable. Yet Barnett (1982:70) concluded that the American population is not easily worked up by this issue, suggesting:

> Possibly the answer is that, at bottom, we do not really consider the reduction of homicide an urgent national priority. While we are terrified at the thought of being murdered ourselves, perhaps we do not view homicide per se as inherently horrible, clearly transcendent in evil to other crimes.

Moreover, as long as most homicide victims continue to be poor and lower-status minorities, those in higher-status positions are unlikely to exhibit a willingness to forfeit some of their liberties which would be necessary to wage an effective campaign.

Hopefully, however, the disparate groups manifesting interest in the problem, regardless of their basis of interest, will be able to come together and coordinate their efforts in a positive fashion. Moreover, efforts to curtail risk may be made more effective if local neighborhood initiative is aroused and the resources available in the public sector are used more effectively in the attainment of a common goal. As a start, researchers might wish to examine the viability of Poussaint's suggestion that homicide prevention centers, which would include programs of prevention, research and treatment, be created in the black community. But even before that formal step is taken, effort should be made to identify a mechanism that would facilitate the promotion of a strong family ethic that has humanitarian concerns as its basis. Failing this, most energies will be devoted to the development of a variety of control mechanisms—selective incapacitation, preventive sentencing—without substantially altering behavioral propensities that serve as a basis of support for heightened levels of risk.

There is hope that the greater number of actors becoming involved in efforts to ameliorate the situation will improve the likelihood of success. If success does not flow from an intensification in effort, the failure generally would be attributable to: (1) a lack of coordinated effort; (2) working at cross purposes; (3) the continued maintenance of a narrow view of the problem; and (4) the simple inability to overcome the joint influence of macroscale forces and individual-level responses to them. Therefore, to guard against the likelihood of failure, additional effort should be devoted to investigating the etiology of the various kinds of behavior that ultimately lead to externally induced fatalities.

From a personality and mental health perspective, efforts are well established (see Kutash et al., 1978; Revitch and Schlesinger, 1981). Yet clinical assessments often provide only weak indicators of behavior outside of controlled environments. Steadman (1986:571), in addressing this point, said, "From the behavioral science standpoint, I would argue that accurate predictions of homicide are impossible because of the low base rate of the behavior, and it is absolutely crucial to recognize that all science is weak in predicting infrequent events." Nevertheless, such assessments are far from useless and are currently being advocated by Dr. Carl Bell, a black psychiatrist who perceives the existing situation of escalating violence as having gotten out of hand (Staver, 1986).

The current status of risk prediction should not be taken to imply that attempts to predict violent behavior or "dangerousness" are not being undertaken. Efforts in that direction are currently being pursued by criminal justice researchers whose primary motivation is protecting society against persons with a prior history of violent criminal behavior (Moore, 1984). However, almost all of this work is directed at individuals with a prior history of offending, who may or may not be experiencing mental health problems. Obviously, these two sets of efforts should be coordinated, on both practical and research grounds. Nevertheless, we should not lose sight of some of the ethical issues that have been raised that relate to the manner in which these research results will be employed (Von Hirsch, 1984). In view of the disparate orientations of mental health and criminal justice practitioners, one concerned with the individual and the other with society, it is of great importance that the welfare of neither target population be compromised by the research outcome.

These issues provide us with one final opportunity to emphasize structural differences and their relationship to risk. Mental health workers more often are called upon to address problems that grow out of primary relationships, whereas criminal-justice-oriented researchers usually direct their research toward behaviors involving secondary relationships. Thus no broad national policy is likely to be presented as a universal risk-reducing mechanism, given the rather wide variation in structure of victimization from place to place. This is certainly not meant to imply that the problem should not be given consideration at the federal level, but simply to highlight differences in risk structure from place to place. The existence of such differences is likely to require the adoption of a set of recommended solutions that reflect the character of place, with emphasis being directed at its economy, culture, and demography.

We reiterate a position stated earlier that the strength of the effort directed toward reducing risk is likely to be strongly influenced by the extent to which the threatening behavior spills over into the mainstream community. Additional support for this position is found in the following statement of Wolfgang (1978:147): "So long as the poor and the black were raping, robbing, and killing one another, the general majority public concern with crimes of violence was minimal." It has become increasingly evident that as instrumentally motivated risk increases, there is a corresponding increase in fear for one's safety that extends far beyond the margins of the nation's larger ghettos. This fear often manifests itself in the growing support for the increased number of programs for career criminals that have recently been developed within selected local criminal justice systems. Because robbery is the quintessential act of violence that has the highest probability of involving a black offender and a white victim, interest in regulating risk in this area has grown. Blacks may benefit from increased attention to the problem, albeit indirectly. Programs that would attempt to lessen risk in conflict-motivated interaction less frequently receive such serious attention. An exception to this is the growing interest in domestic violence programs.

An integral part of the problem of interdicting homicide risk among blacks is that it will require a set of long-term strategies. The U.S. system of government and its citizens are not excited about long-term strategies; the system is only geared to accommodate short-run solutions. The polity wants to see results from its policies and programs, and if things do not change in the short-run, the commitment begins to wane. Any set of strategies devised will have marginal utility in the short-run, but in the long-run may do some good. The desire for short-run results pushes the punishment (criminal justice) response to the problem. Perhaps a more constructive approach is to define the problem in terms of a public health (epidemiological) issue, as suggested by Rosenberg and Mercy (1986), for it is in the area of public health problems that the political system is more inclined to make long-term policy commitments (e.g., cancer and AIDS).

The black community itself must become more involved in programs and efforts designed to reduce risk; otherwise, the indirect benefits mentioned above will not occur without penalty. One would hope that a sense of hopelessness about the situation has not already set in, that the situation is not seen as being already out of control.

In selected high-risk neighborhoods it would be easy to adopt this position. Nevertheless, the need to promote greater internal cohesion has never been greater. But the growing divisions in the black community brought on by the transformation of the urban economy make that task ever more difficult. Brimmer (1986), who recently addressed some of the problems confronting black communities vis-a-vis the economy, had this to say:

> If blacks are to sustain and quicken their renewed economic progress, they will have to overcome a number of handicaps, including some that are self-imposed. Among the latter are the very high rates at which young black men drop out from the labor force and the very high rates at which unmarried black girls bear children (p.92).

Certainly few would deny the implication of Brimmer's statement, and thus deny the need for renewed local community vigor in addressing the issue. But we perceive the problem to be far more complex than his statement implies.

The observed patterns of risk documented here are not likely to show a substantial downward movement until a much larger share of the nation's black population is able to gain a foothold in the new economy. The changes that have occurred in the economy, which are now in full view, have brought in their wake a reordering of national and regional values. The outcome of these changes has been to increase levels of vulnerability to risk for persons on the margins of society, but for black Americans the levels of observed risk are atypical for this time and place. Nevertheless, since 1980 some decline in risk levels have been detected in the largest black concentrations in the nation.

Between 1980 and 1984, the national black homicide risk level declined by more than 25 percent. An incipient upturn, however, was detected as being under way in 1985. Moreover, not all of the fourteen largest black urban concentrations participated in the observed decline; New York, Detroit, and St. Louis experienced higher levels of risk in 1985 than in 1980. What is obvious, based on the observed pattern of decline, is that major Sunbelt centers fared better than their Frostbelt counterparts, a pattern that represents a major reversal in that which prevailed before 1960. All this, we contend, dramatizes the impact of the changing character of the economy and the subsequent inability of a larger share of urban blacks to penetrate growing labor markets.

SUMMARY AND CONCLUSIONS

What has occurred during the period under review that distinguishes it from earlier periods of elevated risk within the nation's larger black communities is a lowering of the age at which risk is heightened, a continuing erosion of expressive dominance, and an intensification of black male involvement as both victims and offenders. These changes generally have occurred in environments in which the transition from an industrial to a post-industrial economy has been most pervasive—in which a large manufacturing labor force exists—and where growth and dependence on an underground economy has reached an advanced stage. This is probably best exemplified by the plight of poor blacks in New York City. McGahey (1986) reports that poor blacks in Brooklyn are recruited into the irregular economy at an early age, a factor that was previously noted by Williams and Kornblum (1984).

Furthermore, ethnic differences allegedly are manifested in the choice of activity that groups participating in the illicit economy perceive as their preferred domain. Robbery and drugs represent the preferred activity of blacks, at least in Brooklyn, according to McGahey (1986). The growing importance of drug-trafficking in the nation's larger black communities has begun to reek havoc across a wide range of dimensions of behavior, while likewise elevating risk. There is little question that the most recent upturn in risk, which began in 1984, represents a maturation and expansion of the irregular economy as a provider of income for the growing segment of urban blacks. The task required to overcome this new outbreak will tax the skills of all who are concerned with issues of equal opportunity and the maintenance of safe and secure residential environments.

On a final note, based on the data we have presented, upturns in risk in the nation's black communities may occur under conditions of both growth and decline. A good case in point is the situation observed in New York and Detroit as recently as 1985. In New York, evidence of economic recovery and growing prosperity was observed, but jobs requiring less than twelve years of formal education continued to decline. Therefore, an intensification in what Kasarda (1988) has chosen to label the "job mismatch" seems to have driven up risk under general conditions of economic growth. Detroit, on the other hand, continued along a downward spiral because new service jobs were not creating opportunities for growth, as was the case in Manhattan. Thus the very wide gap that separated job loss from job gain was such that urban decline was characteristic of Detroit, but not New York.

Needless to say, a growing segment of the black population in both locations has experienced difficulty in attaching themselves to the labor force. Likewise, both places have experienced an elevation in homicide risk since 1980. In light of these trends, Lichter (1988) noted, "The growing marginality of employment among urban black men, particularly young men, is a good place to start when considering reasons underlying the apparent deterioration on black family life, an issue now receiving much attention in the media." But beyond that, a robust effort will be required to demonstrate the linkage between the operation of the macroeconomy and behavior at the level of the neighborhood, if a set of policies is to be devised that will effectively address the problem of elevated risk.

Postscript

After this manuscript had been completed, homicide risk in selected black communities once again began an abrupt upward shift (1985–1988) following a short interval (1981–1984) of decline. By early 1989, the seriousness of the problem had caught the attention of both the print and visual media resulting in increased attention on the nightly news. Moreover, a series of television specials have highlighted the problem by bringing the enormity of lethal confrontations into America's living rooms. The observed outcomes of fatal violent acts were not specifically identified as acts of black violence, but that was unnecessary since the visual images projected demonstrated clearly who the vicitms were. The circumstances associated with death in most of the media presentations were identified as drug-related. Because of the apparent importance of this new round of events, we will briefly attempt to connect them to our previous discussion, and to highlight what seems to represent a never-ending tragedy in the nation's larger black communities.

The incipient elevation of black risk in 1985 now appears to represent the evolution of yet a third window of elevated risk in the nation's larger urban communities. This third window of risk, like its predecessors, is seemingly associated with specific changes taking place in American society. More precisely, its occurrence at this juncture represents the coming together of a number of macrostructural and macrocultural forces that have altered the character of employment, employment location, residential patterns and preferred life-styles. These changes reflect the manifestations of the emerging post-urban era whose impact at the level of the local urban community may range from extremely positive to extremely negative. The social dislocations and growing concentrations of poverty in our larger urban centers, noted earlier by Wilson (1987), tend to represent the negative pole of post-urbanism. But even as the above conditions were becoming more evident, a triggering mechanism was necessary to spark the new wave of violence.

During the second window of elevated risk, traditional motivations for engaging in lethal confrontations were supplemented by non-traditional motivations, as a growing share of victimizations were an outgrowth of instrumental acts, e.g., robbery-homicide. The current wave of elevated risk is associated with the growing importance of drug trafficking as an economic enterprise in low-income urban communities. The triggering mechanism for this new wave of violence, however, is the arrival of a new drug on the market: crack cocaine.

Crack, an inexpensive derivative of cocaine, was first produced in the Bahamas in 1983 (Kleber, 1989). It soon found its way onto the American market and established itself as the drug of choice in a number of low-income communities across the breadth of the nation. The timing of its arrival has varied from one market location to another, but in no location has it produced such overly devastating results as in the nation's capital.

By 1987, crack had become the drug of choice on the streets of Washington, D.C. (*New York Times*, March 28, 1989), and since that time the risk of victimization has quickly elevated. By 1988 that city had the highest homicide rate of any large urban center in the nation, with more than three-quarters of the risk attributed to drug-related killings. It thus appears that a strong association exists between the most recent upturn in black victimization and the growth of the market for crack cocaine, as one black community after another becomes firmly tied into a new form of illicit drug trafficking.

Heightened risk was initially concentrated in those urban centers in which the transformation to post-industrialism had advanced most rapidly, i.e., declining manufacturing dominance and/or the rapid growth of the producer service sector. This, when coupled with locations easily accessible to drug sources from outside the country and the growing presence of immigrant middlemen from drug-producing or distributing countries in the communities, set the stage for a new round of violence.

Not only is this new wave of violence concentrated, at least in this instance, in a selected set of centers, it tentatively appears to favor selected locations within the nation's larger black communities—zones of concentrated poverty (e.g., low-income public-housing complexes). Admittedly, this represents a tentative conclusion based on limited evidence. However, it is not an illogical one as the sale and distribution of crack cocaine at the street level is in evidence at these locations. Thus those left out of the legitimate economy are finding opportunity in a burgeoning sector of the illicit economy, but at an astronomical cost to themselves and the local communities in which they reside.

Hopefully, this new window of violence can be quickly closed; there is evidence that great effort will be made to do so. If not closed quickly, a spillover effect may well lead to an elevation of risk in zones currently beyond those of higher risk (i.e., sectors of the non-poor community). Furthermore, the existing images of some urban centers could be tarnished and, in particular instances, the potential for economic recovery slowed. The stigma of drug-related violence demonstrates that things have gotten out of control and no longer do we simply have a problem that is confined to disadvantaged urban black communities, but one whose tentacles extend globally into an illicit network of activity involving other sovereign nations. The problem has grown more complex over time and easy solutions are difficult to come by. But the end result today is the same as during the preceding intervals of escalating risk–blacks continue to represent the primary targets of victimization.

Notes

Chapter 2

1. Expressive violence is defined as violence which results from a situationally motivated outburst of anger. Domestic violence/family violence are examples of expressive violence.

2. Instrumental violence is defined as violence designed to secure a goal (e.g., money, or other material goods).

Chapter 5

1. Although there were 119 female offenders in the six sample cities for 1975, there were only 117 victims. The percentages of weapons are calculated from the number of victims.

Chapter 7

1. This section is based on observations made of the investigative techniques of homicide crime scenes by the detectives of the Homicide Bureau of the Phoenix Police Department from January 21, 1989 to June 2, 1989. Telephone interviews were conducted on May 18 and 19, 1989, with the heads of the homicide bureaus in Altanta (Lt. Walker), Detroit (Inspector Stewart), and St. Louis (Lt. Hegger) to determine how closely their investigative process paralleled that of Phoenix. With the exception of how the personnel were organized into teams or squads, there was little difference in their investigative techniques.

References

Aakster, C. W. 1974. "Psycho-social stress and health disturbances," Social Science Medicine 8: pp. 77–90.

Adebimpe, Victor R. 1984. "American blacks and psychiatry." Transcultural Psychiatric Research Review 21: pp. 83–111.

Adler, Freda. 1975. Sisters in crime. New York: McGraw-Hill.

Allen, J. 1977. Assault with a deadly weapon: The autobiography of a street criminal. New York: Pantheon Books.

Allen, N., et al. 1980. Homicide, perspectives on prevention. New York: Human Sciences Press.

Altheide, David I. 1979. "The mass media and youth culture." Urban Education 14 (July): pp. 236–253.

Andrews, Howard F. 1985. "The ecology of risk and the geography of intervention: From research to practice for the health and well-being of urban children." The Annals of the Association of American Geographers 75(September): pp. 370–382.

Antonosky, Aaron, 1979. Health, stress and coping. San Francisco, CA: Jossey-Bass.

Archer, D. and Gartner, B. 1976. "Violent acts and violent times: A comparative approach to postwar homicide rates." American Sociological Review 41: pp. 937–963.

Auletta, Ken. 1982. The underclass. New York: Random House.

Austin, Roy L. 1982. "Women's liberation and increases in minor, major, and occupational offenses." Criminology 20: pp. 407–430.

Bailey, William C. 1976."Some further evidence on homicide and the regional culture of violence." Omega 7(2): pp. 145–169.

Baker, Susan P. 1985. "Without guns, do people kill people?" American Journal of Public Health 75 (June): pp. 587–588.

Baldwin, James. 1985. The evidence of things not seen. New York: Holt, Rinehart and Winston.

262 *References*

Ball-Rokeach, S. J. 1973. "Values and violence: A test of the subculture of violence thesis." American Sociological Review 38: pp. 736–749.

Ball-Rokeach, S. J., Rokeach, Milton, and Grube, Joel W. 1984. The great American values test. New York: The Free Press.

Barnett, A., Essenfeld, E., and Kleitman, D. J. 1980. "Urban homicide: Some recent developments." Journal of Criminal Justice 8: pp. 379–385.

Barnett, A., Kleitman, D. J., and Larson, Richard C. 1975. "On urban homicide: A statistical analysis." Journal of Criminal Justice 3: pp. 85–110.

Barnett, Arnold. 1982. "Learning to live with homicide: A research note." Journal of Criminal Justice 10: pp. 69–72.

Barnhart, Kenneth. 1932. "A study of homicide in the United States." Social Science 3: pp. 141–159.

Baron, Larry and Straus, Murray A. 1988. "Cultural and economic services of homicide in the United States." The Sociological Quarterly 29(3): pp. 371–390.

Baum, Andrew, Singer, Jerome E., and Banni, Carlene S. 1981. "Stress and the environment." Journal of Social Issues 37(1): pp. 4–35.

Bengston, V. 1975. "General and family effects in value socialization." American Sociological Review 40(June): pp. 358–371.

Berkowitz, L. 1978. "Is criminal behavior normative?" National Council on Crime and Delinquency 15: pp. 148–161.

Bernstein, I. N., Kelly, W. B. and Doyle, P. A. 1977. "Societal reaction to deviants: The case of criminal defendants." American Sociological Review 42: pp. 743–755.

Berry, Brian J. L. 1979. "Inner city futures: An American dilemma revisited." Transactions of the Institute of British Geographers 5: pp. 1–28.

Biggers, T. A. 1979. "Death by murder: A study of women murderers." Death Education 3: pp. 1–9.

Blassingame, John W. 1972. The slave community. New York: Oxford University Press.

Blau, J. and Blau, P. 1982. "The cost of inequality: Metropolitan structure and violent crime." American Sociological Review 47: pp. 114–127.

Blau, Peter M., and Golden, Reid N. 1986. "Metropolitan structure and criminal violence." The Sociological Quarterly 62(5): pp. 413–425.

Block, C. R. 1985. "Race/ethnicity and patterns of Chicago homicide, 1965–1981." Crime and Delinquency 31: pp. 104–116.

———— . 1985b. "Specification of patterns over time in Chicago homicide: In-creases and decreases, 1965–1981." Illinois Criminal Justice Information Authority (October).

Block, R. 1976. "Homicide in Chicago: A nine-year study (1965–1973)." Jour-nal of Criminal Law and Criminology 66: pp. 496–510.

———— . 1977. Violent crime. Lexington, MA: Lexington Books.

———— . 1979. "Community environment and violent crime." Criminology 45: pp. 565–575.

———— . 1981. "Victim-offender dynamics in violent crime." Journal of Criminal Law and Criminology 2(2): pp. 743–761.

Block, R. and Zimring, F. 1973. "Homicide in Chicago, 1965–1970." Journal of Research in Crime and Delinquency 10: pp. 1–12.

Bluestone, Harvey and Travin, Sheldon. 1984. "Murder: The ultimate con-flict." The American Journal of Psychoanalysis 44(2): pp. 147–167.

Boessel, David. 1970. "The liberal society, black youths, and ghetto riots." Psychiatry 33(May): pp. 265–281.

Bonime, W. 1976. "Anger as a basis for a sense of self." Journal of the American Academy of Psychoanalysis 4: pp. 7–13.

Bourdouris, J. 1971. "Homicide and the family." Journal of Marriage and the Family 33: pp. 667–676.

Bourne, P. 1976. "Alcoholism in the urban black population," in F. Harper (ed.), Alcohol abuse in black America. Alexandria, VA: Douglass Publishers.

Bradbury, Katharine L. 1984. "Urban decline and distress: An update." New England Economic Review (July-August): pp. 39–55.

Bradbury, Katharine L., Downs, Anthony, and Small, Kenneth A. 1982. Ur-ban decline and the future of American cities. Washington, DC: The Brook-ings Institute.

Brantingham, Paul J. and Brantingham, Patricia L. (eds.). 1981. Environmen-tal criminology. Beverly Hills, CA: Sage Publications.

Brearley, H. C. 1930. "The negro and homicide." Social Forces 9: pp. 247–256.

———— . 1932. Homicide in the United States. Chapel Hill, NC: University of North Carolina Press.

Brenner, M. H. and Mooney, A. 1983. "Unemployment and health in the con-text of economic change." Social Science and Medicine 17: pp. 1125–1138.

Brenner, M. Harvey and Swank, Robert T. 1986. "Homicide and economic change: Recent analysis of the joint economic committee report of 1984." Journal of Quantitative Criminology 3(March): pp. 69–80.

Brimmer, Andrew F. 1986. "Trends, prospects, and strategies for black economic progress." The Review of Black Political Economy 17(Spring): pp. 91–97.

Brown, Claude, 1965. Manchild in the promised land. New York: The New American Library.

———. 1984. "Manchild in Harlem." The New York Magazine (September): pp. 36–44, 54.

Bruce-Briggs, B. 1976. "The great American gun war." The Public Interest 45(Fall): pp. 37–60.

Brummit, H. 1978. "Socialization of dyssocial children." The American Journal of Psychoanalysis 38: pp. 31–40.

Bullock, H. A. 1955. "Urban homicide in theory and fact." Journal of Criminal Law, Criminology, and Political Science 45: pp. 565–575.

Bullock, H. A. 1961. "Significance of the racial factor in the length of prison sentences." The Journal of Criminal Law, Criminology and Police Science 522: pp. 411–417.

Bunch, B. J., Foley, L. A., and Urbina, S. P. 1983. "The psychology of violent female offenders: A sex-role perspective." Prison Journal 63: pp. 66–79.

Burke, P. J. and Lurk, A. T. 1975. "Factors affecting postarrest dispositions: A model for analysis." Social Problems 22(February): pp. 313–332.

Cantor, David and Cohen, Lawrence E. 1980. "Comparing measures of homicide trends." Social Science Research 9: pp. 121–145.

Cash, William J. 1941. The mind of the South. Garden City, NY: Doubleday and Co.

Catalano, Ralph and Dooley, C. David. 1977. "Economic predictors of depressed mood and stressful life events in a metropolitan community," Journal of Health and Social Behavior 18(September): pp. 292–307.

Center for Disease Control. 1983. "Violent deaths among persons 15–24 years of age: United States, 1970–1978." Morbidity and Mortality Weekly Report 35(September): pp. 453–456.

Chaiken, Marcia R. and Chaiken, Jan M. 1984. "Offender types and public policy." Crime and Delinquency 30(April): pp. 195–226.

Chesney-Lind, M. 1973. "Judicial enforcement of the female sex role: The family court and the family delinquent." Issues in Criminology 8: pp. 51–69.

Chiricos, F., Jackson, P. D., and Waldo, G. P. 1972. "Inequality in the imposition of criminal label." Social Problems 19(Spring): pp. 553–572.

Chiricos, F. and Waldo, G. P., Jr. 1974. Human activity patterns in the city, things people do in time and space. New York: John Wiley and Sons.

Chiricos, F. and Waldo, G. P. 1975. "Socioeconomic status and criminal sentencing: An empirical assessment of a conflict proposition." American Sociological Review 40(December): pp. 753–772.

Ciotte, Paul. 1987. "The Alexander family murders." Los Angeles Times Magazine 3(August 2): pp. 8–15.

Clark, Kenneth B. 1965. Dark ghetto. New York: Harper and Row.

Clark, Thomas A. 1979. Blacks in suburbs. New Brunswick, NJ: Rutgers University, Center for Urban Policy Research.

Clark, W. A. V. 1986. "Residential segregation in American cities: A review and interpretation." Population Research and Policy Review 5: pp. 95–127.

Cohen, L. E. and Felson, M. 1979. "Social change and crime rate trends: A routine activity approach." American Sociological Review 44: pp. 588–608.

Cohen, L. E. and Kluegel, J. R. 1978. "Determinants of juvenile court dispositions: Ascriptive and achieved factors in two metropolitan courts." American Sociological Review 43(April): pp. 162–176.

Cole, K. E., Fisher G., and Cole, S. R. 1968. "Women who kill." Archives of General Psychiatry 19: pp. 1–8.

Comer, James P. 1985. "Black violence and public policy," in Lynn A. Curits (ed.), American violence and public policy. New Haven, CT: Yale University Press.

Cook, Philip J. 1979. "The effect of gun availability on robbery and robbery murder" in R. H. Haveman and B. B. Zellner, (eds.), Policy Studies Review Annual (pp. 743–781). Beverly Hills, CA: Sage Publications, Inc., 1985.

——— . 1981. "The Saturday night special: An assessment of alternative definitions from a policy perspective." The Journal of Criminal Law and Criminology 72(4): pp. 1735–1745.

——— . 1982. "The role of firearms in violent crime" in M. Wolfgang and N. A. Winer (eds.) Criminal Violence (pp. 236–291). Beverly Hills, CA: Sage Publications.

——— . 1986. "Is robbery becoming more violent? An analysis of robbery murder trends since 1968." The Journal of Criminal Law and Criminology 76(2): pp. 480–489.

Cook, Philip J. and Zarkin, Gary A. 1985. "Crime and the business cycle." The Journal of Legal Studies 14(January): pp. 115–128.

——— . 1986. "Homicide and economic conditions: A replication and critique of M. Harvey Brenner's new report to the U.S. Congress." Journal of Quantitative Criminology 2(March): pp. 69–80.

Cook, Thomas D., et al. 1983. "The implicit assumptions of television research: An analysis of the 1982 NIMH report on television and behavior." Public Opinion Quarterly 47: pp. 161–201.

Crain, R. and Weisman, C. 1972. Discrimination, personality and achievement. New York: Seminar Press.

Crouch, Barry. 1980. "A spirit of lawlessness." Journal of Social History 1: pp. 281–307.

Curtis, L. 1975. Violence, race and culture. Lexington, MA: Lexington Books.

Daly, Martin and Wilson, Margie. 1988. Homicide. New York: Aldine de Gruyter.

Darity, William A., Jr. and Myers, Samuel L., Jr. 1984. "Public policy and the condition of black family life." The Review of Black Political Economy 15(Summer-Fall): pp. 165–187.

Day, Lincoln H. 1984. "Death from non-war violence: An international comparison." Social Science and Medicine 19(9): pp. 917–927.

Dennis, R. 1977. "Social stress and mortality among non-white males." Phylon 38: pp. 315–328.

Dietz, Mary L. 1983, Killing for profit. Chicago: Nelson Hall.

Deskins, Donald R., Jr. 1981. "Morphogenesis of a black ghetto." Urban Geography 2(April-June): pp. 95–114.

Dinman, B. 1980. "The reality and acceptance of risk." JAMA 244(September 12): pp. 1226–1228.

Dohrenwend, Barbara and Dohrenwend, Bruce. 1974. Stressful life events. New York: John Wiley and Sons.

Dohrenwend, Barbara S. and Dohrenwend, Bruce P. 1978. "Some issues in research on stressful life events." The Journal of Nervous and Mental Disease 166(1): pp. 7–15.

Dooley, David and Catalano, Ralph. 1984. "The epidemiology of economic stress." American Journal of Community Psychology 12(4): pp. 387–409.

Drake, S. 1965. "The social and economic status of the Negro in the United States." Daedalus 94(Fall): pp. 771–814.

Dressler, William W. and Badger, Lee W. 1985. "Epidemiology and depressive symptoms in black communities, a comparative analysis." The Journal of Nervous and Mental Disease 173(4): pp. 212–220.

Earls, F. 1979. "The social reconstruction of adolescence: Toward an explanation for increasing rates of youth violence," in H. Rose (ed.), Lethal aspects of urban violence (pp. 51–67). Lexington, MA: Lexington Books.

Ekstrom, Ruth B. 1986. "Who drops out of high school and why? Findings from a national study." Columbia Teachers College Record 87(3): pp. 356–373.

Ellinwood, David T. and Wise, David A. 1983. "Youth employment in the 1970s: The changing circumstances of young adults," in Richard R. Nelson and Felicity Skidmore (eds.), American families and the economy (pp. 59–108). Washington, DC: National Academy Press.

Ellinwood, E., Jr. 1971. "Assault and homicide associated with amphetamine use." American Journal of Psychiatry 127(March): pp. 1170–1175.

Erhardt, C. and Berlin, J. (eds.). 1974. Mortality and morbidity in the United States. Cambridge, MA: Harvard University Press.

Erlanger, H. 1974. "The empirical status of the subculture of violence thesis." Social Forces 22: pp. 280–292.

———. 1976. "Is there a subculture of violence in the South?" Journal of Criminal Law and Criminology 66(4): pp. 483–490.

Estall, R. C. 1980. "The changing balance of the northern and southern regions of the United States." Journal of American Studies 14: pp. 315–382.

Ezekiel, Raphael S. 1984. Voices from the corner: Poverty and racism in the inner city. Philadelphia: Temple University Press..

Farley, Reynolds, 1980. "Homicide trends in the United States." Demography 17(May): pp. 177–188.

———. 1985. "Three steps forward and two back? Recent changes in the social and economic status of blacks." Ethnic and Racial Studies 8(January): pp. 4–28.

Farrell, Ronald A. and Swigert, Victoria L. 1978. "Prior offense record as a self-fulfilling prophecy." Law and Society 14(Spring): pp. 437–453.

Farrington, David P., et al. 1986. "Unemployment, school leaving, and crime." British Journal of Criminology 26(October): pp. 335–356.

Feagin, Joe R. 1985. "The global context of metropolitan growth: Houston and the oil industry." American Journal of Sociology 90(6): pp. 1204–1230.

Federal Bureau of Investigation. 1975. Supplemental homicide reports. Washington, DC: U.S. Government Printing Office.

———. 1976. Uniform crime report. Washington, DC: U.S. Government Printing Office.

Felthouse, Alan R. and Yudowitz, Bernard. 1977. "Approaching a comparative typology of assaultive female offenders." Psychiatry 40: pp. 270–276.

Fisher, J. 1976. "Homicide in Detroit: The role of firearms." Criminology 14: pp. 387–400.

Fox, W. and Wince, M. 1975. "Musical taste cultures and taste publics." Youth and Society 7: pp. 198–224.

Franklin, John H. 1956. The militant South. Cambridge, MA: Beacon Press.

Frey, William H. 1985. "Life course migration of metropolitan whites and blacks and the structure of demographic change in large central cities." American Sociological Review 49: pp. 803–827.

Frisch, Gloria, Morf, Martin E., and Libby, William L., Jr. 1975–76. "The Sandstone experiments: Values of a post industrial community." Interpersonal Development 6: pp. 191–202.

Furstenberg, Frank F., Hershberg, Theodore, and Modell, John. 1975. "The origins of the female-headed black family: The impact of the urban experience." Journal of Interdisciplinary History 6(2): pp. 211–233.

Fusfeld, Daniel R. and Bates, Timothy. 1984. The political economy of the urban ghetto. Carbondale: Southern Illinois Press.

Gastil, R. D. 1971. "Homicide and a regional culture of violence." American Sociological Review 36: pp. 412–426.

———. 1973. "Lower-class behavior: Cultural and biosocial." Human Organization 32(4): pp. 349–361.

Gelles, R. 1978. "Violence in the American family," in J. Martin (ed.), Violence and the family (pp. 169–196). Chichester, England: John Wiley & Sons.

Georgakas, Dan and Surkin, Marvin. 1976. Detroit: I do mind dying. New York: St. Martin's Press.

Gibbs, T. J. 1985. "Black adolescents and youth and endangered species." American Journal of Orthopsychiatry 54(January): pp. 6–21.

Gibson, James L. 1978. "Race as a determinant of criminal sentences: A methodological critique and a case study." Law and Society Review 12: pp. 455–478.

Goldfield, David R. 1982. Cotton fields and skyscrapers. Baton Rouge: Louisiana State University Press.

Goodman, Richard A., et al. 1986. "Alcohol use and interpersonal violence: Alcohol detected in homicide victims." American Journal of Public Health 76(2): pp. 144–149.

Goodwin, D. 1973. "Alcohol in suicide and homicide." Quarterly Journal Studies in Alcoholism 34: pp. 104–111.

Gorn, Elliot J. 1983. "Gouge and bite, pull hair and scratch: The social significance of fighting in the southern backcountry." American Historical Review 90: pp. 18–43.

Gottschalk, L. 1979. "A review of psychoactive drug-involved deaths in nine major United States cities." The International Journal of Drug Addiction 6: pp. 735–758.

Greenberg, David F. 1985. "Age, crime, and social explanation." American Journal of Sociology 91(1): pp. 1–27.

Gwartney-Gibbs, Patricia and Taylor, Patricia A. 1986. "Black women workers' earnings progress in three industrial sectors." Sage 3(Spring): pp. 20–25.

Haberman, P. and Baden, M. 1978. Alcohol, other drugs and violent death. New York: Oxford University Press.

Hackney, S. 1969. "Southern violence," in H. Graham and T. Gurr (eds.), Violence in America (pp. 393–410). Beverly Hills, CA: Sage Publications.

Hagan, John. 1974. "Extra-legal attributes and criminal sentencing: An assessment of a sociological viewpoint." Law and Society Review 8: pp. 557–583.

Halleck, S. 1978. "Psychodynamic aspects of violence," in R. Sadoff (ed.), Violence and responsibility. Jamaica, NY: Spectrum Publications, Inc.

Hannerz, U. 1969. Soulside, inquiries into ghetto culture and community. New York: Columbia University Press.

Harburg, E. 1973. "Heredity, stress and blood pressure, a family set method—I." Journal of Chronic Disease 30: pp. 625–647.

Harburg, E., et al. 1973. "Socioecological stressor areas and black-white blood pressure: Detroit." Journal of Chronic Disease 26: pp. 595–611.

Harburg, E., et al. 1970. "A family set method for estimating heredity and stress—I." Journal of Chronic Disease 23: pp. 69–81.

Harlan, Howard. 1950. "Five hundred homicides." Journal of Criminal Law and Criminology 50: pp. 736–752.

Harries, Keith D. 1980. Crime and the environment. Springfield, IL: Charles Thomas Publishers.

———. 1985. "The historical geography of homicide in the United States, 1935–1980." Geoforum 16(1): pp. 83–83.

Harrington, Michael. 1984. The new American poverty. New York: Holton, Rinehart and Winston.

Harris, Marvin. 1981. America now: The anthropology of a changing culture. New York: Simon and Schuster.

Harris, William H. 1982. The harder we run. New York: Oxford University Press.

Hartnagel, Timothy F. 1982. "Subculture of violence." Pacific Sociological Review 23: pp. 217–242.

Hartshorn, T., et al. 1976. Atlanta, metropolis in Georgia. Cambridge, MA: Ballinger Publishing Co.

Harvey, William B. 1986. "Homicide among young black adults: Life in the subculture of exasperation" in D. Hawkins (ed.) Homicide among black Americans (pp. 153–174). New York: University Press of America.

Hawkins, D. F. 1978. "Applied research and social theory." Evaluation Quarterly 2: pp. 141–152.

———. 1983. "Black and white homicide differentials: Alternatives to an inadequate theory." Criminal Justice and Behavior 10: pp. 407–440.

———. 1985. "Black homicide: The adequacy of existing research for devising prevention strategies." Crime and Delinquency 31: pp. 83–103.

———. 1986. Homicide among black Americans. New York: University Press of America.

Headley, Bernard. 1985. "The Atlanta establishment and the Atlanta tragedy." Phylon 56(4): pp. 333–340.

Heffernan, Ronald, Martin, John M., and Romano, Anne T. 1984. "Homicides related to drug trafficking." Federal Probation 48: pp. 3–7.

Heilbrun, Alfred B., Jr. 1979. "Psychopathy and violent crime." Journal of Consulting & Clinical Psychology 47: pp. 509–516.

Heilbrun, A. B., Heilbrun, L. C. Heilbrun, K. S. 1978. "Impulsive and premeditated homicide: An analysis of subsequent parole risk of the murderer." Journal of Criminal Law and Criminology 69: pp. 108–114.

Heilbrun, A. B. and Heilbrun, K. S. 1977. "The black minority criminal and violent crime: The role of self control." British Journal of Criminology 17: pp. 370–377.

Henderson, Donald. 1964. "Minority response and the conflict model." Phylon 25(Spring): pp. 18–26.

Henn, F., et al. 1976. "Forensic psychiatry: Diagnosis and criminal responsibility." The Journal of Nervous and Mental Disease 162: pp. 423–429.

Henri, F. 1975. Black migration: Movement North 1900–1920. Garden City, NY: Anchor Press/Doubleday.

Herjanic, J. and Meyer, D. 1973. "Notes on epidemiology of homicide in an urban area." An unpublished manuscript.

———. 1976. "Psychiatric illness in homicide victims." American Journal of Psychiatry 133(June): pp. 691–693.

Herzog, A., Levy, T., and Verdonk, A. 1976. "Some ecological factors associated with health and social adaptation in the city of Rotterdam." Urban Ecology 2: pp. 205–234.

Hill, Richard C. 1984. "Economic crisis and political response in the motor city," in Larry Sawers and William K. Tabb (eds.), Sunbelt/snowbelt, urban development and regional restructuring (pp. 313–338). New York: Oxford University Press.

Hirschi, Travis and Gottfredson, Michael. 1983. "Age and the explanation of crime." American Journal of Sociology 89(November): pp. 552–583.

Hoch, I. 1974. "Factors in urban crime." Journal of Urban Economics 1: pp. 184–229.

Hoffman, F. Quoted in Bruce, Andrew and Fitzgerald, Thomas, S. 1923. "A study of crime in the city of Memphis, Tennessee: A report prepared for the American Institute of Criminal Law and Criminology."

Hoffman-Bustamente, D. 1973. "The nature of female criminality." Issues in Criminology 8: pp. 117–136.

Holinger, Paul. 1980. "Violent deaths as a leading cause of mortality: An epidemiology study of suicide, homicide, and accidents." American Journal of Psychiatry 137(April): pp. 472–475.

Holinger, Paul and Klemen, Elaine. 1982. "Violent death in the United States, 1970–1975." Social Science and Medicine 16: pp. 1929–1938.

Holzman, Harold R. 1983. "The serious habitual property offender as moonlighter: An empirical study of labor force participation among robbers and burglars." Journal of Criminal Law and Criminology 73(4): pp. 1774–1792.

Howard, M. 1986. "Husband-wife homicide: An essay from a family law perspective." Law and Contemporary Problems 49(Winter): pp. 63–88.

Howitt, Dennis and Dembie, Richard. 1974. "A subcultural account of media effects." Human Relations 27(1): pp. 25–41.

Huff-Corzine, Lin, Corzine, Jay, and Moore, David C. 1986. "Southern exposure: Deciphering the South's influence on homicide rates." Social Forces 64(June): pp. 906–924.

Huggins, Nathan I. 1977. Black odyssey. New York: Pantheon Books.

Ianni, A. J. 1974. Black mafia. New York: Simon and Schuster.

Imes, James D. 1972. "Homicide and social conditions in the city of Atlanta, 1958–1962." M.S. thesis. Atlanta: Georgia State University, School of Urban Life.

Inciardi, H. 1979. "Heroin use and street crime." Crime and Delinquency 25(July): pp. 335–346.

Iskrant, Albert P. and Joliet, Paul V. 1968. Accidents and homicides. Cambridge, MA: Harvard University Press.

Jacob, Herbert and Eisenstein, James. 1975–76. "Sentences and other sanctions in the criminal courts of Baltimore, Chicago, and Detroit." Political Science Quarterly 90(Winter): pp. 419–428.

Jason, J., Strauss, L. T., and Tyler, C. W., Jr. 1983. "A comparison of primary and secondary homicides in the United States." American Journal of Epidemiology 3: pp. 309–319.

Jason, Janine, Flock, Melinda, and Tyler, Carl W., Jr. 1983b. "Epidemiologic characteristics of primary homicides in the United States." American Journal of Epidemiology 117(4): pp. 419–428.

Johnson, Bruce D. 1984. "Empirical patterns of heroin consumption among selected street heroin users," in G. Serban (ed.), The social and medical aspects of drug abuse (pp. 101–121). Jamaica, New York: Spectrum Publications.

Johnson, C. S. 1934. The shadow of the plantation. Chicago: University of Chicago Press.

Jones, Barbara A. P. 1986. "Black women and labor force participation: An analysis of sluggish growth rates," in Margaret C. Simms and Julianne M. Malveaux (eds.), Slipping through the cracks: The status of black women. New Brunswick, NJ: Transaction Books.

Joyner, Charles W. 1983. The South as a folk culture: David Potter and the southern enigma," in Walter P. Fraser and Winfred B. Moore, Jr. (eds.), The southern engima: Essays on race, class, and folkculture (pp. 157–167). Westport, CT: Greenwood Press.

————. 1984. Down by the riverside: A South Carolina slave community. Urbana: University of Illinois Press.

Kagan, Aubrey B. and Levi, Lennart. 1974. "Health and environment—psychological stimuli: A review." Social Science and Medicine 8: pp. 225–241.

Kagan, Aubrey R. 1974. "Health and environment—Psychological stimuli: A review." Social Science and Medicine 8: pp. 225–241.

Kaplan, John. 1979. "Controlling firearms." Cleveland State Law Review 28(1): pp. 1–28.

Kasarda, John D. 1988. "Economic restructuring and America's urban dilemma," in Mattei Dougan and J. D. Kasarda (eds.), The metropolis era, Volume 1, A world of giant cities. Beverly Hills: Sage Publications.

Kasl, Stanislav and Harburg, Ernest. 1972. "Perceptions of the neighborhood and the desire to move out." Journal of American Institute of Planners 38(September): pp. 318–324.

Kates, Don B., Jr. 1986. "The battle over gun control." The Public Interest 84(Summer): pp. 42–52.

Kelley, Robert F. 1985. "The family and the urban underclass." Journal of Family Issues 6(June): pp. 159–184.

Klebba, A. J. 1975. "Homicide trends in the United States, 1900–1974." Public Health Reports 90: pp. 195–204.

Kleber, Herbert D. 1988. "Epidemic cocaine abuse: America's present, Britain's future?" British Journal of addiction 83(12): pp. 1359–1371.

Kutash, I., et al. 1978. Violence: Perspectives on murder and aggression. San Francisco: Jossey-Bass, Inc..

Ladner, J. 1971. Tomorrow's tomorrow: The black woman. Garden City, NY: Doubleday & Co., Inc.

Lake, Robert W. 1981. The new suburbanites: Race and housing in the suburbs. New Brunswick, NJ: Rutgers University, Center for Urban Policy Research.

Landau, S. 1984. "Trends in violence and aggression: A cross-cultural analysis." International Journal of Comparative Sociology 25(3–4): pp. 133–157.

Landau, Simha F. and Raveh, Adi. 1987. "Stress factors, social support, and violence in Israeli society: A quantitative analysis." Aggressive Behavior 13: pp. 67–85.

Lefer, Leon. 1984. "The fine edge of violence." Journal of the American Academy of Psychoanalysis 12(2): pp. 253–268.

Letcher, M. 1979. "Black women and homicide," in H. M. Rose (ed.), Lethal aspects of urban violence. Lexington, MA: Lexington Books.

Levi, Ken. 1981. "Homicide as conflict resolution." Deviant Behavior 1(April–September): pp. 281–307.

Levi, Lennart and Anderson, Lars. 1975. Psychological stress: Population, environment, and quality of life. New York: Spectrum Publishers.

Levine, Edward M. 1984. "The middle-class and middle-class adolescents in a state of disarray: A social psychiatric analysis." Psychiatry 47: pp. 152–161.

Levine, L. 1977. Black culture and black consciousness. New York: Oxford University Press.

Levy, L., and Herzog, A. 1978. "Effects of crowding on health and social adaptation in the city of Chicago." Urban Ecology 3: pp. 327–354.

Lewis, Dan A. and Maxfield, Michael G. 1980. "Fear in the neighborhoods: An investigation of the impact of crime." Journal of Research in Crime and Deliquency 17(July): pp. 160–189.

Lichter, Daniel T. 1988. "Racial differences in underemployment in American cities." American Journal of Sociology 93(January): pp. 771–792.

Lieberson, Stanley. 1980. A piece of the pie, black and white immigrants since 1880. Berkeley: University of California Press.

Linsky, Arnold S. and Strauss, Murray S. 1986. Social stress in the U.S.: Links to regional patterns in crime and illness. Dover, MA: Auburn House Publishing Co.

Loeber, Rolf. 1987. "The prevalence, correlates, and continuity of serious conduct problems in elementary school children." Criminology 25(3): pp. 615–642.

Loftin, Colin. 1986. "Assaultive violence as a contagious social process." Bulletin of the New York Academy of Medicine 62(June): pp. 550–555.

Loftin, Colin and Hill, Robert H. 1974. "Regional subculture and homicide: An examination of the Gastil-Hackney Thesis." American Sociological Review 39(October): pp. 714–724.

Loftin, Colin, Neumann, Milton, and McDowall, David. 1983. "Mandatory sentencing and firearms violence: Evaluating an alternative to gun control." Law and Society 17: pp. 287–318.

Loury, Glenn C. 1986. "The family, the nation, and Senator Moynihan." Commentary (June): pp. 21–26.

Lowry, Ira S. 1980. "The dismal future of central cities." in A. P. Solomon (ed.) The prospective city (pp. 161–199). Cambridge, MA: MIT Press.

Loya, Ted, et al. 1986. "Conditional risks among Anglo, Hispanic, Black and Asian victims in Los Angeles: 1970–1977," in Secretary's task force on black and minority health (pp. 117–133). Washington, DC: U.S. Department of Health and Human Services (January).

Luckenbill, David F. 1984. "Theoretical observations on applied behavioral science." The Journal of Applied Behavioral Science 20(2): pp. 181–192.

Luckenbill, David F. 1977. "Criminal homicide as a situated transaction." Social Problems 25(December): pp. 176–186.

Lunde, D. 1976. Murder and madness. San Francisco: San Francisco Book Co.

Lundsgaarde, H.P. 1977. Murder in space city. New York: Oxford University Press.

Mancini, Janet T. 1980. Strategic styles: Coping in the inner city. Hanover, NJ: University Press of New England.

Mangun, Garth L. and Seninger, Stephen F. 1978. Coming of age in the ghetto. Baltimore: Johns Hopkins University Press.

Mann, Coramae Richey. 1987. "Black women who kill," in Robert L. Hampton (ed.), Violence in the black family. Lexington, MA: Lexington Books.

———. 1988. "Getting even? Women who kill in domestic encounters." Justice Quarterly 5(March): pp. 33–51.

Mare, Robert D. and Winship, Christopher. 1984. "The paradox of lessening racial inequality and joblessness among black youth: Enrollment enlistment and employment, 1964–1981." American Journal of Sociology 49: pp. 39–55.

Mare, Robert D., Winship, Christopher, and Kubitschek, Warren N. 1984. "The transition from youth to adult: Understanding the age pattern of employment." American Journal of Sociology 90(2): pp. 326–358.

Martin, J. (ed.). 1978. Violence and the family. Chichester, England: John Wiley & Sons.

Massey, Charles R. and McKean, Jerome. 1985. "The social ecology of homicides: A modified life style/routine activities perspective." Journal of Criminal Justice 13: pp. 417–428.

Maxson, Cheryl L., Gordon, Margaret A., and Klein, Malcom W. 1985. "Differences between gang and nongang homicides." Criminology 23(2): pp. 209–222.

Mayhew, B. and Levinger, R. 1976. "Size and the density of interaction in human aggregates." American Journal of Sociology 82(1): pp. 86–110.

McClain, P. D. 1981. "Social and environmental characteristics of black female homicide offenders." The Western Journal of Black Studies 5: pp. 224–229.

———. 1982a. "Black female homicide offenders and victims: Are they from the same population?" Death Education 6: pp. 265–280.

———. 1982b. "Cause of death—homicide: A research note on black females as homicide victims." Victimology: An International Journal 7: pp. 204–212.

———. 1982–83a. "Black females and lethal violence: Has time changed the circumstances under which they kill?" Omega 13: pp. 13–25.

———. 1982–83b. "Environment of risk and determinants of racial attitudes toward gun regulation: A test of the social reality thesis." Journal of Environmental Systems 12: pp. 229–248.

McGahey, Richard M. 1986. "Economic conditions, neighborhood organization, and urban crime," in Albert Reiss and Michael Tonry (eds.), Communities and crime. Chicago: University of Chicago Press.

Mead, M. 1964. "Cultural factors in the cause and prevention of pathological homicide." Bulletin of the Menninger Clinic 28: pp. 11–22.

Megargee, E. I. and Menzies, E. 1971. "The assessment and dynamics of aggressions," in P. McReynolds (ed.), Advances in psychological assessment (Vol. 2). Palo Alto, CA: Science Behavior Books.

Megargee, Edwin I. 1981. "Psychological determinants and correlates of criminal violence." in M. Wolfgang and N. A. Weiner (eds.) Criminal violence (pp. 81–149). Beverly Hills: Sage Publications.

Meredith, Niki. 1984. "The murder epidemic." Scientific American 84 (December): pp. 42–48.

Messner, Steven F. 1982. "Poverty, inequality and the urban homicide rate." Criminology 20(1): pp. 103–114.

Messner, Steven and Tardiff, Kenneth. 1986. "Economic inequality and levels of homicide: An analysis of urban neighborhoods." Criminology 24: pp. 297–317.

Metropolitan Life Statistical Bulletin, November 1974.

Meyers, A., Jr. 1954. "Murder and non-negligent manslaughter: A statistical study." St. Louis University Law Journal 3: pp. 18–34.

Meyrowitz, Joshua. 1984. No sense of place, the impact of electronic media on social behavior. New York: Oxford University Press.

Mieczkowski, Thomas. 1986. "Geeking up and throwing down: Heroin street life in Detroit." Criminology 24(4): pp. 645–666.

Monforte, J. R. and Spitz, W. V. 1975. "Narcotics abuse among homicide victims in Detroit." Journal of Forensic Science 26(January): pp. 186–190.

Moore, Geraldine. 1961. Behind the ebony mask. Birmingham, AL: Southern University Press.

Moore, Mark H., et al. 1984. Dangerous offenders. Cambridge, MA: Harvard University Press.

Moos, Rudolph. 1976. The human context. New York: John Wiley & Sons.

Moulds, E. F. 1978. "Chivalry and paternalism: Disparities of treatment in the criminal justice system." Western Political Quarterly 31: pp. 416–430.

Munford, R., et al. 1976. "Homicide trends in Atlanta." Criminology 14: pp. 213–231.

Murray, Charles. 1984. Losing ground. New York: Basic Books.

Nagel, S. and Weitzman, L. 1971. "Women's litigants." The Hastings Law Journal 23: pp. 171–198.

Neighbors, Harold W. 1984. "Professional help use among black Americans: Implication for unmet need." American Journal of Community Psychology 12(5): pp. 551–566.

Nelson, H. and Clark, W. 1976. Los Angeles, the metropolitan experience. Cambridge, MA: Ballinger Publishing Co.

Newman, O. 1980. Community of interest. New York: Anchor Press/Doubleday.

Newmeyer, J. 1978. "The epidemiology of the use of amphetamine and related substances." American Journal of Psychiatry 127(March): pp. 1170–1175.

New York Times, September 14, 1986.

New York Times, March 28, 1989.

Nielson, David G. 1977. Black ethos northern urban Negro life and thought, 1890–1930 (pp. 63–85). Westport, CT: Greenwood Press.

Nurco, David N., et al. 1985. "The criminality of narcotic addicts." The Journal of Nervous and Mental Disease 173(2): pp. 94–102.

――― . 1986. "A comparison by ethnic group and city of the criminal activities of narcotic addicts." The Journal of Nervous and Mental Disease 174(2): pp. 112–116.

Oliver, Melvin L. and Johnson, James H., Jr. 1984. "Interethnic conflict in an urban ghetto: The case of blacks and latinos in Los Angeles." Research in Social Movements, Conflicts and Change 6: pp. 57–94.

Olweus, D. 1978. Aggression in the schools. New York: Halstead Press.

Openshaw, S. 1984. "Ecological fallacies and the analysis of a real census data." Environment and Planning 16: pp. 17–31.

Parker, R. and Smith, M. 1979. "Deterrence, poverty, and type and homicide." American Journal of Sociology 85(3): pp. 614–624.

Perry, R. W. 1977. "The justice system and sentencing: The importance of race in the military." Criminology 15(August): pp. 225–234.

Pettigrew, T. and Spier, R. 1962. "The ecological structure of Negro homicide." American Journal of Sociology 67: pp. 621–629.

Pettyjohn, Leonard. 1976. "Factorial ecology of the Los Angeles-Long Beach black population." Ph.D. dissertation. Milwaukee: University of Wisconsin-Milwaukee.

Pittman, David J. and Handy, William. 1964. "Patterns and criminal aggravated assault." Journal of Criminal Law, Criminology, and Police Science 55: pp. 462–470.

Police Foundation. 1977. Domestic violence and the police. Washington, DC: Police Foundation.

Poussaint, A. F. 1983. "Black-on-black homicide: A psychological-political perspective. " Victimology 8: pp. 161–169.

Powers, R. and Kutash, I. 1978. "Substance induced aggression," in I. Kutash et al. (eds.), Violence, perspectives on murder and aggression. San Francisco: Jossey-Bass Publishers.

Pulkkimen, Lea. 1987. Offensive and defensive aggression in humans: A longitudinal perspective." Aggressive Behavior 13: pp. 197–212.

Radelet, Michael L. 1981. "Racial characteristics and the imposition of the death penalty." American Sociological Review 46(December): pp. 918–927.

Rainwater, Lee. 1966. "Fear and the house-as-haven in the lower class." American Institute of Planners Journal 32(January): pp. 23–31.

Rappeport, J. 1978. "The violent individual: Mad or bad?—Punish or treat?" in R. Sadoff (ed.), Violence and responsibility, the individual, the family and society (pp. 33–46). New York: SP Medical & Scientific Books.

Rappoport, A. 1978. "Culture and the subjective effects of stress." Urban Ecology 3: 241–261.

Rasko, G. 1978. "The victim of the female killer." Victimology 1: pp. 396–402.

Reed, J. 1972. The enduring South. Lexington, MA: Lexington Books.

Revitch, Eugene and Schlesinger, Louis B. 1981. Psychopathology of homicide. Springfield, IL: Charles C. Thomas Publisher.

Robins, L. 1968. "Negro homicide victims—Who will they be?" Transaction (June): pp. 15–19.

Robins, L., Wish, E., Murphy, G. E., and Breckenridge, M. B. 1971. "The adult psychiatric status of black school boys." Archive General Psychiatry 24(April): pp. 338–345.

Rodgers, Harrell R. 1986. Poor women, poor families: The economic plight of America's female-headed households. Armonk, NY: M. E. Sharpe, Inc.

Rokeach, M. 1973. The nature of human values. New York: The Free Press.

Roncek, D. W. 1981. "Dangerous places: Crime and residential environment." Social Forces 60: pp. 74–96.

Rose, H. M. 1975. "Urban black migration and social stress, the influence of regional differences in patterns of socialization." in G. Gappert and H. Rose (eds.), The social economy of cities (pp. 301–333). Beverly Hills, CA: Sage Publishers.

——— . 1976. Black suburbanization: Access to improved quality of life or maintenance of the status quo. Cambridge, MA: Ballinger Publishers.

——— . 1978. "The geography of despair." Annals of the Association of American Geographers 68: pp. 453–464.

——— . 1986. "Can we substantially lower homicide risk in the nation's larger black communities?" Report of the Secretary's Task Force on Black and Minority Health (pp. 185–221). Washington, DC: U.S. Department of Health and Human Services.

Rose, H. M. and Deskins, D. R., Jr. 1980. "Felony murder: The case of Detroit." Urban Geography 1: pp. 1–22.

Rosenberg, Mark L. and Mercy, James A. 1986. "Homicide: Epidemiologic analysis at the national level." Bulletin of New York Academy of Medicine 62(June): pp. 376–399.

Rossman, David, et al. (1980). "Massachusetts' mandatory minimum sentence gun law: Enforcement prosecution and defense impact." Criminal Law Bulletin 16(March-April): pp. 150–163.

Ruben, Elizabeth R. and Leeper, James D. 1981. "Homicide in the five southern states: A firearms phenomenon." Southern Medical Journal 74(3): pp. 272–277.

Rushforth, N., et al. 1977. "Violent death in a metropolitan county: Changing patterns in homicide (1958–1974)." New England Journal of Medicine 297: pp. 531–542.

Sampson, R. J. 1984. "Group size, heterogeneity and intergroup conflict: A test of Blau's inequality and hetergeneity." Social Forces 62: pp. 618–639.

——— . 1985a. "Structural sources of variation race-age-specific rates of offending across major U.S. cities." Criminology 23: pp. 647–673.

——— . 1985b. "Race and criminal violence: A demographically disaggregated analysis of urban homicide." Crime and Delinquency 31: pp. 47–82.

——— . 1985c. "Neighborhood and crime: The structural determinants of personal victimization." Journal of Research in Crime and Delinquency 22(1): pp. 7–40.

——— . 1987. "Urban black violence: The effects of male joblessness and family disruption." American Journal of Sociology 93(September): pp. 348–382.

Sargent, Edward D. 1986. "The plague of blacks killing blacks." Washington Post—National Weekly Edition (March 17): pp. 7–8.

Savitz, Leonard. "Black Crime," in K. Miller and R. Oreger (eds.) Comparative Studies of Blacks and Whites in the United States. New York: Seminar Press.

Schlesinger, Louis W. and Revitch, Eugene. 1980. "Stress, violence and crime," in I. Ervin and L. B. Schel (eds.), Handbook on stress and anxiety. San Francisco: Jossey-Bass.

Schultz, Leroy G. 1962. "Why the Negro carries weapons." The Journal of Criminal Law, Criminology, and Police Science 53(December): pp. 476–483.

Shin, Y., Jedlicka, D., and Lee, E. 1977. "Homicide among blacks." Phylon 39(December): pp. 398–407.

Shin, Yongsock. 1981. Differentials in homicide in the United States, 1930–1975: A demographic study. Ann Arbor, MI: University Microfilms International.

Silberman, C. E. 1978. Criminal violence, criminal justice. New York: Random House.

Silverman, L. and Spruill, N. 1977. "Urban crime and the price of heroin." Journal of Urban Economics 4: pp. 80–103.

Silverstein, B. and Krate, R. 1975. Children of the dark ghetto. New York: Praeger Publishers.

Simon, R. 1975. Women and Crime. Lexington, MA: Lexington Books.

––––––. 1976. "American women and crime." Annals of the American Academy of Social and Political Science 423.: pp. 31–46.

Sinclair, R. and Thompson, B. 1977. Detroit, and anatomy of social change. Cambridge, MA: Ballinger Publishing Co.

Skogan, Wesley G. and Maxfield, Michael G. 1981. Coping with crime, individual and neighborhood reactions. Beverly Hills, CA: Sage Publications.

Smith, Anthony. 1985. "The influence of television." Daedalus 114(Fall): pp. 1–15.

Smith, M. Dwayne, 1987. "Patterns of discrimination in assessments of the death penalty: The case of Louisiana." Journal of Criminal Justice 15: pp. 279–286.

Smith, Susan J. 1982. "Victimization in the inner city." British Journal of Criminology 22(October): pp. 386–402.

Spergel, I. 1963. "Male young adult criminality, deviant values, and differential opportunities in two lower class Negro neighborhoods." Social Problems 10(3): pp. 237–250.

Spindler, George D. 1977. "Change and continuity in American core cultural values: An anthropological perspective," in Gordon J. Direnzo (ed.), We the people, American character and social change. Westport, CT: Greenwood Press.

Spivak, Lee N. and Marcus, Janet 1987. "Marks and classroom adjustment as indicators of mental health at age twenty." American Journal of Community Psychology 15(1): pp. 35–55.

Spohn, Casia, Gruhl, John, and Welch, Susan. 1987. "The impact of the ethnicity and gender of defendants on the decision to reject or dismiss felony charges." Criminology 25(1): pp. 175–191.

Stamps, Spurgeon M., Jr. and Stamps, Miriam B. 1985. "Race, class and leisure activities of urban residents." Journal of Leisure Research 17(1): pp. 40–56.

Staples, Robert. 1987. "Social structure and black family life: An analysis of current trends." Journal of Black Studies 17(March): pp. 267–286.

Staver, Sari. 1986. "Male stresses, position role, and stopping murder." American Medical News (July 11): p. 25.

Steadman, Henry J. 1986. "Predicting violence leading to homicide." Bulletin of the New York Academy of Medicine 62(5): pp. 570–578.

Steffensmeier, Darrell J. 1978. "Crime and the contemporary woman: An analysis of changing levels of female property crime, 1960–75." Social Forces 57(December): pp. 566–583.

Stern, A. 1979. Me, the narcissistic American. New York: Ballantine Books.

Sternlieb, George and Hughes, James W. 1983. "The uncertain future of the central city." Urban Affairs Quarterly 18(June): pp. 455–472.

Sternlieb, George and Hughes, James W. 1977. "New regional and metropolitan realities." Journal of the American Institute of Planners 43(3): pp. 227–241.

Streiford, David M. 1974. "Racial economic dualism in St. Louis." Review of Black Political Economy 5: pp. 63–81.

Stroman, Carolyn A. 1984. "The socialization influence of television on black children." Journal of Black Studies 15(September): pp. 79–100.

Stuckey, Sterling. 1987. Slave culture, nationalist theory, and the foundations of black America. New York: Oxford University Press.

Swersey, W. 1981. "Homicide in Harlem and New York City." Unpublished paper, 24 pp., September.

Swidler, Ann. 1986. "Culture in action: Symbols and strategies." American Sociological Review 51: pp. 273–286.

Swigert, V. and Farrell, R. 1977. "Normal homicides and the law." American Sociological Review 42(February): pp. 16–32.

Swigert, V. and Farrell, R. 1976. Murder, inequality and the law. Lexington, MA: Lexington Books.

Tardiff, Kenneth and Gross, Elliot M. 1986. "Homicide in New York City." Bulletin of the New York Academy of Medicine 27(June): pp. 413–425.

Tardiff, Kenneth, Gross, Elliot, and Messner, Steven F. 1986. "A study of homicides in Manhattan, 1981." American Journal of Public Health 76(February): pp. 139–143.

Temin, C. E. 1973. "Discriminatory sentencing of women offenders: The argument for ERA in a nutshell." The American Criminal Law Review 11: pp. 355–372.

Thomas, Charles W. 1987. "Pride and purpose as antidotes to black homicidal violence." Journal of the National Medical Association 79(2): pp. 155–160.

Thornberry, T. P. 1973. "Race, socioeconomic status and sentencing in the juvenile justice system." Journal of Criminal Law, Criminology, and Police Science 69(1): pp. 90–98.

Thornberry, Terrence, Moore, Melanie, and Christenson, R. L. 1985. "The effect of dropping out of high school on subsequent criminal behavior. Criminology 23(1): pp. 3–18.

Thorne, F. 1975. "The life style analysis." Journal of Clinical Psychology 31(April): pp. 236–248.

Toch, H. 1969. Violent men. Chicago: Aldine Publishing Co.

Totman, J. 1978. The murderess: A psychosocial study of criminal homicide. Palo Alto, CA: R&E Research Associates.

Trachte, Kent and Ross, Robert. 1985. "The crisis of Detroit and the emergency of global capitalism." International Journal of Urban and Regional Research 9(June): pp. 186–217.

Turner, Charles W. 1977. "The stimulating and inhibiting effects of weapons on aggressive behavior." Aggressive Behavior 3: pp. 355–378.

Turner, Charles W., Fenn, Michael R., and Cole, Allen M. 1981. "A social psychological analysis of violent behavior," in Richard B. Stuart (ed.), Violent behavior (pp. 31–67). New York: Brunner/Mazel Publishers.

Ueshima, Hirotsugu, et al. 1984. "Age specific mortality trends in the U.S.A. from 1960 to 1980: Divergent age-sex-color patterns." Journal of Chronic Disease 37: pp. 425–439.

Uhlman, Thomas M. and Walker, N. Darlene. 1980. "He takes some of my time; I take some of his: An analysis of judicial sentencing patterns in jury cases." Law and Society Review 14(Winter): pp. 323–341.

U.S. Census Bureau. 1975. The social and economic status of the black population in the United States, 1974. Washington, DC: U.S. Government Printing Office.

Unnever, J. D., Frazier, C. E., and Henretta, J. C. 1980. "Race differences in criminal sentencing." The Sociological Quarterly 21: pp. 197–205.

Unnever, James D. and Hembroff, Larry. 1988. "The prediction of racial/ethnic sentencing disparities: An expectation states approach." Journal of Research in Crime and Delinquency 25(February): pp. 53–82.

Valentine, B. 1978. Hustling and other hard work. New York: The Free Press.

Von Hirsch, Andrew. 1984. "The ethics of selective incapacitation: Obersvations on the contemporary debate." Crime and Delinquency 30(April): pp. 175–184.

Waldron, I. and Eyer, J. 1975. "Socio-economic causes of the recent rise in death rates for 15–24 years olds." Social Science and Medicine 9: pp. 383–396.

Wallace, Phyllis A. 1980. Black women in the labor force. Cambridge, MA: MIT Press.

Ward, D., Jackson, M., and Ward, R. R. 1969. "Crimes of violence by women," in D. J. Mulvihil and M. M. Tumin (eds.), Crimes of violence. Washington, DC: U.S. Government and Printing Office.

Watts, Ann D. and Watts, Thomas M. 1981. "Minorities and urban crime: Are they the cause or the victims?" Urban Affairs Quarterly 16(June): pp. 423–436.

Webster, S. 1974. The education of black Americans. New York: John Day Co.

Wehlage, Gary G. and Rutter, Robert A. 1986. "Dropping out: How much do schools contribute to the problem?" Columbia Teachers College Record 87(3): pp. 374–392.

Weis, J. G. 1976. "Liberation and crime: The invention of the new female criminal." Crime and Social Justice 6(Fall/Winter): pp. 17–27.

Weiss, J. and Borges, S. S. 1973. "Victimology and rape: The case of the legitimate victim." Issues in Criminology 8: pp. 71–115.

Weiss, Noel, 1976. "Recent trends in violent deaths among young adults in the United States." American Journal of Epidemiology 103: pp. 416–422.

Weisheit, R. A. 1984. "Female homicide offenders: Trends over time in an institutionalized population." Justice Quarterly 1: pp. 471–489.

Wellford, C. 1975. "Labeling theory and criminology: An assessment." Social Problems 22(February): pp. 332–345.

Wenk, E. A., et al. 1972. "Can violence be predicted?" Crime and Delinquency (October): pp. 393–402.

Wideman, John E. 1984. Brothers & keepers. New York: Holt, Rinehart and Winston.

Wilbanks, W. 1983a. "The female homicide offenders in Dade County, Florida," Criminal Justice Review 8: pp. 9–14.

———. 1983b. "Female homicide offenders in the U.S." International Journal of Women's Studies 6: pp. 302–310.

Williams, K. R. 1984. "Economic sources of homicide: Reestimating the effects of poverty and inequality." American Sociological Review 49: pp. 283–289.

Williams, Kirk R. and Flewelling, Robert. 1988. "The social production of criminal homicide: A comparative study of disaggregated rates in American cities." American Sociological Review 53(June): pp. 421–431.

Williams, Melvin D. 1980. "Belmar: Diverse life styles in a Pittsburgh black neighborhood." Ethnic Groups 3: pp. 23–54.

Williams, Terry and Kornblum, William. 1984. Growing up poor. Lexington, MA: Lexington Books.

Wilson, James Q. and Herrnstein, Richard J. 1985. Crime and human nature. New York: Simon and Schuster.

Wilson, W. J. 1985. "The underclass in advanced industrial society." in Paul E. Peterson (ed.), The new urban reality. Washington, DC: Brookings Institution.

———. 1987. The truly disadvantaged: The inner city, the underclass, and public policy. Chicago: University of Chicago Press.

Wilt, G. and Bannon, M. 1974. A comprehensive analysis of conflict-motivated homicides and assaults. Final report. Washington, DC: The Police Foundation.

Wolfgang, M. E. 1978. "Perceived and real changes in crime and punishment." Daedalus 86(Winter): pp. 143–158.

———. 1986. "Homicide in other industrialized countries." Bulletin of the New York Academy of Medicine 62(June): pp. 400–412.

———. 1958. Patterns in criminal homicide. Philadelphia: University of Pennsylvania.

Wolfgang, M. and Ferracuti, F., 1973. Psychological testing in the subculture of violence. Rome: Bulzoni.

Wolfgang, M. E. and Ferracuti, Franco. 1967. The subculture of violence. London: Lavistock-Social Science Paperbacks.

Wolfgang, M. E. and Riedel, M. 1973. "Race, judicial discretion, and the death penalty." The Annals of the American Academy of Political and Social Science 401(May): pp. 119–133.

Wright, James D., Rossi, Peter H., and Daly, Kathleen. 1982. Under the gun: Weapons, crime and violence and America. New York: Adline Publishing Co.

Wyatt-Brown, Bertram. 1982. Southern honor, ethics and behavior in the old South. New York: Oxford University Press.

Yinger, J. 1977. "Characterological change among black Americans: A contextual interpretation." in G. DiRenzo (ed.), We, the people, American character and social change (pp. 195–219). Westport, CT: Greenwood Press.

Zahn, M. A. 1975. "The female homicide victim." Criminology 13: pp. 400–415.

Zatz, Marjorie S. 1985. "Pleas, priors, and prison: Racial/ethnic differences in sentencing." Social Science Research 14: pp. 169–193.

——— . 1987. "The changing forms of racial/ethnic biases in sentencing." Journal of Research, Crime and Delinquency 24(February): pp. 69–92.

Zatz, Marjorie S. and Hagan, John. 1985. "Crime, time, and punishment: An exploration of selection bias in sentencing research." Journal of Quantitative Criminology 1: pp. 103–126.

Zimring, F. E. 1968. "Is gun control likely to reduce violent killings?" University of Chicago Law Review 35(Summer): pp. 721–737.

——— . 1976. "Street crime and new guns: Some implications for firearms control." Journal of Criminal Justice 4: pp. 95–105.

——— . 1979. "Determinants of the death rate from robbery: A Detroit time study," in H. Rose (ed.), Lethal aspects of urban violence (pp. 31–50). Lexington, MA: Lexington Books.

——— . 1984. "Youth homicide in New York: A preliminary analysis." "The Journal of Legal Studies 13(January): pp. 81–99.

Zimring, F. E., Eigen, Joel, and O'Malley, Sheila. 1976. "Punishing homicide in Philadelphia: Perspectives on the death penalty." The University of Chicago Law Review 43(Winter): pp. 227–252.

Zimring, F. E., Mukherjee, S. K., and Van Winkle, B. 1983. "Intimate violence: A study of intersexual homicide in Chicago." University of Chicago Law Review 50: pp. 910–930.

Zimring, F. E., and Zuehl, James. 1986. "Victim injury and death in urban robbery: A Chicago study." Journal of Legal Studies 15(January): pp. 1–40.

Index